IT HAPPENED TO ME

Series Editor: Arlene Hirschfelder

Books in the It Happened to Me series are designed for inquisitive teens digging for answers about certain illnesses, social issues, or lifestyle interests. Whether you are deep into your teen years or just entering them, these books are gold mines of up-to-date information, riveting teen views, and great visuals to help you figure out stuff. Besides special boxes highlighting singular facts, each book is enhanced with the latest reading lists, websites, and an index. Perfect for browsing, there are loads of expert information by acclaimed writers to help parents, guardians, and librarians understand teen illness, tough situations, and lifestyle choices.

1. *Epilepsy: The Ultimate Teen Guide,* by Kathlyn Gay and Sean McGarrahan, 2002.
2. *Stress Relief: The Ultimate Teen Guide,* by Mark Powell, 2002.
3. *Learning Disabilities: The Ultimate Teen Guide,* by Penny Hutchins Paquette and Cheryl Gerson Tuttle, 2003.
4. *Making Sexual Decisions: The Ultimate Teen Guide,* by L. Kris Gowen, 2003.
5. *Asthma: The Ultimate Teen Guide,* by Penny Hutchins Paquette, 2003.
6. *Cultural Diversity—Conflicts and Challenges: The Ultimate Teen Guide,* by Kathlyn Gay, 2003.
7. *Diabetes: The Ultimate Teen Guide,* by Katherine J. Moran, 2004.
8. *When Will I Stop Hurting? Teens, Loss, and Grief: The Ultimate Teen Guide to Dealing with Grief,* by Ed Myers, 2004.
9. *Volunteering: The Ultimate Teen Guide,* by Kathlyn Gay, 2004.
10. *Organ Transplants—A Survival Guide for the Entire Family: The Ultimate Teen Guide,* by Tina P. Schwartz, 2005.
11. *Medications: The Ultimate Teen Guide,* by Cheryl Gerson Tuttle, 2005.
12. *Image and Identity—Becoming the Person You Are: The Ultimate Teen Guide,* by L. Kris Gowen and Molly C. McKenna, 2005.
13. *Apprenticeship: The Ultimate Teen Guide,* by Penny Hutchins Paquette, 2005.
14. *Cystic Fibrosis: The Ultimate Teen Guide,* by Melanie Ann Apel, 2006.
15. *Religion and Spirituality in America: The Ultimate Teen Guide,* by Kathlyn Gay, 2006.
16. *Gender Identity: The Ultimate Teen Guide,* by Cynthia L. Winfield, 2007.

CREATIVITY

THE ULTIMATE TEEN GUIDE

ARYNA RYAN

IT HAPPENED TO ME, NO. 43

ROWMAN & LITTLEFIELD
Lanham • Boulder • New York • London

Published by Rowman & Littlefield
A wholly owned subsidary of The Rowman & Littlefield Publishing Group, Inc.
4501 Forbes Boulevard, Suite 200, Lanham, Maryland 20706
www.rowman.com

Unit A, Whitacre Mews, 26-34 Stannary Street, London SE11 4AB

British Library Cataloguing in Publication Information Available

Library of Congress Cataloging-in-Publication Data

Ryan, Aryna M., 1952–
    Creativity : the ultimate teen guide / Aryna M. Ryan.
      pages cm. — (It happened to me ; 43)
    Includes bibliographical references and index.
    ISBN 978-0-8108-9223-1 (hardback : alk. paper) — ISBN 978-0-8108-9224-8 (ebook)
  1. Creative ability in adolescence. 2. Creative ability—Problems, exercises, etc. I. Title.
    BF724.3.C73R93 2015
    155.5'1335—dc23   2014039268

Printed in the United States of America

To the teens whose views are in this book,
to the teens this book may help,
and, of course, to Stephen

Contents

Acknowledgments

For many years I've known I'd write a book, but I never had the yen to pen the great American novel. For giving me the opportunity to write my first book, all kudos and lots of kisses go to my brother Steve. (I owe you 9,573 1/2 foot rubs.) We may not agree about tennis—eek!—but we both *love* books.

It's been said that no one writes a book alone; not until I wrote this did I understand that statement. There is so much that an author does *not* do, and I must give so much credit to my editor, Arlene Hirschfelder, who's been a peach. The week my book proposal was due, her home was hit by Hurricane Sandy and she simply carried on. Arlene has been knowledgeable about the book-making process and over-the-top kind and encouraging to a new author. I hope, if I ever write another book, I have the wonderful blessing to have her expertise and positivity again. Thanks also to her friend Julia Breer for sending me creativity questionnaires filled out by teens.

Very special thanks to Rosemary Mallett, who sent me the first questionnaires filled out by her own (and other teachers') students. Thanks to Lisa Blue at the Winter Park Public Library for allowing me to distribute the questionnaire at two events, and to Dion Fletcher for her sons' input and help finding more teens for the questionnaire.

Thanks to *all* the teens who filled out the creativity questionnaires and returned them with permission slips. Every bit of your input was greatly appreciated.

Thanks to the Bookends and Between the Liners for all the book sharing we've done. A great big hug to Carrie Morgan, gal novelist, for the writing program.

Thank you, Mom (Anne, the artist) and Dad (Jack, the writer), for the creative blend. A kiss to Amy Ryan-Rued for the Vision Boarding tips. A tip of the fedora to both artistic grandfathers, particularly John L. Ryan, who complimented me on grammar and punctuation in my preteen letters to him, and to Marguerite (grandma).

Huge hugs to my best girlfriend Linda Suskie, who led me to the graduate creativity program so I had the "cred" to write this book. (Yay, International Center for Studies in Creativity!) As an author herself, she knew the process I was undertaking. I even used a tiny portion of her latest book in the education chapter.

Thank you so much, Ed, for everything you did to support me on this book: coffee and donuts, bringing home dinners, helping me organize chapters, finding photos, locating forgotten page numbers, figuring out the endnote function, and so much more. You are a magnificent blessing.

Always and forever, enormous appreciation to my husband, Neil, who always encourages me—sometimes with a firm nudge. He supplied the drawings, contacted sources for reprint requests, nudged the endnotes into shape, and formatted the final manuscript. I could not have created this book without your ever-present, always-generous, and often hilarious support.

Introduction

On the day I wrote this introduction (August 21, 2014), there were 418,260 books available on Amazon with titles that contained one or more of the following words: *create, creative, creativity, innovate, innovation, invention*. (Some titles represent fiction and other titles overlap, but this is still an overwhelming number.) Of these nearly 420,000 books, the only creativity books written for teens are ones that teach techniques for making arts or crafts, plus a twenty-four-year-old pamphlet on creative problem solving. None of these books describe how creativity relates specifically to teens.

The purpose of this book is to show how creativity is *especially* impactful at this time in teens' lives. At this stage in your psychological development, you are deeply motivated to explore your unique identities. Creativity is a powerful force to unlock and showcase this uniqueness. Although the following is a quote from a man whose life spanned the mid-nineteenth to the mid-twentieth century, it is still the perfect motto for teens. As George Bernard Shaw declared, "Life is not about finding yourself. Life is about *creating* yourself."

The other reason teens like exploring creativity is that the topic intrigues them. The word *creativity* can be found in many languages, and creative activities exist in every culture; however, until the last sixty years or so, creativity itself has been almost a complete mystery. This book will show you what's been discovered about creativity in general and how those discoveries apply to you.

One mystery you can clear up right away: why did you pick up this book? It's probably because you saw the word *creativity* in the title. You might've thought, "Cool. This should be interesting" or something like that. You sure *didn't* think, "Jeez, this book sounds boring. I don't want to know any more about *that*." You were right. Simply hearing the words *create, creative,* or *creativity* conjures up images of color and fantasy, of sound and movement—and most of all, of fun. Being creative *is* fun, no question, but you'll also realize that creativity is more than fun—it is essential to life.

What This Book Is and Isn't About

While it is essential for you to know what this book is about, it is equally important for you to be clear about what this book is *not* about. First, this book or any other book on creativity *can't* teach you to be creative. (Any person who claims that she or he can *teach* you to be creative is not telling the truth.) A book that claimed it could teach you to be creative would be as dishonest as one that claimed it could teach you how to love.

This book is also *not* designed for you to learn an art or craft. There are a few exercises included to "loosen you up"; however, this book won't give you *specific* techniques for drawing, painting, sculpting, throwing pottery, designing in glass, or for any other arts and crafts you might be interested in. This book won't give you tools for making music, whether you sing, play an instrument, or compose. This book won't give you the secrets for becoming a better actor, director, scene designer, lighting designer, or costumer. For you aspiring writers, this book won't give you detailed tips on how to write better, whether you are (or want to be) a journalist, novelist, poet, playwright, or screenwriter. Those of you who are intrigued with inventing something small or maybe something so huge it will, like Steve Jobs's inventions, change the world—don't look for guidance on how to invent in these pages. This book won't give you direction in your art, advice on how to be a great inventor, or even show you *how* to be creative.

So what *will* this book give you?

What this book is designed to do is help you *remove* the barriers to your creativity. This book will not only tell you what creativity is *and* isn't; it will also help you maximize your creative potential. You'll get the chance to explore what creativity means to you, how to develop more of it in yourself, and how to assist yourself when you have trouble being creative.

The first chapter, "Creativity: Myth, Mystery, and Method," examines creativity's myths, defines creativity in depth, and explains *why* you're creative. In chapter 2, "Teens' Growth and Mastery," you will learn about the special relationship teens have with creativity. Chapter 3, "Creativity's Roots and Branches," provides both the history and the offshoots of creativity. Chapter 4, "Creativity Guidelines and Assessments," demonstrates how some aspects of creativity *can* be measured. Chapter 5, "Creativity: Everyday and Play," introduces the concept of everyday creativity and submits new research about play. Chapter 6 will show you how to crush your creativity, and chapter 7 will show you how to cultivate it. Chapter 8 illustrates the connection between creativity and happiness. Chapters 9 and 10 both focus on creative problem solving: "Divergent and Convergent Tools for Creative Problem Solving" (chapter 9) and "Creative Problem Solving Session" (chapter 10). Chapter 11, "Creativity and Learning," scrutinizes how creativity is and isn't a factor in current educational systems. Chapter 12 investigates the link between creativity and change leadership. "Creativity Catchall" (chapter 13) offers some fun, some useful, and some fun *and* useful creative activities and techniques. The final chapter allows you a glimpse into creativity and your future.

In other words, this book is designed to help you learn about the nature of *your* creativity. Everyone is distinctive in how she or he expresses creatively. You are not a one-size-fits-all type of person. Neither is anything you have already created, that you might be creating now, or you might create in the future. You—and all your creations—are unique.

As you read this book, many of the chapters feature teen views on aspects of creativity. These were gathered from teens from various geographical locations, of all ages, who filled out the questionnaire at the end of this introduction.

Years ago, I heard a speaker claim that if a person remembered three points from a speech, the speech was exceptional. If the person remembered only two points, that was significant. And if a person remembered just *one* point from the speech, it had been worth the listener's time and attention. So make it easy on yourself—try to find *one* memorable point from this book—a phrase or idea that works for you. Whatever that is, it will be enough to keep your creativity growing.

Questionnaire[a]

Teen Views on Creativity

Please write your FIRST NAME and your AGE ONLY. *If you want to contact me, my e-mail address is aryna@stateofyourheart.com*

NAME _____ AGE _____

Please answer in your own words (no Googling :-). If you wish, you can write in a six-word format. (*Example*: "Rain. Two strangers. One umbrella. Love.") *You're welcome to write on the back!!*

1. What is *your* definition of creativity?
2. How do you feel when you are being creative? What stops you from being creative?
3. How is your creativity different now than when you were younger?
4. How do you think everybody else is creative? How could creativity be measured?
5. How you think creativity can help solve problems?
6. How do you think creativity could be included in education?
7. How do you think creativity relates to play?
8. How do you think creativity could be useful for leaders?
9. How do you think creativity is important in everyday life?
10. How do you think creativity could play a role in your future?

CREATIVITY: MYTH, MYSTERY, AND METHOD

The Big Picture

There are many misconceptions about the subject of creativity. Since some of these misconceptions are centuries old, they've attained the status of myths. A myth is defined as "an unproved or false collective belief that is used to justify a social institution."[1]

Basically, a myth is false, but it is widespread. A myth appears to be believed by everyone; therefore, it has great power in influencing society. As Mark Twain once said, "A lie can travel halfway around the world while the truth is putting on its shoes."[2]

However, Lenin unwittingly described just how powerful myths are when he stated, "A lie told often becomes the truth."[3]

While creativity itself is not exactly a social institution, no great human endeavor has been achieved without it. Yet creativity has been surrounded by many false beliefs.

Dismantling Creativity Myths

Beginning with Myth 1, "Creativity is mysterious," let's examine what we know about other fields of knowledge that were once considered mysterious. When humans didn't know much about how life actually functioned, all we could do was imagine how it might. Eventually, these imaginative ideas evolved into myths.

For thousands of years, myths abounded regarding the function of the heart, particularly the human heart. Until the early seventeenth century, doctors believed that blood was one of four liquids, or "humors," in the body. (The other humors were black bile, yellow bile, and phlegm.)[4] Doctors also thought that the

Myths Humans Have Held about Creativity over the Centuries

Myth 1: Creativity is mysterious.

Myth 2: Creativity just "happens."

Myth 3: Creativity comes from muses (or divine inspiration).

Myth 4: Creativity can't be measured.

Myth 5: Some people are creative, others aren't.

Myth 6: Artists are the creative ones.

Myth 7: To be creative a person must have special talents.

Myth 8: Creative people are eccentric.

Myth 9: Creative people are "airy-fairy."[a]

heart turned food into blood, the heart warmed the blood, and the heart manufactured "vital spirits."[5]

Then, in 1619, William Harvey, an English physician, made a simple calculation. He estimated that every heartbeat ejected two ounces of blood. At an average seventy-two heartbeats per minute, this meant that the heart would have to eject 135 gallons of blood an hour! Of course, no human body could contain 135 gallons of *any* liquid, so Harvey theorized the heart was reusing (recycling) blood. After nine years of experimenting with animals, Harvey published his findings in 1628. As usually occurs when new information upsets myths, Harvey's work was initially rejected. By the time he died nearly thirty years later, however, doctors in the Western world had accepted Harvey's conclusions.[6] A mystery was solved and long-entrenched myths were erased by scientific fact.

Creativity has gone through a similar process. Before the 1950s, less than 2 percent of psychological studies (creativity is a branch of psychology) focused on creativity; therefore, early creative studies are about sixty-five years old.[7] That time span is very short in the scientific arena, only half of the 125 years that psychology has been considered a science. Imagine how much more will be known about creativity in 2055! (Maybe some of you will discover new facts that will make myths out of what we "know" about creativity today.)

What we do know now is that creativity is *not* completely mysterious,[8] although we're still discovering new truths about it because we're still exploring the brain. We're also learning more about how people affect other people's creativity.

She thinks creativity is a mystery!

We know that creativity doesn't just "happen" (Myth 2).[9] It may appear that way, but just as Harvey's evidence dispelled the myths about the heart in his day, there is much psychological evidence that dispels this creative myth.

Of course, when people can't figure out how something happens, a default position is to credit unseen beings. The Greeks believed in muses—goddesses who were supposedly the daughters of Zeus, ruler of the gods, and a mortal mother. The function of these goddesses was to protect and inspire all arts and knowledge. Seven muses were assigned to the arts alone: epic poetry (or sagas), lyric (love) poetry, tragedy, comedy, dance, hymns (to the gods), and song. History and astronomy also had muses, as did geography, mathematics, and philosophy.[10] It wasn't until the Renaissance that humans caught on to the fact that creativity (although that word wasn't invented yet) actually abided in humans themselves.[11] Once Christianity took hold, artists switched their allegiance from Greek muses to a Catholic—and later a Protestant—God. Myth 3, that creativity springs from muses or divine inspiration, was a logical progression; people were still ignorant about the brain's function and how social influences worked on creativity. In the Middle Ages (sixth to thirteenth century), if nobody could unravel a mystery, then the default position was to connect it to divinity.

Regarding Myth 4, that creativity can't be measured, we know that the *results* of creativity can be.[12] So can people's creative styles[13] and the environment[14] in which individuals will be most creative. We have a great deal of research about which elements crush and which elements cultivate creativity. (Some of them may surprise you.)

On to Myth 5: "Some people are creative, others aren't." Actually, while this belief has been true for centuries, the impact of this myth is waning. When I began teaching creative enrichment classes in 2000, many people claimed they *weren't* creative. Today, I hardly ever hear that statement. It's not clear why this shift in attitude has occurred. Maybe the demand for innovation in business has spurred people to chance being creative to make a profit. Maybe there are more books, magazine articles, and videos on creativity. (Although it's a mystery to know which came first: people's desire to become creative, so they bought a book or watched a how-to video? Or vice versa?) The proliferation of imaginative websites, original products, and YouTube videos on the Internet may have inspired people's creativity. ("Hey, if that person can make jewelry and sell it on Etsy, why can't I?") Whatever the reasons, this myth is approaching its expiration date.

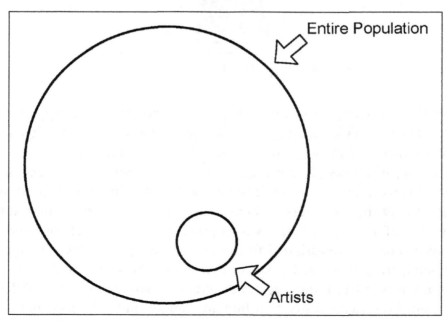

Artists, the creative ones. *Drawing by Neil Battiste*

Related to Myth 1 is Myth 6: "Artists are the creative people." To be truthful, however, it seems that people are making that statement less and less in the last ten years.

Many times when people claim they are not creative, what they usually mean is they aren't *artistic* (Myth 5). It might be true that they have no artistic ability. No one really knows how much of the population is actually talented in the visual or even performing arts, but it's important to note that this number is way, *way* less than the total population of the planet.

Myth 7, "Creativity comes from having special talents," is tricky because it depends on how you describe talent. If you are referring only to people who have *exceptional* talent in the arts (visual or performing), or for instance, in a specialty like math, then yes, creativity would be limited to those people. As you will see in chapter 4, "Creativity Guidelines and Assessment," and chapter 11, "Creativity and Learning," however, *everyone* is born with talent in at least one area and those talents are easy for others to spot. ("She's a cat whisperer." "He's great with kids." "He can build anything." "She's terrific at planning.") If this is true, it's starting to sound like *every*one might be creative.

Myth 8, "Creative people are eccentric," depends on exactly what we call eccentricity. Eccentricity is defined as "deviating from the recognized or customary character, practice, etc.; irregular, erratic, peculiar, odd."[15] This means eccentricity is relative. If you're in South Africa and you're wearing an outfit suited to the South *Pole*, you're going to look eccentric (and sweat off a few pounds). If you're in the South Pole, you're not only toasty but also you're smart *and* a stylish entry in the frozen fashion parade.

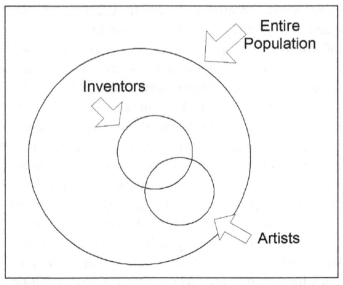

Or maybe inventors and artists? *Drawing by Neil Battiste*

The point is, looking or acting eccentric is not a valid measure of creativity. That belief is as valid as someone who offers the following syllogism: "All shirts have arms. I have arms. Therefore, I'm a shirt." (For you teens who might appreciate a spicier syllogism: "All cats eat mice. My cat eats mice. Why is there blood on my mouse pad?")

Myth 9, "Creative people are airy-fairy," is a common myth that creativity is "flighty." There's no rationality or organization, no analytical aspect to it. Actually, the creative process includes analysis, which is described later. The process of creative problem solving is actually a combination of convergent thinking, which means you're walking down the beaten path; and divergent thinking, which means you're making your own path.[16] One of the best-known examples of divergent thinking is brainstorming. Convergent thinking analyzes the ideas from a brainstorming session and selects the ones most appropriate for solving a problem. Here's a real-life way to distinguish between these two thinking modes: if you're at the store standing in front of shelves of body products, trying to decide what to buy (body lotion? body butter? beeswax lip balm? salt rub?), you're using convergent thinking. If you're at home concocting your *own* body butter, beeswax lip balm, body lotion, and salt rub (like my niece did for a science project), you're using divergent thinking. While you cannot think divergently and convergently *at the same time* (that would be similar to simultaneously stepping on the accelerator and brake), both are necessary thinking processes for solving problems.[17]

The truth is we are *all* creative. We all have talents. We all use convergent and divergent thinking every day. The crucial point is that we are all creative because we all solve problems. This is vital for you to understand: *we are all creative* because *we all solve problems*. Because you each have certain talents, you often solve problems in the areas of your life related to those talents.

Since most of you reading this book are students, you're solving the problem of how to take in what you hear, understand what you see and read, demonstrate what you've learned, and finally, know how to use what you've learned. You're constantly solving the problem of how to maximize your learning. If you're on a sports team, you're solving the problem of how to score the most points using the athletic and strategic talents of your team. If you're an artist, you're using your visual talent (which includes hand-eye coordination) to solve the problems of what image to produce, which materials to use, how to make the image look the way you want it, and even provide the message you want the image to convey. If you're a leader, you're solving the problem of how to influence people and guide them in order to accomplish a task or possibly an entire agenda. Whether you're aware of it or not, you apply problem solving to all areas of your life, from figuring out large issues like what career to go into to more common ones like deciding what movie to see, where, when, and with whom. (And are you going to buy popcorn or a hot dog?) You get *creative* in your problem solving when you utilize new ideas or combine conventional ideas in a new way.

Creative Mystery Is Still Afoot

We don't know everything about creativity. We know creativity originates in the brain, but even neuroscientists admit that the mind is not part of the physical brain. Research into what occurs during meditation confirmed this. "The mind is created within the interaction of internal neurophysiological processes and interpersonal experiences."[18] In simpler words, this means that your mind is more than the brain's cells, chemicals, and functions. Your mind includes what you have felt, known, and experienced in your life and can include what you are *capable* of experiencing. (That's why people say "expand your mind.") If this weren't true, we would be cyborgs, programmed machines unable to have original thoughts. (Yes, Data on *Star Trek* often had original ideas; we're talking real life here.)[19]

Even though creativity researchers have demystified many aspects of creativity, there is a great deal that is not known. For example, we don't know what exactly happens in the brain in the creative process (and what happens may be different for each person, who knows?).

It may be beneficial to have creativity remain somewhat of a mystery. In *Proof of Heaven*, a neurosurgeon who underwent a "near-death experience" realized that human beings have powers in the mind that are far beyond our comprehension.[20]

The psychologist Carl G. Jung proposed that all humans share a "collective unconscious,"[21] which links us to communal ideas and experiences, and which manifest themselves in universal myths. While the idea that creativity comes "from nowhere" or from "thin air" has been debunked by creativity researchers,[22] we still don't know how creativity emerges. For instance, how do connections made during sleep or downtime when *not* focusing on the problem lead to an "aha" discovery? This process remains a mystery in creative research.

Of course, no one has grabbed a hunk of creativity; hacked off a slice; pared it down to a tiny, almost translucent sliver suitable for mounting on a slide; and taken a look at it, even under a very powerful electron microscope. So far. You're smart enough to know that not everything can be seen under microscopes or through telescopes—not everything can be measured. However, measuring is not the only test for reality. We can't actually see intelligence, pain, and joy, yet they're all real. We can measure and see the results of intelligence. We can assess pain levels. As for joy, while no "joy-o-meter" has yet been invented, we have no problem observing joyful behavior in children or animals, or even ourselves. ("We won!" "I got an A plus!" "She'll go out with me!")

Even fiction has reality. To children, the Dr. Seuss's fantasy characters Sam-I-Am and the Lorax are very real ("Look, Mom, there are pictures of them!"). Onstage, actors, wearing the costumes of similar people who lived in Edwardian England in a production of *My Fair Lady*, are real to the audience. This is because audiences "make" the characters real, employing a "willing suspension of disbelief."[23]

Some aspects of creativity have been explained and measured. We can see artwork and use the inventions that result from creativity. We can see people being creative. We can recognize a creative environment.

Right now, however, some aspects of creativity are still a mystery. That's all right. Those aspects keep us curious and searching.

The Larger Scene

So what *else* do psychologists know about creativity? Since research into creativity as a science has spanned the past sixty-five years (with some influential articles and books reaching back to the 1920s, '30s, and '40s), it is not possible to include all the theories and people who made them here, nor all the creative studies conducted with children, adults, and to some extent, teens. So we'll only cover some basics, starting with the most widespread, accepted definition of creativity:

Creativity is novelty that's useful (or appropriate).[24]

Seems pretty simple, doesn't it? It actually took years of sifting through many definitions of creativity to reach this one, which included everything creativity was, *and* it didn't contain a lot of restrictions so creativity could "breathe." There are other definitions of creativity, as you will learn later. However, let's look at what's involved when we define creativity in a scientific manner.

The Four Ps

So now you know the most accepted creativity definition. But what else is involved in creativity? That question can't be answered simply. The answer depends greatly on which aspect of creativity you're referring to. Do you mean who's a creative *person*? Or what is a creative *product*? How about what constitutes a creative *process*? Or maybe you want to know what the elements of a creative environment are, or *press*.

First, we start with you, the *person*.[25] Obviously, without you and others like you, nothing can be created. So, what are the qualities of a creative person? Take a minute and guess before reading on. See how close you get to the ones researchers

The Four Ps of Creativity

Person: Who created it?

Product: What was created?

Process: How was it created?

Press: What was the environment in which it was created?[b]

have observed.[26] Be aware that this is only a list of the *sixteen categories* of characteristics (see the list on this page). Each category contains multiple characteristics.

The first category, Aware of Creativeness (*creativeness* doesn't sound like a real word, does it? It is.) could also be labeled *creativity consciousness*. Gary Davis, a creativity professor and author, claims that we can increase this consciousness. He believes that "improving our own creativity and teaching creativity to others is the number one trait to develop."[27]

While each one of these categories contains personality characteristics, the number of characteristics in each category varies. For instance, the Thorough category contains only three: "disciplined, committed to one's work; organized; perfectionist." The High Energy category contains *thirty-nine* characteristics, including "ambitious; impulsive; gets lost in a problem;" and "drive to produce."[28]

Categories of Creative Personality Traits

1. Aware of Creativeness
2. Original
3. Independent
4. Risk-Taking
5. High Energy
6. Curious
7. Sense of Humor
8. Capacity for Fantasy
9. Attracted to Complexity, ambiguity
10. Artistic
11. Open-Minded
12. Thorough
13. Needs Alone Time
14. Perceptive
15. Emotional
16. Ethical[c]

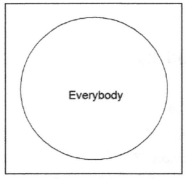

Who in the world is creative?
Drawing by Neil Battiste

Certain categories include characteristics that contradict personality traits in other categories; for example, under Emotional is "selfish" and under Ethical, you will find "altruistic."[29] However odd these contradictions might seem, they are consistent with the truth that creativity—and people—are complex.

Be clear: not everyone's personality has *all* these characteristics. For instance, the category Artistic not only includes "good designer"; it also holds "sensitive to beauty" and "enjoys art, music, creative dramatics."[30] Many people enjoy beauty and the arts without being able to produce either.

Given these characteristics of creativity, which quality, in your humble opinion, is the most important? (Hint: It's not the first on the list.) How many of these qualities would you say that you have? Of course, you've already learned from this book that you are creative. (If you don't think you have some of the listed qualities that you'd *like* to have, you can develop them.)

The Threshold Theory

This theory states that you must have a certain level of intelligence to be creative, but being *more* intelligent doesn't mean you're *more* creative. The only problem is that some creativity researchers love this theory, others are so-so about it, and some can't stand it!

All we can say is that there *is* a relationship between creativity and intelligence. We're just not sure what it is. (Maybe this is one of those mysteries about creativity you might explore.)[d]

So now you know. A creative *person* is one who engages in the process of creativity. This actually counts everyone in the world (yes, even babies). Why? *Because we all solve problems.* This is crucial for you to understand: the *reason* we are all *creative* is because we *all solve problems.* As psychologists were exploring the creative person, they got to wondering about the relationship of intelligence to creativity.

You can remember about being creative in your childhood. You didn't have to be smart or funny or particularly clever to be creative. Some tests have indicated that a person needs to have a "moderately superior" intelligence in order to be creative.[31] Moving up the IQ scale, however, doesn't mean you'll be *more* creative. It's more complex than that. It's kind of like saying that to play basketball you need to be able to carry a ball, walk, run a little, and jump. That's all true. However, simply because you can walk, run faster, or jump higher doesn't mean you'll be a great, or even a *good*, basketball player! There's much more to becoming a Michael Jordan than walking, running, and jumping. By the way, he is considered to be the most creative player ever. (In chapter 7, "How to Cultivate Your Creativity," you'll find out some of the reasons why.)

Creativity is the same. A person has to have a certain *level* of intelligence to have the capacity to be creative, but smarter people have no guarantee that they'll be *more* creative.

So you are talented (everyone has talent to a greater or lesser degree), you can be gifted, you can be talented *as well as* gifted, you can be a genius, *and* you can be all three. Whichever of these categories applies to you, or even if none of them do, remember, you are *always* creative.

In fact, your creativity can become *more* than a way for you to express yourself or to solve problems. Creativity can become a way for you to grow as a person, and ultimately, creativity can help you become all that you can be or, as Abraham Maslow termed it, to achieve "self-actualization."[32]

The humanistic psychologist Carl R. Rogers claimed that creativity was similar to self-actualization because both had "an urge to expand, extend, develop,

Thumbnail Biography of Abraham H. Maslow

Abraham H. Maslow (1908–1970), American psychologist and educational theorist, most known for his hierarchy of human needs (often seen in a pyramid shape), also wrote and lectured on the connection between self-actualization and creativity. He observed that "the concept of creativeness and the concept of the healthy, self-actualizing, fully human person seems to be coming closer and closer together, and may turn out to be the same thing."[e]

Tolerance of Ambiguity

Ambiguity is "doubtfulness or uncertainty of meaning or intention." *Tolerance of ambiguity* means to accept uncertainty. For the moment, you don't know your direction. So relax and breathe.[f]

mature, the tendency to express and activate" all of a human being's capabilities.[33] Connecting creativity to self-actualization has become known as a "growth theory of creativity."[34]

To be creative, however, takes a *process*, which is the next topic. *Process*[35] is being involved in the creation of something, even if you are at the beginning point of only creating ideas and have nothing to show for it yet. This is the trial-and-error part of creativity.

Explaining how *process* works is more complex. Plus we don't know everything involved in the creativity process. We do know, however, that you must utilize certain skills in order to create.

For example, it is helpful to have a *tolerance of ambiguity*.[36] This means that when you aren't sure, you are able to deal with the discomfort of not being sure. This may sound odd, but the ability to handle "not knowing" will propel your creativity because it is *a creativity skill*.

At this time in your life, you're already questioning who you were as a child, and you're not sure of who you'll be as an adult. You're uncertain of your identity. Because you're already in this mental and emotional phase, you might as well employ a tolerance of ambiguity in your life. It will propel your creative process. If you are already creative, you already utilize the tolerance of ambiguity. If you want to expand your creativity, you must increase your tolerance of ambiguity.

In addition, it's helpful to have a *tolerance for complexity*;[37] in other words, you can handle a lot happening, many choices, oodles of options. (You could almost call this ability a tolerance of chaos, and at times, this label will make sense!) A tolerance of complexity is vital because when there's controlled chaos (not the running amok kind) or complexity, you have the opportunity for many choices. The truth is, if you can't hang out with complexity, if you need to go down a

Tolerance of Complexity

This means maintaining direction, while deferring judgment. Momentarily accepting all options.[g]

> ### Incubation
>
> Incubation "may be best viewed as a period of preconscious, fringe-conscious, off-conscious or perhaps even unconscious mental activity that takes place while the thinker is (perhaps deliberately) jogging, watching TV, playing golf, eating pizza, walking along a lakeshore, and even sleeping."[h]

well-worn path, you can't possibly make anything new. This newness won't just pop up at you, however; it has to be nurtured like tending plants. Tolerance of complexity is *also a creative skill.* Tolerance of both ambiguity and complexity are necessary to generate new ideas.

Creativity also involves incubation, which means "gestation, development, cultivation, nurturing."[38] To incubate means "to develop, grow, take form."[39] Synonyms include "hatch, sit on, keep alive, protect, nurture, develop, simmer, brew, gather strength."[40] One of the most vivid definitions of incubate is "keep warm."[41] This definition most likely refers to keeping eggs or babies warm, but why can't it apply to *keeping your ideas warm*? Keeping them warm is just that simple. It means not tugging on your ideas and pushing them to burst forth, or teasing or nagging them, but allowing your ideas to rest and develop on their own.

If you've ever watched a butterfly emerging from a cocoon, you know you need patience to allow the butterfly to struggle. Some people who have been uncomfortable watching this process break the cocoon to help the butterfly get out. Their help is misguided, however, because the struggle getting out of the cocoon is what strengthens the butterfly's wings. Those butterflies that get help do not do well; they certainly don't fly well, if at all.

This situation parallels your relationship with incubation during your creative process. You can't "break the cocoon" of creation that's struggling to come forth. You have to keep it warm, let it rest, let it be.

It's time to move onto *product.*[42] Of the four Ps, product is the easiest to describe. We're all familiar with the products of creativity: paintings, music, movies, inventions, e-books, Rubik's cubes, singing bass, Minecraft, dancing Santas, dump cake recipes . . .

Or you may have produced a creative product yourself. It may have been a project for class, a web page or blog, a science experiment for a science fair, or something you've constructed, baked, painted, sewn, sculpted, written, or composed; the list goes on of items that you could have made.

As you might have figured out by now, a creative product must be both novel *and* useful (or appropriate). To be clear: Novelty is not enough—a product must be useful, which means it must be *appropriate* for the problem it solves. A category of

Incubating through the problem.

products called chindogu aptly illustrates why newness—novelty—is not enough to qualify a product as creative (read more on page 15).

Even though amazingly, often amusingly inventive, chindogu contradicts the accepted definition of creativity, which is originality *plus* usefulness. While most chindogu are fascinating and many are hilarious, they are deliberately fashioned to be inappropriate and impractical. So they can't pass the test for being a creative product.

The last category, which is easy to explain, is the circumstances *under which* you create. To have this term start with a *p* so it'll match the others, we call it *press*. [43] The word *press* refers to the environment around you, and the word *press* fits because your environment can *press* on you. Hopefully, it is a positive pressure that challenges and encourages you. As you already know, however, often pressure is not so benign. (You'll see how to handle tough "press"—or environment—in later chapters.)

Possibly researchers called it *press* because it's a shortened version of *pressure*. More likely, they wanted a fourth *p* to finish their list! (Alliteration is also fun and handy for memorization.)

In the realm of creativity, press means the environment in which a creative person (and by now you know that's all of us) creates. It'd be great if this environment—press—always supported the process of creativity. Press, however, is a

Chindogu

Chindogu is a Japanese term for *useless* inventions. Remarkably, chindogu inventors must adhere to ten tenets (rules) for fashioning chindogu, the first of which is that the invention *cannot be for real use*. The second tenet is that *it must exist*. These inventions may be useless, but they are not fantasies. Check out the Honest Husband Hat (#44) and the Zen Litter Box (#163) on under "Exhibition Hall A" on Chindogu.com (www.chindogu.com/tenets.html). Then take a peek at the Baby Mop, the Full Body Umbrella, and the Noodle Cooler at www.weirdasianews.com/2009/10/19/chindogu-weird-useless-japanese-inventions/. Enjoy![i]

neutral term; it can indicate a supportive or detrimental environment. (Billy Joel wrote a song about pressure called appropriately, "Pressure," which describes how a negative environment affects a person.)[44] Another way to describe press is "creative climate."[45] Although this term sounds positive, creative climate is actually another *neutral* term to describe whether the environment supports or detracts from people's creativity. A positive creative climate would allow people to indulge in trial-and-error experiments and make mistakes in an arena of non-judgment. This climate would also allot people sufficient time to go through the trial-and-error process. As you can imagine, having plenty of unhurried time is absolutely essential to creativity. Remember the last time you were rushed on a project that required you to be creative? Under that time pressure, how creative were you?

The creative environment, of course, is wholly different than the ecology of air, water, grass, and trees; however, it is just as vital to developing creativity as those elements are to keeping you alive and healthy. The environment for creativity is partly physical, definitely psychological, social, and emotional, and for some, may include spiritual aspects.[46]

There are criteria for determining whether people are working in a creative climate, and these apply to *any* situation in which people need to use creativity. These criteria, or dimensions, are listed on page 16.

If there is an activity that you enjoy, it's challenging but not too difficult, and you have freedom to do it, these are the basics of creative climate. If some of

Dimensions of a Creative Climate

Challenge: emotional investment of people in goals

Freedom: independence of behavior

Idea Support: how new ideas are treated

Trust and Openness: emotional safety

Dynamism and Liveliness: eventfulness

Playfulness and Humor: spontaneity and ease

Debate: various ideas and viewpoints clash

Risk Taking: tolerance of ambiguity!

Idea Time: for elaboration of new ideas

Conflict: idea tensions or people tensions?

All dimensions are considered positive, *except* conflict among people. There *must* be a conflict of *ideas*, not personalities.[j]

your ideas are supported, you can be open and trust the people you're with, and the place is alive with energy and possibility, with people joking and having fun, these are more plusses. Finally, if debate about ideas is allowed but not conflict among people, and it's all right to take risks with new ideas that you have time to develop, you're going to create a lot of meaningful "work." (There are quotation marks around the word *work* because if you're in an environment like this, what you'll be doing every day won't feel like work!)

This is what is called a positive "creative climate."

Have you been wondering what the number one creative characteristic is? Here you go: curiosity. Don't you wanna know why? (Think about it.)

A few famous people have made observations about curiosity, among them Dorothy Parker (1893–1967), who was an author, poet, critic, screenwriter, and wit (basically, a person who makes spontaneous funny statements or what you might call the "class clown"). She once said, "The cure for boredom is curiosity. *There is no cure for curiosity.*"[47]

Someone you've all heard of, Albert Einstein, explained curiosity from a different vantage point when he advised, "The important thing is not to stop questioning."[48]

All four Ps: people painting porch playfully.

When you were a child, you asked questions—lots and *lots* of questions. In fact, you probably drove adults around you *nuts* with all your questions! Well, as a teen, you are also asking questions. Only the questions have changed from, "Why do cats purr and dogs don't?" to "Why is the world the way it is? Why are people so cruel to each other? What am I going to do with my life?" ("Why is my mom on my case all the time?")

Don't all these questions confirm that the number one creative characteristic is curiosity? A UCLA study shows that five-year-olds ask sixty-five questions a day; adults in their mid-forties ask only *six*.[49] If you compare children's creativity levels to adults, you can see a direct link to curiosity. No wonder children are so creative and adults often aren't. If you don't exercise your curiosity, you lose your creativity.

Here's why: When you are curious about *anything*, even something as simple as looking up a word in the dictionary, a subject on Wikipedia, or even the name of an actor on IMDb (Internet Movie Database), there is a neural pathway in your brain that "fires" from your specific question. Your brain's creativity is not limited to that particular question, however.[50] In addition to the neural firing *from* your specific question, you also have a general neural pathway that *looks* for—or goes *toward*—new information. This general pathway, called SN, or *seeking new-ness*, also fires up. Every time you are curious, you prime your SN pathway to fire up more easily the next time. So if you want to increase your creativity, keep seeking new information and keep asking questions.[51]

Because this question-asking comes from a place in you that doesn't know, isn't that a simple way of stating that you possess a tolerance of ambiguity? When you get answers that lead to more complicated questions or complex answers, isn't that when your tolerance for complexity kicks in? In case you were wondering how the heck you were going to incorporate those two creative skills in your life, this is how: by asking questions. By the way, asking questions doesn't necessarily mean that you need to ask them of other people. You can use your questioning nature when you're by yourself, such as taking something apart to see inside. Or asking how those two objects would work together. Or wondering what it would look like to try that color on your painting. Or seeing how those two words might combine in your haiku.

The more you exercise your "I wonder" muscle, the more your brain will continue seeking new information, building those pathways that lead to original and useful products—to creativity as it is purely defined.

Although this thirteen-year-old (Thomas from Virginia), may have not realized it when he said, "Your creativity is used during something as simple as asking a question," he was absolutely correct. (Maybe *he'll* be famous someday.)

People who produce a lot of creative products (music, inventions, paintings) are very curious. They wonder why something can't be better. They wonder if something could be done in a different way. That wonder leads to them trying various ways to solve their problems. That wonder comes *from* as well as leads *to* creativity.

TEENS' GROWTH AND MASTERY

··

The Big Picture

So what's the big deal about being a teen? "Are you kidding?" you probably shrieked (if only in your mind). "What *isn't* a big deal?"

You're right, of course. You've got hormone levels constantly fluctuating, you're thinking about sex *all* the time (girls, too), your parents are *always* on your case, you've got to straighten out this friendship or dump that one; there's so much to do at school, you don't look as good as the other girls (or guys), you've got hassles with a teacher (or with two or with the vice principal), you've got another breakout . . . and don't anyone even *dare* ask what you're going to do when you grow up! (Check out YouTube to hear what Logan LaPlante says about growing up on TEDx.)[1]

Oh, and that's just the normal stuff. If you're a teen with a single parent who has to work a lot, or there's tension or abuse at home, or you're a foster teen, or someone at home has a substance abuse problem (or you do), or your family's broke or worse, or you're all homeless, or one of your parents is deployed overseas, or someone in the house has a chronic illness (maybe you have the medical problem), or you're part of a gang (or trying to get out of one), or someone close to you is in jail, or you have a learning disability, you have much more to deal with than "normal" teenage issues.

So those last two paragraphs were depressing to read, right? They might have been, but the points made were to direct you to the *real* purpose of being a teen: establishing your *own* identity in the world. You do that first in your family (which is why the parents you probably got along with in the past seem so tough to deal with now), at school (where you have an image to project to your friends, your teachers, the guys or girls you like and the ones you don't), out in the world at your job (if you have one) with your boss and coworkers. You even have to maintain a cool image at the mall or in front of cops you see and who see you when you're driving.

Does it help to know that your job at this age is not to simply figure out who you are; it's to *create* who you are? One of the best ways to create your identity is to self-express, and one of the most effective ways to express yourself is through creative ventures.

Because, of course, you want to be a unique person (by the way, you already *are*, but you may not realize it yet), creativity can help you achieve your goal. By definition, creativity is novelty, or in the case of human beings (since we're referring to the *person* here, not the *product*), to be creative is to be exploring, experimenting, finding new ways to exist. (This is what is behind style and the reason there is change that shows up not only in fashion styles, but in society, in thought, and eventually in evolution.) The nature of creativity demands novelty. It can't work if it depends on the past, or if it only comes from fixed ways of doing things, or if it stays in that "box." Creativity can be directed, it needs to be supported, but it cannot be *molded*. Creativity is unchained; it's always out of jail—or trying to break out. Not in reality, of course, but the word *creativity* implies freedom. Don't *expressiveness, novelty*, and *freedom* sound like concepts you want in your life?

These concepts absolutely align with the way teens need to be going in their lives. It could be that creativity helps you be a little bit selfish—not in a negative way, but in a way that helps you bring out your *self*. Can you remember anyone saying to you, "Oh, just be yourself" and then wondering what the heck that meant? Maybe it means being the way you want to be in the moment in whatever situation you are in. The truth is, though, to be that way will require a lot of energy because you'll need to pay attention to your feelings moment to moment so that you *can* be yourself.

Well, how can you do that when you're so confused? Not only feeling confused about yourself, but also about the world. Actually, *confusion* is not an emotion. It's *a conflict between two value systems*. You don't have to think about that much to realize that you're in conflict about lots of values now. You like the memories of being a kid and not having to be as responsible as you are now, but you want to be thought of and treated as a young adult. You're probably confused about what you used to feel and what you feel now. You probably have a conflict between needing the emotional and financial support from your parents and frustration at not having all the freedom you want. You might be confused about how you feel about the guy or gal you're attracted to and how he or she has responded to you. You're probably confused *and* distressed about why people treat each other the way they do, how the world can seem so hypocritical, and on and on. Actually, one negative synonym for being a teen might be the word *confusion*.

This is exactly why Erik Erikson, a psychologist who charted the psychological stages of all humans across a normal life span, called this adolescent stage Identity vs. Identity Confusion.[2] The good news is you're absolutely normal. This is the one time in your life you are *supposed* to be confused.

Of course, knowing this doesn't make you feel any better. In sorting through this confusion to create an identity, you have to include your family's DNA, the sum of all your experiences in life: what you've seen, heard, done, eaten; where you've lived and traveled; who you've loved and hated; and what you've loved doing (and hated), *plus* all your talents, your dark side, skills, mistakes, aspirations, sense of humor, failures, desires, bizarre thoughts, and goals—take *all* this, and form it into a unique *you*.

So how the heck does creativity fit itself into all this mess? Actually, creativity belongs to teens *more than to any other age on the human timeline*.[3] This makes sense, right? Because you are creating yourself more at this time than at any other time in your life. Since you were twelve, you've been able to think cognitively, which means you can reason.[4] Now you are better able to *think* through your choices: what you like (clothes, music, movies, food—all that stuff), what you want to do with your time, and how you want to present yourself to the world.

Repeat: You *are* actually creating yourself. That's *much* tougher than creating art, inventing a machine, or solving a problem. Creating yourself is going to take time (and will extend beyond your actual teens until about age twenty-four),[5] yet it is the task you need to complete before you can go into adult life (which, frankly, may not look all that appealing right now!). One positive synonym for teen could be *creativity*. (Hmmm, both *confusion* and *creativity* begin with c. . .)

So how can this book help you with all of the confusion and creation? Mostly, by validating what you're going through and by giving you facts that explain why adolescence is an unsettling age.

You'll be getting guidelines on how to be more creative, which will help you be more expressive, which will help you with your identity creation. Other books in this series have talked to you about how to handle dating and sex, and parents, and issues at school, and friendships, and have explored topics such as money, social networking, and body image. This book, however, will support you in the fact that you are creating yourself and your sense of how you want to be in the world.

Center Stage: The Teen Brain

The main reason that teens are so creative (and confused) at this time in their life span is due to the way their brains are developing. Teens' brains are actually re-creating themselves.[6] This is necessary, so they not only do grow up, but they *can* grow up.

What do all these brain changes have to do with creativity? At this age—your age—the teen brain is pruning brain cells (like gardeners prune trees) and adding new ones. This pruning results in your brain becoming more "integrated," which simply means your brain can make more connections.[7] Having more connections

Book: *Brainstorm: The Power and Purpose of the Teenage Brain*

Daniel J. Siegel, MD. New York: Jeremy P. Tarcher/Penguin, 2013, 307 pages. A must read for you, as a teen (which Siegel defines as from twelve to twenty-four years of age) to help you understand why you feel and act so differently than you did at eleven. Even though the book is based on neuroscience, it is written for teens. *Brainstorm* discusses the essence of adolescence, the teenage brain, of course, relationships, and how to meet the challenges of being a teen. Also featured are MindSight Tools, which provide mind-calming and focusing exercises.[a]

means there are more possibilities for putting ideas together. Consequently, many of those connections are going to be *original*—or as people also call them, "creative." As a teen, you are thinking in new ways. Rather than thinking only in facts or fantasy like young children, however, teens are now capable of *conceptual* thinking. If you want the fancy term for this new ability, it's called *formal operational thinking* (FOT).[8]

Let's put a little of that FOT in action right now. Let's explore the meaning of the word *creativity*. What do *you* think about creativity? Is there a definition that's meaningful to you? Of course, the dictionary has its views on the topic:

> Creativity: "the ability to transcend traditional ideas, rules, patterns, relationships, or the like, and to create meaningful new ideas, forms, methods, interpretations etc.; originality, progressiveness, or imagination."[9]

Now what does this definition of creativity mean exactly? The definition mentions ideas. It mentions rules. It mentions patterns. It mentions relationships and transcending them. It also includes the word *meaningful*.

But back to you—how would *you* define creativity?

Would you do a tiny experiment right now? Please close your eyes and simply think about it. You don't have to direct your thoughts; whatever you come up with is fine. When you've got some ideas and you decide you're ready, please open your eyes.

What thoughts did you have? What do you notice about your definitions? Did they mention anything about being original or having fun? How about expressing yourself? If so, you are on the track of creativity researchers. They, too, had to come up with a workable definition of creativity so they could conduct studies about it (which, you may remember, was "novelty that's useful"). However, creativity researchers have also agreed that there are as many definitions of creativity as there are people. So your definition(s) are completely valid—for you. (When

Teens' Views on Creativity

Question 1: "What is *your* definition of creativity?"

"Being creative is to have unique ideas, creations, and artistic abilities or talents. You show creativity through your writing, your thoughts and your art."—Jordan, 13, Maryland

"My definition of teen creativity can relate to art, music, photography, being with friends or finding and being in love."—Kimberly, 15, California

"It is something that you feel your raw emotion being released in a way that you feel best expresses it."—Arianna, 18, California

"The ability to think and solve problems differently than the norm."—Justice, 17, California

"The effort to think of the original."—Max, 16, California

"The ability to create something from nothing and having it be unique."—James, 15, California

"Any way you can express yourself, your ideas, confronting obstacles in a way that's different than how most people would do so."—Melanie, 14, California

"To express yourself through unique ways."—Ashley, 17, California

"Viewing the world differently. Being able to make/see something out of nothing."—Sam, 16, California[b]

I was in school learning about creativity, each semester we had to invent a new definition for it that we hadn't used before. You might find this a challenging and fun exercise.)

If you want, you can record your ideas in a notebook, phone, or computer file. There's no need to write complete sentences—single words or phrases are fine.

Compare what you thought (or wrote) about creativity to the teens' definitions on page 23. Do you notice any similarity between your ideas of creativity and these teens' views? How are yours different?

The Larger Scene

Just as creative studies are relatively new, so are studies on teenagers. (Far more research has been conducted on children than on teens.) Besides both being relatively new fields of study, creativity and teens have other aspects in common.

Those of you who are older teens saw the introduction of avatar games; you younger ones have never known a world without these. If you're reading this, chances are you were born between 1995 and 2001, which puts you in the thirteen-to-nineteen age category. Obviously, we think of teens as between thir*teen* through nine*teen*, and technically, these numbers are the true "teens." Research has shown, however, that teen brain development actually spans ages twelve to twenty-four.[10] So if you're twelve or if you're between twenty and twenty-four, the information on the teen brain and creativity also applies to you.

So what does the "digital native" designation have to do with creativity? *You are going to create new forms of creativity.* Some of you have already learned how

Talkin' about Your Generation (Born 1995–2012)

You have been called the "digital natives" because all your lives you've had access to cell phones, laptops, the Internet and World Wide Web, iPods and iPads, MP3 players, smartphones, iPhones, and of course, CDs, DVDs, TiVo, Netflix, YouTube, Hulu, Facebook, IM, and on and on! You've also been called Generation Z, the Homeland Generation, Gen Tech, Gen Wii, Gen Next, TwoKays (or 2Ks), the Conflict Generation, Net Gen, Post Gen, Generation I (or iGeners or iGens), the @generation, the Swipe Generation, the Tweenials, and Screeners. Take your pick; create your own label, or skip all labels.[c]

to program code and through "creative coding" you've designed websites for yourselves or others. Or you've created your own anime. You are as familiar with YouTube, Internet searches, and e-tail as you are with your toothbrush (which probably has a charger). You've been helping your parents and grandparents with their computer glitches since you could talk and reach their keyboards. (When my nephew was a year and a half, my mother and sister were babysitting at his house. They wanted to watch TV but couldn't get it to turn on. They figured the cable was out. My nephew, pacifier in his mouth, watched them fiddle with the TV and remote for a while, then calmly toddled behind the TV and plugged it in! Now thirteen, he plans to attend MIT. The signs were there . . .)

How many teens use books nowadays.

You are also a unique population because you are the *first teens* to possess specialized knowledge about the teen brain.[11] We now know that the teen brain goes through more changes than at any other time in life.[12]

Alongside your familiarity and comfort with technology is your brain, which by pruning brain cells and integrating others, is leading you to more connections in your thinking. Plus you have a *drive* to make those connections. It's too complicated to describe here, but there's actually a place in your brain that *rewards* you for taking risks—in other words, for seeking novelty. This place in your brain doesn't stay active after the age of twenty-four unless you nurture it.

So why not use this brand-new brain for new ideas? For sure you're already thinking, "Why are we here? Why is society this way? Why are my parents still treating me like a kid?" Teens notice situations involving prejudice, spirituality, patriotism, fairness, and power. Teens look at all kinds of life issues that they didn't think about before—actually, that they *couldn't* think about very well, not until their teen brain developed into a new model. (You could think of it as Brain 2.0.)

Brain 2.0 is able to think in new abstract and conceptual ways, which leads to the message of that very-old-now, so-decades-ago slogan, "Thinking outside the box." Not only do you know what that means, but you're more capable of it than at any other time in your life. The kind of thinking that's creative, that leads to creative endeavors, not only in art, but in music, drama, science, society, and solving problems, is now yours. *Really* yours, not some fancy talk at the end of a speech.

This is the time for you to begin experimenting with creative thinking: to get involved in the trial-and-error process that is the *essence* of creative production.

You, as a teen, are able to perceive and reason and problem solve in ways that are totally new to you. Plus that "reward drive" in your brain gives you more pleasure doing exactly what your brain is designing itself to do! This also answers the question, "Why do such risk-taking, limit-testing, sensation-seeking behaviors happen?"[13] Or, as parents put it, "What possessed you to *do* that?" (The answer is that Brain 2.0 is still in "beta" testing. It won't be complete for years yet.)

At this time of your life, not only is your brain urging you to think in original ways, you are also able to connect more socially. When you do that, you are ab-

> "Adolescence is a golden age for innovation because it is during this time of growth and change that the [brain] shifts in the reward centers . . . encourages creative thought and drives adolescents to explore the world in new ways."—Daniel J. Siegel (1957–), USC psychology professor, author[d]

sorbing more impressions, more data from people. This data is raw material that becomes ideas and impressions. Whether you realize it or not, you're using those ideas and impressions and combining them with your own concepts. This makes you an amazing source of creativity.

You haven't been aware of why you're thinking and acting differently, but you have been aware of changes in yourself since you were younger.

Teens' Views on their Creativity as Children

Question 3: "How is your creativity different than when you were younger?"

"I know how to express myself in more ways."—Ashley, 17, California

"It has a freer reign in my life; it's more creative, and I have more skill to set it free."—Skye, 18, California

"It's much more abstract."—Dakota, 17, California

"When I was younger I'd use my imagination. Now I just connect a couple of ideas together."—Angel, 16, California

"My ideas have changed and become more complex."—A.J., 16, California

"In my case I think I've gotten more creative than when I was younger. I've been exposed to more situations and as a result have new ideas and more things to be creative about than ever."—Darius, 16, Florida

"I'm bolder and more imaginative."—Justice, 17, California

"My creativity today has more ideas than I had when I was young."— Klarissa, 16, California

"When I was younger, I used to think I was creative, but I was really just following others. Now I use other people's ideas and build on them while using my own ideas."—Nina, 15, New York⁶

Well, you're not that child (kid) any more. You're a teen (or a little beyond) and you've created at a certain level before, but you're on a new adventure now. Adventuring means you'll discover some courage and some spirit and some unknown events and some danger and some exhilaration. Your teen years will be filled with all of these. You can set up a "creative climate" for yourself at the perfect time you need one, to establish a creative threshold into your future.

At the Intersection of Teens and the Creative Process

Ira Glass (1959–), the host of *This American Life* on Public Radio International, gave this talk to his audience on August 18, 2009:

> Nobody tells this to people who are beginners and I really wish somebody had told this to me. All of us who do creative work, we get into it because we have good taste.
>
> But it's like there is this gap. For the first couple years that you're making stuff, what you're making isn't so good. It's not that great. It's trying to be good, it has ambition to be good, but it's not that good. But your taste, the thing that got you into the game, is still killer. And your taste is good enough that you can tell what you're making is kind of a disappointment to you. A lot of people never get past that phase. They quit. Everybody I know who does interesting, creative work, they went through years where they had really good taste and they could tell that what they were making wasn't as good as they wanted it to be. They knew it fell short. Everybody goes through that.
>
> And if you are just starting out or if you are still in this phase, you gotta know it's normal and the most important thing you can do is do a lot of work. Do a huge volume of work. Put yourself on a deadline so that every week or every month you know you're going to finish one story. It is only by going through a volume of work that you're going to catch up and close that gap. And the work you're making will be as good as your ambitions.
>
> I took longer to figure out how to do this than anyone I've ever met. It takes a while. It's gonna take you a while. It's normal to take a while. You just have to fight your way through that.[14]

Can you relate to any part of this speech? Did it bring up any feelings? Did it "hit you in the heart" or "where you live?" Did Mr. Glass's words help you? (You can listen to Glass give this talk about taste and creativity at jamesclear.com/ ira-glass-failure. Scroll down to the video.)

Chances are if you are reading this book, you sensed the impact of Mr. Glass's words before you ever read them here. I wanted you to read them because what Glass said was so true for me as a teen. What he described was *exactly* what happened to me in high school. I started writing little articles based on the style of a satiric columnist who was very popular at the time. I wasn't frustrated that I couldn't make my pieces funny; I could and did. What drove me nuts was that they were so much *like* the columnist's pieces. I wanted mine to be original, I wanted them to be really good, I wanted people to notice, and I wanted all this at fifteen years old! I also had this notion that if I couldn't do it perfectly the first time, then I had no talent, and it was pointless to keep trying. (Any part of that last sentence sound familiar?) So I got frustrated and quit. I sidelined my writing; except for assignments and letters, I didn't write for years.

I wish someone had told me then what Mr. Glass said in his talk. Maybe I wouldn't have listened, but maybe those words might have made an impact. (By the way, he's wrong about being the oldest person to get this message. I know how old he is and I know my age; I got it *way* later than he did. At least I finally got it.)

I suspect that many of you reading this have been just as frustrated with the gap between your taste and your creative output as Glass and I were. To be honest, it was my frustration at fifteen that was my primary motivation for writing this book. I want to save you some time, to prevent at least some of you from going through the same angst, of misunderstanding that when you start out, "copying" another's style is not only perfectly acceptable, it's *how you learn*. It's a necessary step to creating your own style, your own way of communicating to the world what you want, and doing that authentically. Be clear: you're not less authentic because you can't do what you love well; you're simply less skilled. That's all that's going on, so cut yourself some slack. Toss a little compassion your way.

Also, you are more than likely confusing your taste, which Glass referred to, with your judgment. This is very common with teens. (To be honest, the judgment capability of your brain isn't fully formed until you're about twenty-four.

! The Difference between Taste and Judgment

(Expressions of) *taste* describe internal states and preferences. No one can argue with your taste because it's personal. It's your choice and you're unique in how you express it. *You don't need to defend your taste.*

(Expressions of) *judgment* assert the truth of things or the wisdom of a course of action. *Judgments have to rely on evidence.* People have a right to challenge your judgment.— Vincent Ryan Ruggio, *The Art of Thinking*[f]

That is why brain researchers stretch the adolescent time span from twelve to twenty-four years old.)[15]

Everyone's taste is personal. No one has the right to criticize you for it—although they do and will, as if you haven't already noticed! We all like what we like and hate what we do. That's fine.

Where teens get in trouble is that they judge aspects of their lives from an incorrect stance. As you read earlier, sound judgment is not a strength for teens. (Not that you get to blame your mistakes of judgment on your brain; it simply helps to know what's going on with it and to create ways to manage the gap between your ability to judge and your choices.)

The first place you need to manage that gap is in judging yourself. Right now choose something you're *really* bad at doing. It won't be hard because no one—child, teen, or adult—on this planet is good at doing everything. (Even if we were, when would we get the time to do it all?)

OK, you've thought of something you're bad at. Now, by tomorrow, you need to be *good* at doing this "thing," this activity. You need to be good enough to get into a contest and place at least second. What? Not possible?

Why? Oh, because you're not good at it yet? And you can't be good by tomorrow? Now you get the point here. It's no biggie for you to say you can't do this. Hopefully, it hasn't hurt your pride or self-esteem to be involved in this little experiment because usually when you're bad at something, it isn't a big deal. (Unless you're not good at math—that's problematic.)

Now, look at, think about the things or activities you really want to do, have some skill in, have maybe gotten some recognition for. Pick one. Now, get good at *that* by tomorrow, enough to win that second place prize.

Can you do it? (Maybe some of you already have.) But if you can't, how do you feel about it? Probably not so calm as you were about the other activity you didn't do well. On this activity you judge yourself, and if you're a typical teen (and who says you are?), you probably feel much worse about not being good at this. Your judgment about how good you "should" be at this point in your life is faulty. (Not just because you're a teen, by the way; most people's judgment is not good—not accurate—when assessing themselves.)

First off, you don't have enough information to be able to be a good judge. Second, unless you've been a ballerina since three years old and you practice five or six days a week (substitute any activity for ballet and use the same time frame), you simply haven't had enough *time* to get good.

Malcolm Gladwell, a sociologist who writes about striving and success, says that it takes a person ten years or 10,000 hours of investment in a skill to master it.[16] Those skills span from clothing design to forestry management. They include perfecting the art of negotiation to baking superb soufflés.

Ten years?? Yup. So if you're fourteen, that means you would have had to start at four years old and put in 10,000 hours to master your activity. Here's the math on that: There are 168 hours in a week. If you sleep 56 hours a week (8 hours x 7 days) that leaves you with 113 hours. Take away 30 (6 hours x 5 days) school hours and you have 83 hours. By the time you deduct hours for travel, homework, eating, grooming, chores, TV, video games, surfing the web, hanging out with friends and family, texting, being at worship, and a few miscellaneous hours, you'll probably be left with at *most* 12 to 15 hours a week. (I did the math twice.)

You have those 12 to 15 hours to practice Buddhist basketball or Goth guitar or Sith skateboarding or Godzilla graphic design or caramel castles. Multiply 12 hours/week times 52 weeks/year, you'd only be able to practice 644 hours annually. You'd have those 644 hours, however, only if you were consistent, took no vacations or other time off, and there were no emergencies or changes in your schedule. (And how likely is that?)

You can look at the figures: ten years of 644 hours adds up to 6,440 hours, which means you're still less than two-thirds of the way to becoming a master at whatever you're doing.

By the way, having twelve to fifteen hours to practice weekly not only assumes you'll have no glitches in your practice hours, it also assumes you have an almost ideal "creative climate"—all the support and space and finances you need. Only you probably won't. Maybe there's no room to do your favorite activity at home. Maybe you need lessons or a new instrument and can't afford either, or you dislike your teacher's style if you can afford one. Maybe your family makes fun of what you do or you have a little or big brother who messes with your stuff. Any of these and more are going to cut deeply into the time you spend practicing what you love.

As Gladwell notes,

Ten thousand hours is an *enormous* amount of time. It's all but impossible to reach that number all by yourself by the time you're a young adult. You have to have parents to encourage and support you. You can't be poor because if you have to hold down a part-time job on the side to make ends meet, there won't be time left in the day to practice enough. In fact, most people can reach that number only if they get into some kind of a special program . . . or they get some kind of extraordinary opportunity that gives them a chance to put in those hours.[17]

If you pay attention to what Glass said and Gladwell wrote (plus my math), you'll realize that you will not be able to achieve mastery quickly. In fact, you can bypass the idea that you *need* to achieve it that fast—that there's something wrong with you if you don't. Glass is right about the process; Gladwell is correct about the time span.

To be excellent at anything, even in an area in which you have talent or possibly genius, not only do you have to put in the time and do a lot of work, you have to accept that your work *may not be good for a long time*. Chances are you are not going to be an expert at anything by the time you get out of high school.

As Glass said, this is normal.[18] As Gladwell wrote, this is what happens on the road to mastery.[19] What I'm saying—and writing—is, *get off your own case*. You'll get to where you want; if you keep going, you will. So ride a compassionate pony to the castle you're seeing up ahead. The pony won't get you there any faster, but

Mastery: 10,000 hours spent doing what you love.

you'll have a much smoother ride and you'll be able to appreciate the landscape as you pass through.

It's also true that it'll take stamina to go through the process of mastery. In the Middle Ages, becoming a master worked like this: Boys or girls (who were allowed to be trained as seamstresses,[20] tailors, makers of soft shoes, bakers, and makers of paper and books)[21] would be apprenticed to an expert who was a pro, a master, at a skill—baking, blacksmithing, tanning, shoemaking (cobbling), whatever.[22] These children, who might be as young as ten were often teens, would spend *seven years* as an apprentice,[23] day in and out. They lived in the master's household and their "pay" was room and board. After seven years as apprentices, the "young man" or "young lady," who was between seventeen and twenty-two years old, became a "journeyman."[24] (The term *journeywoman* doesn't seem to exist—big shock.) This meant they left the master's home, often to travel to continue their training. Or they might marry, but they were not allowed to have apprentices.[25]

As a journeyman, a man could register with the appropriate town organization or "guild" and could make a wage, but could not take on apprentices.[26] Women were not required to register, but they made much less money and often had to give up their trade when they married.[27] (Or they might work from home.) Men and women spent *four to seven more years* as journeymen, learning their trades and turning out superior bread, dresses, or shoes—for horses or humans.[28] If they had learned all they could and were making excellent horse harnesses or men's clothing (nearly as good as their masters), they *could* become masters if the guilds accepted their work. Many journeymen did not pass the guilds' tests and never set up their own workshops.[29]

Notice that this mastery didn't happen in a few months, certainly not in the teen years from twelve to nineteen. The process of mastery took stamina; paying attention; doing the degrading, menial work; and making piece after piece until they got it right, often under the direction of a grouchy, impatient master or mistress. What was even tougher was that often the boys or girls didn't even *choose* the skill they were mastering! (People didn't get a lot of choice in their work in those days; children had none.) At least in this century you get the chance to pursue what you love doing.

You can't speed up the process to get good at it, however. Yes, Mozart was writing music as a child. There's some debate, however, about his reputation as a child prodigy.[30] Mozart put in years of work in music before he wrote his first symphony at eight.[31] (Also, his father wrote down his early works and probably improved them.) By eight, when Mozart wrote his first symphony, he had already spent over six thousand hours practicing! He did not finish his earliest "master work" until he was twenty-one; he'd already put in ten years of composing practice.[32] So make sure you don't use Mozart or anyone like him as a standard to make you feel worse about yourself and your lack of mastery at your age.

Sure, it's not particularly fun to not be as good as you want in the beginning and middle stages. (Glass told you that many people quit.) It's a blow to your pride; it's frustrating, even maddening to try so hard to be excellent and to not reach that goal—on the first, on the second, even on the ninety-third try. Everyone knows that if you are trying to become very good, expert at a skill, an art, a life passion, as the saying goes, you gotta keep "paying your dues." Actually, *going through this process is the dues*, though it takes courage to keep paying them, particularly when you can't see the "payoff."

Whatever it is that you're striving for, in the way you're approaching solving the problems of your art or sport or science or skill, it's connected to creativity.

Because even with all the electronics, which makes it easier for us to communicate, bank more efficiently, make reservations, send photos, set up appointments, check out the weather and the latest game scores, order food, and send gifts—with all of that capability in hand-held devices—there's no way around the fact that creativity can't be ordered up by entering the right user name and password. In other words, "There's no app for that."

(As some of you know, all those apps rely on codes based on algorithms that are programmed into our phones and laptops and iPods.) Creativity can't be programmed. If you'll pardon the pun, creativity marches to the beat of a different Hummer.

No one yet has invented a way to shortcut the process of making art or getting an invention accepted in the marketplace (despite what happens on those business "reality" shows).

Because mastery takes so long, you had best select a skill, an art, a sport, a training, or a professional track you want to devote ten years—and more—of your life to. When you get into the 3,417th hour of your "apprenticeship" and you did it all wrong that day, and you got reprimanded, and the pay stinks, and you're missing your friends, the only motivation that will keep you from quitting is your own love of the "game."

This love is the primary item you have to bring to the mastery table. You're acquiring the skills of what you love through solving the problems (the creative part), and in 6,583 hours—or less than seven years—these will add up to give you what you've wanted all along: the ability to match your own taste.

CREATIVITY'S ROOTS AND BRANCHES

The Big Picture

This chapter will present a *very* brief history of creativity. You're already familiar with the myths surrounding creativity from chapter 1, so you know that humans have been fascinated by creativity for millennia.

In ancient China, India, and Greece, people did not believe that mankind was actually capable of creating.[1] Muses were supposed to have inspired humans to create.[2] In the European Dark Ages and Middle Ages, pretty much anyone who had an original idea, whether in the arts, music, literature, science, or medicine, attributed it to the divine.[3] If a man's "divine" new idea clashed with official Catholic Church teachings, however, as Galileo Galilei's (1564–1642) did when he supported Nicolaus Copernicus's (1473–1543) theory that the earth revolved around the sun, he could be declared a heretic, forced to recant, and put under house arrest.[4]

During the Renaissance (fourteenth through seventeenth centuries), mankind's view of creativity shifted. For the first time, people recognized that certain exceptional people were themselves creative, and the concept of divine inspiration lost significance.[5] This led to appreciation of artists such as Michelangelo Buonarroti, Sandro Botticelli, Titian (a.k.a. Tiziano Vechelli), and Raphael (a.k.a. Raffaelo Sanzio da Urbino), all from Italy. Of course, Leonardo da Vinci (Italy) led the pack with his original contributions to art, science, and technology. Notably, all these men were from various parts of what we now call Italy, which hints at the incredible creative climate present in those regions during the Renaissance.

By the 1700s, people realized that imagination was key to creativity.[6] Genius was also recognized, and a distinction was made between talent and genius.[7] However, creativity itself received little attention until after Darwin published his groundbreaking work on evolution. Scientists observed how much individual

Jesters: symbols of fun and creativity in the Middle Ages.

differences mattered, and one result was establishing a link between intelligence and creativity.[8]

There were no scientific studies on creativity at this point, which is not surprising, as psychology itself was not a science until just before the twentieth century. In 1926, Graham Wallas proposed one of the first models of creative thought. It involved preparation, incubation, illumination, and verification (for more details, see page 37). Wallas did not use the word *creativity* anywhere in his model. That was because he had never heard of it. No one had. It didn't come into use until a year later (see page 37).

Except for Abraham Maslow's and Carl Rogers's papers and speeches on self-actualized—meaning reaching one's full potential—and specialized talent creativity,[9] the study of creativity waned from 1927 until 1950. (No doubt the

Wallas's Problem Solving Model

Graham Wallas (1858–1932), English sociologist, social psychologist, and cofounder of the London School of Economics, developed the following model, which, for almost ninety years, has remained the best analysis of the creative process.

Preparation: the person focuses on a problem, looking for a solution

Incubation: the problem is internalized in unconscious mind; seems like nothing's happening (includes *intimation*; i.e., person gets a "feeling" that a solution is "on its way")

Illumination (or insight): creative solution/idea "bursts" forth from preconscious to conscious mind

Verification: the idea is validated, elaborated, and applied[a]

Thumbnail Biography of Alfred North Whitehead

In 1927, Alfred North Whitehead (1861–1947), an English mathematician and philosopher, coined the word *creativity* in his Gifford Lectures at the University of Edinburgh, Scotland. Whitehead later published the term *creativity* in his book *Process and Reality* (1928/1978).[b]

Great Depression and World War II stalled it some.) At the half-century mark, two pivotal events revolutionized the field of creativity.

The Modern Era

The first event that changed the direction of creative exploration occurred at the American Psychological Association (APA) convention in 1950. The APA's new president, Joy Paul (J. P.) Guilford, protested that "psychologists have seriously neglected the study of the creative aspects of personality."[10] At that time, less than 2 percent of all psychological research focused on creativity; Guilford's speech launched serious scientific studies into creativity. J. P. Guilford, who challenged psychologists to expand their creative research, explored the differences between convergent and divergent thinking.[11]

As psychologists responded to Guilford's challenge on creativity, many were unaware of a breakthrough process that had been developing on Madison Avenue since the 1940s. Alex Osborn, co-owner of the successful New York advertising agency BBDO, led many creative teams during his career. Osborn had invented numerous techniques to encourage his teams' creativity. In 1953, Osborn described a practical and effective creativity model, the Creative Problem Solving (CPS) process, in his book *Applied Imagination*.[12] In an earlier book, *How to Think Up*, Osborn had described a key technique of this creative model—the most famous creative technique in the world: brainstorming.[13]

Osborn, who traveled regularly from his agency in New York City to his home in Buffalo, began collaborating with Dr. Sidney Parnes on further developing CPS. In 1954, he and Parnes established the Creative Education Foundation at Buffalo State College.[14] Osborn also cofounded the Creative Problem Solving Institute (CPSI), which promotes the longest-running creativity conference in the world.[15]

CPS has been researched since its inception in the 1950s, and it continues to be the most well-known technique used in education and business. (CPS will be described further in chapters 9 and 10.)

The Larger Scene

Since 1955, CPSI has held training programs in CPS. By 1967, Buffalo State College had begun to offer graduate courses in CPS, and in 1975 it offered a master

Creative Problem Solving

Alex Osborn (1888–1966) was the inventor of brainstorming and the father of Creative Problem Solving (CPS). He was cofounder of the Creative Education Foundation and the Creative Problem Solving Institute. Osborn, an actual "mad man," knew the financial potential of CPS. Instead of copyrighting CPS, however, Osborn chose to put it into the public domain. You might say that Osborn utilized "open source" long before the term was coined.[c]

of science degree based on the study of CPS. In 2002 that program expanded into an international master's (MS), the only graduate degree program in creativity in the world.[16]

There were many other creativity researchers who were exploring new aspects of creativity. One, Edward de Bono, developed lateral thinking using a metaphor of Six Thinking Hats, whose individual colors were linked to certain *directions*: blue (managing), white (information), red (emotions), black (discernment), yellow (optimistic response), and green (creativity). A person could actually or metaphorically switch "hats" as he went into a new thinking "direction."[17] Arthur Koestler coined the word *bisociation*, which means combining two very different items to determine if they will form something original and useful, that is, creative.[18]

Margaret Boden called creative people who were well known "h-creative" (*h* for historical). Those who were unknown she named "p-creative" (*p* for personal).[19] Robert Sternberg proposed a three-facet model of creativity consisting of intelligence, cognitive (thinking) style, and personality motivation. He concluded that "people are creative by virtue of a combination of intellectual, stylistic, and personality attributes."[20] Mark Runco observed that there are "implicit theories of creativity," that is, theories that exist about creativity in each person's mind. These function as a model for each person and also help to define creativity for others (e.g., children's creativity is "adventurous, enthusiastic, active, curious, artistic, and imaginative").[21] Dean K. Simonton conjectured that chance plays a role in producing innovative ideas and products and in how society accepts them. He called this phenomenon "chance-configuration theory."[22]

One key researcher, who became known as the "Father of Creativity" for his prolific and groundbreaking work on creativity, was Dr. E. Paul Torrance.[23] He conducted the first scientific tests of creativity on human beings. You may be surprised to discover what those first "creative guinea pigs" did professionally. (The answer is at the end of this chapter. In the meantime, see if you can guess who they were. Hint: They were not artists or inventors of any kind.)

However, Torrance's most prominent work focused on a segment of the population that had no professions at all—children. He created the Torrance Tests of Creative Thinking (TTCT), which included all sorts of verbal and figural (drawing) puzzles.[24] Through the TTCT, Torrance wanted to determine the following:

1. Fluency: How many relevant, meaningful ideas were generated? (You want lots.)
2. Originality: How statistically rare were these responses? (The rarer, the better.)
3. Elaboration: How detailed were the responses? (The more detailed, the better.)

Definitions of Creativity: The Four Cs Model

James C. Kaufman and Ronald A. Beghetto developed this model:

Mini-c: learning that is meaningful and transformational to the individual

Little c: creative expression and everyday problem solving and creative expression

Pro-c: creativity used by people in their professions and vocations (these people are not well known)

Big C: creativity significant in its field (e.g., famous art and inventions)[d]

In order to observe how these children developed their creativity, Torrance re-interviewed them every five years until they were well into adulthood; this method is called a "longitudinal study."[25]

During this expansive era of creativity research, various definitions of creativity were offered. Some are still valid; others have been disproved or updated.

Setting the Tone

As promised, here is the profession of the subjects on whom Torrance conducted the first scientific study on creativity: test pilots, and to top that, test pilots in Texas. (Did you guess correctly? Did you get close?) Torrance was trying to determine if and how pilots would use creativity if/when faced with an emergency (a bail out, crash landing, parachuting behind enemy lines, capture, etc.). This study took place right after Guilford challenged psychologists to increase research into creativity, and so it qualified as the first scientific research on creativity.[26]

By the time the 1970s arrived, creativity researchers had reached five conclusions: (1) Everyone is creative in his or her own way. (2) Everyone can learn to solve problems better. (3) Creativity skills can be taught, so . . . (4) People can become more creative. (5) Creative Problem Solving works.[27]

CREATIVITY GUIDELINES AND ASSESSMENT

Guidelines: The Big Picture

There are no rules for creativity because there is no formula, which scientists call an *algorithm* (al-go-rith-im; the last two syllables are pronounced "rhythm"), no way to add a + b + c and achieve a creative result. Instead, creativity relies on heuristics (hyer-is-tiks), or guidelines. If there *was* a creative formula, that would mean that there would be no room for exploration, and exploration and experimentation are at the heart of creativity.

The guidelines that creativity follows are different than rules. In science, rules are based on algorithms, or formulas. If there are no formulas, the path to solutions can be scary. There are not going to be definite signposts to measure how you're doing. Without the benefit of formulas, researchers have examined what happens *around* creativity and learned that certain conditions—in the mind and the outer environment—are necessary for creativity to thrive. While creativity itself cannot be taught or transferred, there are learnable skills that will help you increase your creative output.

Guidelines: Creative Process

This is a description of the *creative process*, not necessarily the path to a creative product. You might not get a creative product every time you're involved in the process. You might not even get a workable idea. These are facts that are essential for you to know. This is the first guideline for creativity: you can't predict the results.

Because you can't predict, this is when you need to call on your *tolerance of ambiguity*, which you could call a tolerance of the unknown. You'll not only have to accept that you don't know what you'll get; you'll have to tolerate that you can't control *when* and *how* you'll get it. The perk to being willing to tolerate ambiguity is that you'll get more comfortable not knowing. That comfort will increase your creative capacity.

The next creative tool is called the *tolerance of complexity*. Often, after you've brainstormed (or ideated), you have too many ideas to handle, or you wonder how to sort them, or there are so many directions to go, so the process gets—complex. OK, now pull out your magic *tolerance of complexity* cape and flap it over the situation. Let all those ideas and questions and directions mill around for a while. Don't look for "premature closure"—a fancy way for saying, "Don't take the first answers you get." Accept that chaos is what's supposed to be happening now. It's like cleaning a closet jammed with winter clothes, sports equipment, and all kinds of junk. After you've pulled everything out, it's all over the floor. Closet cleaning is a metaphor for tolerance of complexity. Leave the contents of your "mental closet" strewn around for a while. You'll get to sorting later, after you use the last creativity tool.

Now it's time to take a nap. No kidding. When you've had to make a tough decision, people probably advised you to "sleep on it." Or maybe when you were frustrated with an exasperating problem, you walked away. In the creative process, sleeping or walking away is not avoiding the problem. It's giving *incubation* a chance to get its hands on your ideas or wrestle with your problem. Your subconscious brain needs this "vacation" to sort your ideas, mix them back up, and come up with a new answer, unlike what your conscious mind would have devised. The answer may be a perfect solution. At the very least, it will give you a new direction. (If you don't want to take a nap, then take a walk or a run. Take a relaxing shower or bath. Wash the dishes, sweep the floor, do any task that's easy or habitual for you, to keep your body busy and allow your brain to do the real work.) You can't rush this process. Think of it like growing plants. Once you sow seeds, you can't keep digging into the soil to see how much they've grown!

In addition to these creative tools, you will need to have an *openness to experience*, which means exactly like it sounds. Finally, you need time to ideate and develop your ideas. The entire process of creativity cannot be rushed. (Quick! You have ten seconds to come up with five ideas for making your school better. One, two, three . . . ten. Time's up. How did *that* work?) The last requirement for creativity is a nonjudgmental environment. You'll learn much more detail about nonjudgment throughout the book. At this point, simply remember that judgment—from others and yourself—is an incredibly powerful deterrent to creativity.

Creativity Assessment

Unraveling Talented, Gifted, and Genius

These terms often confuse people when they consider who's creative. You know now that everyone is creative, but would it surprise you to know that *everyone* is talented? Each person is. You are. It's more accurate to say, however, that everyone is born with strengths in certain areas. We usually reserve the word *talented* for people who have a greater degree of ability in a certain area such as music, design, or dance.[1] In fact, when most people refer to a talented person, they almost always mean someone who has ability in the visual or performing arts. They are right, but they need to include people who are adept at math, people who are good with words (either written or spoken), those with superior ability for cooking, gardening, caring for animals, for athletics, for organization, even for listening to people's problems.

Gifted is the next term on the list and this one's easy. A gifted person has high intelligence determined by a certain cutoff point on an IQ test, usually 120 to 130.[2] Of course, gifted people will also have some talent in one or two areas, but their overall *intelligence* is what distinguishes them from a person with an unusually high *talent* in one field.

A *genius* is a person with an IQ of 140 or above.[3] Einstein is the one person everyone can point to and call a legitimate genius. However, we often call a person with exceptional talent in one area a genius.

So you can see how these terms have gotten all mixed up. We've said that someone is *a genius* in the kitchen, or he has a *talent* for getting into trouble, or that she is *gifted* with children. Of course, if we were using our terms more correctly, we'd say the chef has a cooking talent, the troublemaker needs help identifying and developing his actual talents, and the woman's intelligence level has nothing to do with her ability to relate to children. The truth is, the terms *talent*, *gifted*, and *genius* have been used as synonyms for each other for so long that it's unrealistic to expect people to change how they habitually use them. Now that you know the difference, however, maybe once in a while you'll remember to use them appropriately.

Time is another factor that confuses the talent/gifted/genius issue. If you meet a seven-year-old boy who plays the piano, he might have only an average music talent. If you meet him when he's twenty, after he's spent his childhood playing the piano twenty to twenty-five hours a week, he'll have accumulated well over 10,000 hours. When you hear him play you might call him a musical genius. He might or might not be one; what he has demonstrated is years of dedication and discipline to practice all those hours. He developed whatever innate musical talent he had as much as he could. He simply kept playing, and anyone gets better with practice.

You see how challenging it would be to determine this pianist's innate talent? It would depend on when you met him.

To summarize: You and everyone else have talents, you and many others may be talented to a superior degree in one area, some of you are gifted, and a few of you are geniuses. Whichever one or combination of these describes you, remember, you *always* have the capacity for creativity.

Tools for Assessing

How can creativity be assessed? Isn't assessment a synonym for testing? How can you test a concept like creativity, which can't be seen, heard, tasted, touched, smelled, or sensed in any way?

To begin, assessment is *not* a synonym for testing or for measurement. The best synonym for assessment is "evaluation,"[4] which means looking at what is true about a topic or situation. Since truth is the goal of an assessment, or evaluation, there are no right or wrong answers when evaluating. While it's true that everything can't be measured, it's difficult to think of a subject that can't be assessed or evaluated, which includes creativity.

Now that you know what assessment is, you're probably wondering how you'd go about using it to evaluate creativity.

One approach is to utilize the Four Ps.[5] Obviously, you can't measure creative people, but you can evaluate how they go about the creative process. You can also assess how they feel when creating. Of course, you can measure their creative products by applying relevant criteria. The truth is, you evaluate creative products every day. You go to movies and decide if they've been well acted, well directed, well written. You loved, hated, or were bored by the film. You either gasped at or were underwhelmed by the CGI (computer-generated imagery) effects. And a musical's memorable only if you're humming its tunes as you leave the theater.

You often apply similar criteria for assessing music, video games, or phone apps. You're constantly evaluating clothes, websites, and cars. The trickiest part of creativity assessment, however, is evaluating *process*. Since process involves so much trial and error, does it make sense to say that a process that involved the most errors was the most creative? (If this is true, then Thomas Edison, who experimented with 10,000 materials to make the filament for the first light bulb, won the prize for most creative process!) What if a trial-and-error process *doesn't* lead to a creative result? Does that mean the process wasn't creative?

If you think the trial-and-error process is creative no matter what the result, woo hoo! Using trial and error is creative *regardless of the outcome*. So you can see how tricky it would be to measure process by product.

Teens' Views on Measuring Creativity

Question 4: "How could everyone's creativity be measured?"

"People are creative in many ways; for instance, I build things, my acting friends create characters, and my brother films. Nobody's creativity should be measured; there are no limits."—Chandler, 13, Florida

"Many people aren't. Creativity is measured maybe by in how much [sic] different thoughts are than the [statistical] mean."—Skye, 18, California

"I think everyone is creative by the work of art or way of thinking. I don't think something original is creative. Creativity should be measured by originality."—Alicia, 16, California

"Creativity can't be measured, because it all applies to every aspect in life, no matter what age."—Sam, 16, California

"I think that some people are more creative than others. There are many different ways to test creativity. Giving people scenarios to get themselves through can test creativity."—Meagan, 16, California

"Everybody else is creative through their style and preferences. It could be measured by how well they are confident."—Shai, 16, California

"I think people are creative by choosing clothes, decorating their homes or creating music or art. Creativity could maybe be measured by giving people a problem and see now they solve it."—Sofia, 17, Minnesota

"Everyone is creative in their own ways. Writing, art, and music are all different mediums. Teens also use creativity to solve problems. It can be measured by how they solve their problems."—Aspen, 16, Florida

"Results of creativity could be measured, but so many facets may have to be specified."—Gregory, 18, Florida

"Everyone is creative in their own unique way. There is no single way to measure creativity."—Justin, 12, Florida[a]

In my questionnaire, I asked how creativity could be measured (see some answers on page 45). All the teens who responded that creativity *can't* be measured were correct. It can't. Twelve-year-old Justin from Florida went one better when he said that, "There is no single way to measure creativity." There are actually quite a few ways, Justin. There are literally hundreds of measures for creativity. Wait a minute, how can there be *hundreds* of measures to measure something that *can't be measured*? That makes no sense!

True, creativity *itself* cannot be measured; however, as you've already learned, creative *products* can be. Plus people's *style and approaches* to creativity can be measured.

By the way, for you to understand how assessments work, you'll need a tiny statistics lesson. (It'll be painless.) All assessments are built on two requirements (criteria): validity and reliability. An assessment is *valid* if it evaluates what it's supposed to. It's *reliable* if results are consistent over time. To illustrate: Pretend you and nine friends decide to go to dinner at a BBQ restaurant that's just opened—the PigOut Pantry. By the end of the meal, everyone agrees that the ribs and chicken, sides and desserts are terrific; the service good; and the prices reasonable. So two weeks later you all return. Everything is as satisfactory as the first time. A month later, on your third visit, all is still good, so you give it a "thumbs up," deciding that the PigOut will be your go-to spot for BBQ.

You get why PigOut Pantry made the cut, right? All ten of you rated the food, service, and prices—all *valid* criteria for evaluating a restaurant. (You didn't eat there because you liked the waitpersons' *shoes*. It would make no sense to rate a restaurant on that irrelevant detail.) The fact that on all three visits, the PigOut Pantry offered the *same* BBQ items in the same portions, at the same prices, served in a similar manner demonstrated that the PigOut delivers a *reliable* dining experience.

Let's change the scenario. What if at your third visit you discover the PigOut is now a sushi bar? Whoa. Or PigOut still serves BBQ, but the portions are *way* smaller *and* the prices are jacked up—what a rip-off! Or the portion sizes and prices are the same, but the service is rude, sloppy, and slow. No tip that night. Even though in each scenario, only one of the criteria changed, you are bummed. The PigOut just lost ten BBQ-loving customers.

*Every*one looks for validity and reliability in life; there's simply less emotion in using a scientific method, such as an assessment, for evaluation.

Alicia, Meagan, Shai, Skye, Sofia, Aspen, Justin, and Gregory's responses about measuring creativity came closest to understanding that *certain aspects* of creativity *can* be measured (see page 47). These are (1) creativity styles and (2) how people could use their creativity in the future.

The assessments—sometimes referred to as measures—are important because they will help you find a direction for using your creativity in ways that work best for you.

Select Teen Views about Creativity Assessments

Alicia: "Creativity should be measured by originality."

Meagan: "There are many different ways to test creativity. Giving people scenarios to get themselves through can test creativity."

Shai: "It could be measured by how well they are confident."

Skye: "Creativity is measured maybe by how many different thoughts are than the [statistical] mean."

Sofia: "Creativity could maybe be measured by giving people a problem and see now they solve it."

Aspen: "[Creativity] can be measured by how they solve their problems."

Justin: "There is no single way to measure creativity."

Gregory: "Results of creativity could be measured, but so many facets may have to be specified."[b]

Measuring Creative Thinking

FourSight, the Kirton Adaption-Innovation Inventory (KAI), and Torrance Tests of Creative Thinking (TTCT) are included in this chapter because their validity and reliability are well established.

In addition to reading an explanation of each assessment, you'll find websites, links, and other information. Sometimes books or other materials are available. Also included is information about who developed the assessment and for what purpose. If available, directions for taking the measure—how, where, in what time frame—are provided, along with any prices (current as of September 2014).

FourSight

This assessment will give you insight into your strengths in *creative problem solving*. FourSight was developed in 2004 at Buffalo State College by Dr. Gerard Puccio,

Creativity Assessments

FourSight

Kirton Adaption-Innovation Inventory

Torrance Tests of Creative Thinking[c]

department head of the International Center for Studies in Creativity.[6] FourSight was developed to assist people in business, organizations, and communities in understanding how people think when solving problems creatively. FourSight is also enormously useful for putting together teams. The premise of FourSight is that everyone solves problems, of course, but to solve them, everyone uses one (or two) of four thinking modes. You may be an Ideator, who generates ideas and makes connections; a Clarifier, who identifies the right problems to solve; a Developer, who finds the most elegant solutions for problems; or an Implementer, who puts solutions into action. Usually, you will be strong in two thinking modes; however, you will discover your aptitude in all four areas.

If you take this assessment, you'll answer thirty-six questions, and will soon know your approach to creative problem solving, as well as how you will fit in a team situation.[7]

The truth is, you're going to be working in many groups in your lifetime (you've probably already been in school groups), and it is invaluable for you to know how you work best in them. If you ever get into any kind of management—business, hospitality, retail, and theater are examples—you will know how to use your knowledge of people's creative problem solving styles to create effective teams that will be capable of producing excellent results.[8]

For more information, go to www.foursightonline. Cost: $25.

Kirton Adaption-Innovation Inventory

Developed by Dr. Michael J. Kirton, the Kirton Adaption-Innovation Inventory (KAI) doesn't ask the question, "*Are* people creative?" Kirton started with the premise that everyone is creative. What the KAI assesses is "*How* are people creative?"[9]

Unfortunately, you cannot take this valid, reliable, and effective assessment online nor can you have it mailed to you. Only certified KAI professionals can buy, administer, and score the KAI. Because the training to become a KAI professional is pricey, there aren't many available and they only administer the KAI to groups. The good news is that if and when you locate a certified KAI professional, your KAI index—or assessment—would be part of his or her fee.

So what's the point of discussing the KAI if you can't take it? Because it's simply too important a creativity measure to ignore. And because someday you might be in a group—a creativity class, a work seminar, a weekend retreat—that offers the KAI and you can take it. Or you might meet a KAI professional. In the meantime, here's an explanation of how KAI works.

The KAI measures the creative approaches people use. Dr. Kirton chose the words *adaptor* and *innovator* to describe these approaches (Adaption-Innovation Inventory—duh).[10] You almost certainly know what innovators are—OK, here's a refresher—they generate original ideas, create original products, and make breakthrough discoveries. Adaptors are people who modify, develop, and improve those ideas, products, and discoveries. Of course, many people believe that the innovator has the "cooler" role. Adaptors, however, are just as essential to creative production.

For example, some long-ago caveman innovator created the wheel. Since then, adaptors have made other improvements to it. Another example: Consider how much planes have changed since the Wright brothers. If creative adaptors didn't exist, aviation would have ended with the first powered plane, the Wright Flyer I.[11] Unless you were willing and able to learn how to fly *that* particular model, you would never experience flight. The Wright Flyer I model had no room for passengers. (Of course, the Wright brothers themselves adapted ideas from other aviation inventors. They did, however, invent the flight control system, which played an enormous role in achieving the first manned flight. They were also smart enough to bring a photographer on-site to record that historic flight.[12])

If there were no creative adapters, then we would only have planes like the Wright brothers built. Our 747s, Learjets, rockets, and space vehicles would not exist. In one sense, of course, *all* inventions are adaptations of previous ones. Some inventions, however, are such divergent departures from what currently exists that we must call them innovative.

Here's how KAI works: A KAI certified professional hands you the KAI index. You rate yourself according to a series of statements. (These statements have been carefully worded to eliminate as much bias as possible.) The KAI professional scores your index. Your score will range from 32 to 160; you get 32 points for simply writing your name on the paper.[13] (There's a statistical reason for setting up the index this way, which isn't important for you to know.)

What *is* important is that the midpoint of the KAI (shown on a bar graph) is 98. People who score to the left of 98 are adaptors. The further left your score is on the bar, the more adaptive you are. People who score to the right are innovators, and, of course, if you score further right from 98, you're more innovative. (No one has ever scored 160, by the way—another statistical weirdie.)[14]

It's useful to know your approach to creativity, not only for you as an individual, but for understanding how you will fit into groups. For managers, knowing employee's KAI scores would assist them forming successful groups that will consist of both adaptors and innovators. If you are ever in a seminar, college, or at your job and the KAI is offered, jump at it.

Torrance Tests of Creative Thinking

The Torrance Tests of Creative Thinking (TTCT) are online, and what's even better, they're less than $10 each. The TTCT were developed by Dr. E. Paul

Creativity assessments shouldn't make you feel small.

Torrance in the 1970s to evaluate the level of people's creativity. Torrance began testing children, and when possible, he retested the same ones every five years until they were adults—some in their thirties. (When people are evaluated repeatedly over a long period of time, we call this *longitudinal*.[15]) Torrance was trying to determine if the tests they took as children predicted their creativity later in life.[16]

These tests have been backed by a great deal of research and they've been adapted and polished for all ages in the twenty-first century. There are Verbal and Figural assessments. On the Verbal portion, the test taker simply has to reflect on his or her own life. The Figural portion requires some simple drawing, but artistic ability is not being assessed; creativity is.

These are enjoyable assessments, so give them a try at ststesting.com/2005gifttct.html. Cost: $7.10 for student TTCT Figural booklet and scoring and $8.75 for student TTCT Verbal booklet and scoring.

Additional Assessments: Personality

The assessments in this section do not measure creativity per se. They look at personality characteristics. All have existed for years and all have been well researched.

True Colors

This assessment measures your personality and places you into one of four categories, each represented by a color.[17]

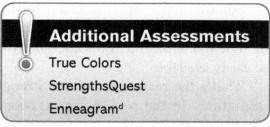

If you take the assessment and find your best "color," which represents your strengths, you can see how you operate in life, particularly toward problem solving. You can also understand that in groups you will need to be with people who have different colors as their strengths. This is necessary so that the group can see all aspects of solving a problem, achieving a goal, or making a project.

Even if you've already taken True Colors online, if you ever get a chance to take this assessment again in a group situation, do it! Usually, after everyone has discovered his or her true colors, the presenters will ask all the people of one color to form their own group. The presenters will then give the same challenge to all four color groups. When each group provides its solution to the challenge, the results are eye-opening. That's because all the people who are in one color group—let's call them the Purples—try to solve the challenge only from their viewpoint. They don't notice (or barely notice) other important details about the problem. They certainly ignore any solutions that don't fit their group's approach toward challenges. When the Purples' solution is compared to the other color groups' solutions, every group sees its own gaps and tunnel-vision thinking. When people realize how polarized their problem-solving approach is, most of them are chagrined. Then they usually find it hilarious. They understand how they need to include thinking from the other color groups, and the best way to achieve that is to have a variety of colors in a single group.[18]

To take True Colors, go to truecolorsintl.com/about-us/. Cost: $34.50.

StrengthsQuest

Before you read the description of StrengthsQuest (SQ) and how it can help you, would you try something very simple? Even if you're reading this book online, you probably have a pen or pencil and some scrap paper nearby. (Use a crayon, an old envelope, anything you've got—you're not going to keep this.) All you have to do is write your signature five times, as fast as you can. Then look at what you wrote. Now, put the pen or pencil in your *non*dominant hand and again, as fast as you can, write your signature five times. It's obvious that your dominant hand did a much better and faster job of signing your name (unless you're one of the rare ambidextrous people who *writes with both hands an equal amount of time*).[19]

So now what? Are you going to stop writing with your dominant hand and switch to your other one? Of course not—that doesn't make any sense. It's a waste of time to concentrate on something you don't do well when what you do well is so easily available.

That's the reasoning behind StrengthsQuest. Everyone is born with certain strengths.[20] In the past, however, people—and unfortunately, that included the education system—have focused on people improving their weaknesses. That strategy made about as much sense as asking people to write with their non-dominant hands. (By the way, this practice happened too often in schools until the 1970s. There was a notion that writing with the left hand was "bad." Forcing a left-hander to write with the right hand was a pointless and traumatic experience for many students, including my sister. The nuns tried for years to get her to use her right hand. It was awful and frustrating and it didn't work. She still writes with her left hand.)

Think about it: Isn't it easier and much more psychologically healthy for people to focus on their strengths? Of course. Does this mean people will never improve? Of course *not*. They will focus on getting *better at their strengths* instead of wasting time upgrading their weaknesses. This is a two-pronged truth: the first half is that *no* one has every strength. The second half is that no one is *supposed* to be "a well-rounded individual." Even if you singled out the most talented and accomplished people who ever lived (or are living now), you'd see how true this is. Let's look at two. Albert Einstein formulated the theory of relativity, which revolutionized the field of physics, and he articulated many insightful, meaning-ful observations about life. Now, imagine Einstein on a pro basketball court. How about being a hair stylist for the Oscars? Or look at Mother Teresa—a wonderful woman who not only helped the poor directly but also began and maintained an organization, which included worldwide fund-raising, to continue her charitable mission. Now picture Mother Teresa starring in a Broadway musical. Would *you* have paid $200 plus to see her wear a slinky costume, sing, dance, and spout funny lines? (I wouldn't.) She may have been declared a saint but she'd suck as a star.

The same is true of you. You already have some idea of what you're good at—and what you're not! If you aren't sure what you excel in, that's an excellent reason to take the StrengthsQuest. It is a very effective, well-researched assess-ment that will rate you according to thirty-four attributes, or "themes." When you get your "score," instead of a number, you'll receive your top five themes (of the thirty-four).[21] The *order* in which your themes are listed is very important. The top theme is your strongest and on down.

Here are some examples of StrengthsQuest themes: harmony, competition, discipline, communicator, positivity, plus twenty-nine others. In case you're won-dering how individualized the SQ is, the odds of any one person having the same top five themes as another person are only 1 in 240,000. Those odds mean that you will not be exactly like anyone else among your family, friends, or classmates. You are, for all practical purposes, unique.[22]

The thirty-four strengths are arranged in categories—or "domains" (headings): Executing, Influencing, Relationship Building, and Strategic Thinking. Returning to Einstein and Mother Teresa, can you predict which domains they would fit in? For Einstein, one would have to be Strategic Thinking. Relationship Building would have be one of Mother Teresa's domains. You've probably already figured out that if you have a top five, at least two of your themes will come from the same domain. Some people's strengths will cluster in only two domains.[23]

After you've taken SQ and learned your top five, what about the other twenty-nine themes? They're there, also arranged in order of influence on your life. In fact, if you repeat the SQ measure at *least three* years later, you will often have a few different themes in your top five. No, you haven't changed personalities; it's simply that you might, in your current circumstances, be drawing upon your second five themes. The top ten themes can rotate, but they will *never* include your bottom ten. Those themes at the bottom are *not* your strengths and never will be. Except for satisfying your curiosity, it isn't even important for you to know what your bottom ten are.

One last point: SQ is *not* a career test. It's not going to tell you that a certain list of themes is what you need to be a doctor, teacher, professional skateboarder, physicist, fashion designer, Broadway star, or saint (kidding). Any combination of themes can help you succeed in *any* career. For instance, if you want to be an army general and have no themes in the Strategic Thinking domain, you might figure you're out of luck. You know generals need to think strategically to move troops, plan campaigns, and win wars. You can still be a general, however, because you'll learn how to capitalize on your top five themes to reach that rank.[24]

To take StrengthsQuest, you'll need to buy a *new* copy of the book *Strengths-Quest: Discover and Develop Your Strengths in Academics, Career, and Beyond* by Donald O. Clifton and Edward Anderson (www.amazon.com/Strengths-Quest -Discover-Develop-Academics/dp/1595620117/ref=sr_1_1?s=books&ie=UTF 8&qid=1408603535&sr=1-1&keywords=strengthsquest+2nd+edition+with+id +code). Inside the front cover you'll see a code for the SQ website. *You need that code to take the assessment.* The code can only be used once, so if you buy a used copy, the code is useless. Cost: $50–$55 (as of August 2014).

Enneagram

This assessment determines which of nine personality types you fit into. Each type, in addition to being assigned a number from 1 to 9, also has a name.[25] Most people, however, refer to themselves by their numbers rather than the names.

Two Enneagram Books

Enneagram Made Easy: Discover the Nine Types of People by Renee Baron and Elizabeth Wagele. San Francisco: Harper, 1994, 161 pages. You'll enjoy reading and looking at the cartoons in this book, which describes the nine personality types of the Enneagram. You can learn all the basics about your personality type, as well as the other eight.

The Enneagram Advantage: Putting the Personality Types to Work in the Office by Helen Palmer and Paul B. Brown. New York: Random House, 1998, 282 pages. With this book, which describes the nine personalities in great depth, you'll see how they "work together"—literally.[e]

("I'm a 1." "He's a 7.") There is an additional component to your type, which will be explained after you take the assessment.

The name Enneagram (ANY-a-gram) stems from the Greek words *ennea* for "nine" and *gram* for "a drawing," so *Enneagram* means "a drawing with nine points." These points represent the nine personality types. The nine types are Ones (Perfectionists), Twos (Helpers), Threes (Achievers), Fours (Romantics/Dramatics), Fives (Observers), Sixes (Questioners), Sevens (Adventurers), Eights (Asserters), and Nines (Peacemakers).[26]

Here are two links for the Enneagram:

www.enneagramquiz.com/quiz.html
www.enneagramtest.net

(Note: Be careful Googling or Binging for other Enneagram links. I ended up in an ad vortex on one search.)

HeartMath

Would you be surprised to learn that even love can be assessed? While it's true that love itself cannot be measured, the energy the heart emits can be gauged.[27] The ability to measure heart energy shouldn't be earthshaking news; there has been biofeedback equipment since the 1970s. Researchers have determined that there are five heart "energy levels." In ascending order of vibrational strength,

Myers-Briggs Type Indicator

If you are familiar with the Myers-Briggs Type Indicator (MBTI) or simply Myers-Briggs, you know there are sixteen personality types. If you aren't familiar with Myers-Briggs, it has existed since the 1930s and is the *gold* standard for personality assessment. You can Google/Bing "Myers-Briggs" or "MBTI" and take a shorter version online for free, but if you want a professional to score yours, it'll cost $150 (includes personal feedback). The sixteen MBTI types relate to the nine Enneagram types.[f]

they are nonjudgment, care, forgiveness, compassion, and appreciation. To recap, nonjudgment emits the lowest energy and appreciation the highest. Researchers call this study of the heart's energy "HeartMath."[28]

While HeartMath techniques are extremely valuable in managing stress and promoting harmony in your body and between others, it is not a creativity assessment. I present this information on measuring heart energy, however, solely to show you an example of how an intangible like love—or creativity—can be assessed. You are already aware that intelligence can be measured by a variety of assessments.

Using biometric equipment, the heart's electromagnetic field is measured, and a person's energy is determined to be "coherent." Being coherent means her

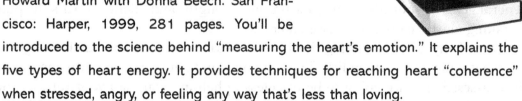

Two HeartMath Books

The HeartMath Solution by Doc Childre and Howard Martin with Donna Beech. San Francisco: Harper, 1999, 281 pages. You'll be introduced to the science behind "measuring the heart's emotion." It explains the five types of heart energy. It provides techniques for reaching heart "coherence" when stressed, angry, or feeling any way that's less than loving.

The Hidden Power of the Heart by Sara Paddison. Boulder Creek, CA: Planetary Publications, 1988, 294 pages. This book explains HeartMath with *no* math![g]

or his heart energy is positive and at one of five love levels—nonjudgment, care, forgiveness, compassion, and appreciation. When incoherent, the person experiences frustration, sadness, anger, even illness.

There are several HeartMath techniques to return your heart to a coherent state.[29] The first is Freeze-Frame, which outlines a series of steps that you can use in the middle of a stressful situation.[30] When you are really stuck in a pattern of negative emotion, Cut-Thru provides a way out.[31] Heart Lock is a twenty-minute focus on positive heart energy.[32]

Although HeartMath is not directly related to creativity, you can imagine how being able to de-stress quickly and get to a loving state can only enhance it (you can read more about HeartMath at www.heartmath.com).

The Larger Scene

There are many other personality measures (and others for creativity) on the market. Not all are reliable or valid, so be careful what you find on the Internet.

The last assessment has its own section *at the end of this chapter* and is very easily taken and scored. You can take it yourself using pencil/pen and paper. When you've added up the checkmarks in the four columns, look at the beginning of chapter 13, "Creativity Catchall," for an explanation of your score.

After you've taken all these assessments, you'll probably notice a pattern. You can't change your personality, your talents, your "bent" for what you do. You are the same person from one day to the next—in how you think and respond, that is—so you'll see similarities in the results across several of your assessments.

You'll emerge as a similar "type" on them. Now, these tests will *not* show you *how* to use your creativity, or in what form. You still have that choice. These tests are not dictating to you. You're the one who took them, after all. They're simply tools, and you can use them or not. A wise philosopher (Socrates) once said, "Know thyself." These assessments are one way to do that. If you don't know what you like or can do well, it's really hard to pick a direction. These tests are more like MapQuest. You know where you want to go—in this case—toward success and happiness. The assessments give you a route—how to achieve those general goals in your life using your unique strengths and talents. That's the point of taking all these creativity assessments.

One of my goals in writing this book is to save you time and hassle in figuring out what you want to do in life. Though you won't get to careers until chapter 14, these assessments are going to be priceless in helping you plan your future. Your future relies on enjoying what you are doing. If you are in work you love, it's play. It's actually "pay for play," and who wouldn't want a future like that?

Personal Strengths Survey

The last assessment is the Personal Strengths Survey.[33] If you're reading this online, get a pen and print the next page. If you're reading this in a library, use your own paper and pen. Either way, set your phone timer or any available timer for only *three minutes.*

In this survey, there are four sections, each containing eighteen strengths. Quickly check off (or keep track on paper) every character trait that you consistently display in *each section*. Don't overthink your answers—go with your gut reaction. (This is why you set your timer for only three minutes.)

Tally up the numbers in *each* section—you can write the numbers next to the motto line. (*Do not* add up the numbers from all sections!) Notice which two sections reflect your first and second highest level of attributes. Where are these on the paper? That is, are they upper left (UL), upper right (UR), lower left (LL), or lower right (LR)? The positions on the paper link to the personality types.

Finally, turn to the Personal Strengths Explanation in chapter 13, "Creativity Catchall," to read about each type that fits you. (The reason the results are in chapter 13 is so you won't be tempted to look a few pages ahead in this chapter *before* you take the assessment.) Look for the sections (UL, UR, LL, or LR) that correspond to your highest numbers. You'll see what your highest scores represent as well as an explanation of each section.

This is an easy measure to take and the results are easy to grasp. It is quite effective in describing your personality, including your motivations, values, and how you function in the world.

If you like taking this survey, pass it along to your friends. (Be careful not to give away the names of the categories in chapter 13 before they take it. Also, make sure they give themselves only three minutes.) You'll be amazed at the insights you'll get about one another.

Personal Strengths Survey

Upper Left: UL
___takes charge
___likes authority
___determined
___confident
___firm
___enterprising
___competitive

Upper Right: UR
___enthusiastic
___takes risks
___visionary
___motivator
___energetic
___very verbal
___likes variety

___enjoys challenges
___problem solver
___productive
___purposeful, goal-driven
___bold
___decision-maker
___adventurous
___strong-willed
___independent, self-reliant
___controlling
___action-oriented
#_____ Motto: "Let's do it now!"

___friendly
___enjoys popularity
___fun-loving
___spontaneous
___enjoys change
___creative
___group-oriented
___optimistic
___initiator
___infectious laugher
___inspirational
#_____ Motto: "Trust me—it'll work out."

Lower Left: LL
___loyal
___sensitive
___calm
___non-demanding
___avoids confrontations
___dislikes change
___warm and rational
___gives in
___indecisive
___dry humor
___adaptable
___sympathetic
___thoughtful
___patient
___tolerant
___nurturing
___good listener
___peace maker
#_____ Motto: "Let's keep things the way they are."

Lower Right: LR
___enjoys instruction
___accurate
___reserved
___controlled
___predictable
___orderly
___factual
___conscientious
___perfectionist
___discerning
___detailed
___analytical
___inquisitive
___precise
___persistent
___scheduled
___likes routine
___meticulous
#_____ Motto: "How was it done in the past?"

CREATIVITY: EVERYDAY AND PLAY

....

Picturing Everyday Creativity

So what did you do that was creative today? Did you draw or paint something? Did you write a new song, poem, or story? Did you work on a website or do some "creative coding"? Did you make part of an outfit or work on a page in a scrapbook?

What? You can't claim any creative output today? The truth is, you're probably overlooking the fact that you *were* creative today and you probably didn't realize it. You probably did something that would fit in the Everyday Creativity category.[1]

What is everyday creativity? It's pretty much what it sounds like. It's a type of creativity that is not part of a big or even a medium-sized project. Instead, you might think of it as an original act that solves a small problem. It can also be an original expression that is meaningful only to the expresser.[2] So you can understand everyday creative small problem solving, here's an example: One rainy afternoon at a Copenhagen train station, rows and rows of bicycles were parked, uncovered, getting soaked. All the bike seats were also wet except for one. One seat was covered in plastic—not a fancy cover bought at a bicycle shop; this seat cover was homemade. The cyclist had fashioned it from a fast-food plastic bag, the company logo prominently displayed. At some point on that rainy day, the cyclist was going to get off the train, walk to her bike, pull the wet plastic off, and unlike every other cyclist in the lot, ride home on a dry seat. (Though it's possible the others had towels.) Maybe this cyclist would save the fast-food bag cover or maybe she'd toss it and make another for the next rain. Either way, she demonstrated a perfect example of one type of everyday creativity: a novel way to solve a small problem

No one except the cyclist profited from this tiny solution; the clever fast-food plastic seat cover solution never got advertised on TV (though it might have appeared on Twitter). Most likely, however, this bit of everyday creativity remained anonymous.

> "Everyday creativity has two criteria: originality and meaningfulness."
> —Frank X. Barron (contemporary), psychology professor emeritus,
> University of California at Santa Cruz, creativity expert[a]

What about the other definition of everyday creativity—a meaningful expression?[3] For a moment, think about something that's yours: your room, your backpack, your cell phone, your shoes, your vehicle or locker (if you have either). Ask yourself, "What did I do that was creative today or yesterday or last week or month?" Maybe you doodled in the margins of your notebook. Maybe you put together an outfit in a new way. Maybe you blogged or wrote a poem or a song for someone you care for. Maybe you added steps to a cheerleading or a dance routine you were practicing. Maybe you decorated a T-shirt, wrapped a birthday or holiday gift in a special way, made a greeting card, created a plastic or bead bracelet. Maybe you gave some advice to a friend that turned out to be really helpful. You might have designed your own tattoo! Any of these are meaningful expressions and perfect examples of everyday creativity.

"So what?" you might think. A little embellishment here and there isn't enough to start a career, to make a project, even to brag about. It's so small. Agreed—it is a little thing. If you think about it, though, little things mean a lot. Did someone give you an unexpected smile today? How did you feel when you saw that smile? You probably felt better, right? That was a small gesture from someone, but it had a memorable impact on you. For a minute, pretend you got unexpected smiles all day. Can you imagine how you'd feel by the end of the day? Wouldn't that feeling tend to flow over into the next day?

The same is true with everyday creativity: all your little everyday creative acts add up, though not necessarily into a big obvious creations. At the very least, however, practicing everyday creativity *makes your life more meaningful*. It helps you solve small, even pesky, problems. For those of you who want everyday creativity to have more impact, you may realize that practicing everyday creativity keeps you in practice for "bigger" acts of creativity—your "significant" poems and songs, artwork and inventions. Never forget, though, that "little" acts of everyday creativity are valuable in themselves.

There are four ways to increase your everyday creative output: (1) notice when you do little creative acts, (2) look for opportunities to do those acts, (3) be open to new experiences, and as you already know, (4) stay curious! Suggested opportunities for you to increase your everyday expression: If you walk, bike, or drive to school, take a different route home. (Probably a good idea to text or tweet your new route so someone knows where you're going.) You could style your hair dif-

Thumbnail Biography of Julia Cameron

Julia Cameron (March 4, 1948–) is a playwright, scriptwriter, novelist, journalist, poet, filmmaker, and songwriter who gained fame with her 1992 publication of *The Artist's Way: A Spiritual Path to Higher Creativity*. The book provided a twelve-step model to "recover" a person's inner artist, giving "closet" artists user-friendly tools to remove barriers (primarily self-criticism) to self-expression. The *Artist's Way* (*AW*) spawned an international proliferation of self-help or facilitator-led "artist's way" groups. Cameron wrote myriad *AW* sequels, exploring creativity at work, raising a creative child, and how to *avoid* making art. While her books have a "higher power" theme and are not based on research, they draw on her thirty years of experience as a writer and creativity teacher. She currently leads online courses on creativity at juliacameronlive.com.[b]

ferently a few times a month—or week. (Many of you already do this—and not only you girls.) You could listen to and try to learn the lyrics to a song that's unlike the music you usually listen to. Taste a new food. Teach your pet a new trick. All these little acts keep the brain chugging away. They all, as Julia Cameron likes to say, "fill the well" so you can draw from it later.[4]

Did you also know that reading can be a creative act? (Except if you're reading to avoid homework, chores, or anything else you don't want or are afraid to do.) Reading fills your brain with new connections.

As for problem solving, look for small ways to make your life easier or more fun—like that person who covered the bicycle seat. If you're having trouble keeping your room clean (at least 50 to 80 percent of teens have this issue!), think of ways to get yourself motivated to keep it from health hazard territory. You can bet that no adult thought up the idea to hang a basketball hoop over the trash can! Maybe you'd like to hang a lot of hooks on your walls so it's easy to hang your clothes. Or place crates on the floor for the dirty ones? You're already hanging posters and souvenirs and photos on the walls—what else can you do to make it your original space?[5] (Most likely you're gonna have to ask permission to paint the walls eggplant purple or camo.)

Look at the little problems in your life. Really, for everyday creativity, *don't* pick the hard problems—not at first. To begin with, the hard ones are outside the realm of everyday creativity. Also, if you can't solve the hard ones right away (and you probably won't—that's why they *are* hard problems), you'll get discouraged. Solving the little problems with your ingenuity will develop your creative

Everyday creativity: doing the ordinary is meaningful to you.

confidence. Small problems *can* be solved with a little effort. Look at how many times you've had to change passwords. You had to think up strong ones, plus you had to make them memorable. You had to be ingenious to do both but it wasn't earthshakingly *hard*.

Some further examples of everyday creativity: decorating your laptop, mobile phone, iPod, and backpack to suit yourself. Organize music in your phone in a way that's unique to you.

Since no one knows your little (and big) problems as well as you do, it's tough to cite more specific examples in this book. So make a list—grab your cell phone (or here's an original idea, a piece of paper!)—and write down some of your smaller problems. Doodle some ideas for fixing them or draw out your answers rather than writing them! No one's stopping you from singing or dancing them out—simply look at the characters in musicals (*High School Musical, Glee, Camp*).

Because no one knows your life, with its big and little problems, like you do, your solutions will be unique. They will be *your* solutions and therefore as unique as your situations. Your solving them in your own particular style for *your own particular reasons* will only help you feel better about your abilities and your self-esteem, and provide one more slice to your self-identity.

As you know, that's your job as a teen—creating your own identity. If creativity isn't about self-esteem, then what's the point of self-expression? Self-expression is *all* about you creating yourself.

As you get comfortable being cre-ative about solving little problems or simply being a little bit creative every day or a few times a day, you'll be building creative "muscles," you'll have creative "capital," you'll have . . . well, you finish this with your own metaphor!

> "Life isn't about finding yourself. Life is about creating yourself."
> —George Bernard Shaw (1856—1950), playwright, critic, political activist[c]

Why dwell so much on the subject of everyday creativity? Well, partly it's to demystify the entire concept of creativ-ity—to take it out of this notion that it is something special that very few people can use or have access to. The other part is to help build your "creative toler-ance." We used to say in creativity classes, "Nothing is more dangerous than an idea when it's the only one you have."[6] Why is one idea dangerous? Not because, as you might think, it will cause change—though it might.

Usually what happens, however, is that a person—you, for example—has a good idea and then becomes attached to it. You like it because it is *your* idea. Often, because you get so attached to it, you aren't open to exploring it further, adding to it, taking suggestions about it, looking at in other ways, turning it up-side down—doing anything other than holding onto it tightly.

Not that there's anything wrong with your idea—your grasping it tightly is not meant to invalidate you. The intent behind these suggested explorations is to make your idea stronger, test it out, see how it'll work in a real application.

Why do people get so attached to their "aha" thoughts? Partly because they're theirs, of course. But why else? Isn't it often because people are afraid that one good idea is all they've got? They believe there's a scarcity. They truly don't think they're going to ever have another really good inspiration!

Nothing could be less true. By practicing everyday creativity, you'll soon see that you're generating new notions all the time. You'll get so used to generating them that at some point you'll realize that brilliant insights are available for the taking (or making). Then you won't become attached to any one of them. You'll be confident that you'll always have another good one. You'll also see that almost every original thought—even a great one—needs stretching, sanding, polishing, or adapting in some way. By the time you realize this, you'll be open to volunteering your idea—not just one, but many—for adaptation.

You'll get comfortable with the process of brainstorming ideas (divergent thinking),[7] as well as selection and adaption (convergent thinking),[8] and finally, the plan to take your idea—excuse me, your many, *many* ideas—out in the world to work, or better yet, to play.

The other reason to indulge in everyday creativity is to build your confidence in yourself as a creative person. You don't have to limit your creative output to only one or two areas, such as art and journalism. You can have ideas in many areas, about many different situations in life.

This doesn't mean you'll be equally creative and original in every area you choose. No one is talented in all categories. What about the painter, sculptor, architect, inventor Leonardo da Vinci or Thomas Edison, the inventor of the electric light bulb, phonograph, and movie camera, and a shrewd businessman? Sure, they each had great talent, an ardent interest in what they were doing, and highly developed creative skills. However, they may not have had any more ideas than others. They were more comfortable than most at asking questions, recognizing original ideas, and were willing to spend an exhaustive amount of time and energy developing them. And even da Vinci and Edison had their limitations. (da Vinci probably wasn't much of a cook, it's a sure bet Edison didn't build his own house, and certainly neither one was an Olympian!)

In addition, both of these men worked very hard at reworking their theories—doing all that stretching, sanding, polishing, and adapting. Their interest and curiosity kept them working on similar problems in their respective fields until they became experts.

In the practice of everyday creativity, however, you don't have to be an expert. You're being creative in small ways *every day*, which is why this creativity is called that name. You need to be open to practicing a little bit—or a lot—of creativity every day. If you don't practice every day—at the very least asking questions about topics that intrigue you—you can't generate new ideas *and* be comfortable with the creative adaptation and assessment process. You can't do that anymore than you can expect a great checkup at the dentist when you've only brushed your teeth a few seconds each morning. Creative thoughts and teeth both have to be managed with daily attention.

You *have* to practice creativity. That's especially true if you haven't figured out what you're good at in life. We know so much more about the brain than we used to. We know that it can be trained—at least parts of it can. We do know that the portion that comes up with ideas—mostly areas on the right side—can definitely

> "The opposite of play isn't work. It's depression. To play is to act out and be willful, exultant, and committed."—Brian Sutton Smith (1924–), play theorist, professor emeritus of education, University of Pennsylvania[d]

be "molded." With the practice of everyday creativity *every day*, you can build your creative mind.

Playing in the Sandbox

What is play? While you may not be able to give a dictionary definition, you know play when you see it, and you certainly knew it when you experienced it.

Let's look at some definitions. Play is "an exercise or activity for fun and amusement" and "fun or jest, as opposed to seriousness."[9]

When you think of play, what images come to your mind? What feelings show up in your body?

Play not only is a part of creativity, it a *huge* function of creativity. In fact, it would not be possible for creativity to be as effective as it is, to have the impact it does without the element of play. In fact, it could be said that creativity is really play.

Although there are many techniques for bringing forth your creativity in order to achieve a goal, it is vital to simply create with no goal at all. Creativity's power has to emerge freely. It can't be leashed or made to perform like that (trained) dog. It doesn't take orders, or conform to rules.

What creativity *does* require, however, is time. Creativity wants you to sit with it, to try out lots of materials—clay, fabric, cake batter, colors, philosophies, wood, musical notes, computer code, magic tricks, puns, swimming strokes. It wants you to let it play with you at its leisure and for you not to push it toward your ends. Look at this way: If you already knew the end of where you wanted to go, you would have no need for creativity. You could just plug in a pattern and out would come your product all made up, a copy (maybe in a different color) of the

> "To play is to listen to the imperative inner voice that wants to take form and be acted out without reason. It is the joyful, spontaneous expression of one's self."—Michele Cassou (contemporary), painter, teacher, author[e]

Every day in every way there's always play.

pattern you input. You'd have a formula! (And you'd have a 3-D printer, which Chuck Hull, while *playing around*, invented.)[10]

What you wouldn't have is creativity. Or play. Instead, creativity has to soak up your hidden thoughts, your emotional fingerprints in order to give up its secrets. You cannot master creativity, nor can you cage it. It has to be in partnership with you in order to fulfill its purpose.

Play is important because it's about time and freedom. You get to be aimless. You get to forget any agendas. You can't rush creativity. You can't say, "I am going to be creative between three and four." You can't say, "I'll come up with seven creative products by such-and-such time." You have to give your creativity time to come out. It's not shy; it has tremendous power, only it can't be coerced. Creativity has to be coaxed and charmed. It can't be beaten into achieving because achievement is not the aim of creativity. Being itself is its only aim. Creativity isn't magic but it isn't all science either. Its power lies somewhere between. As Tom Robbins wrote, "Humanity has advanced, when it has advanced, not because it has been sober, responsible, and cautious, but because it has been playful, rebellious, and immature."[11]

A New View of Play

There is recent research that play may be one of the main *emotions* of the human brain.[12] Dr. Jaak Panksepp has investigated how play works in the brain. He charted seven networks of emotion in the brains of cats and rats. These seven emotions are seeking, rage, fear, lust, care, panic/grief, and play. These emotions are true for humans as well.[13]

Note what Jaak Panksepp said—that play is "the foundation of the nature of joy."[14] His observation springs the jack-in-the-box on the reason why we like playing! While the idea of joy being a product of play seems logical, had you ever thought of play as an *emotion?*

Panksepp reveals that a main benefit of play is its ability to "take away the psychological pain of separation."[15] Panksepp refers to "animal" in his description of play because he observed depression and play in the brains of rats. Except these rats were lucky. To get a response from the rats, Panksepp actually *tickled* them, which they naturally enjoyed very much. In fact, Panksepp claims that the rats laughed.[16]

> "Play is a brain process that feels good, that allows the animal to engage fully with another animal . . . if you understand the joy of play, you have the foundation of the nature of joy."
> —Jaak Panksepp (1943–), Estonian-born American psychologist, psychobiologist, neuroscientist[f]

I imagine this idea of play as a "brain process" and an emotion is news to you. However, this view demonstrates how inborn play is. It is as inborn as "care," which is a form of love and only a biological step away from play.[17]

So creativity brings forth our free and playful side, and as humans, we like that. We never grow out of play, and we seem to produce very well from indulging in it. The greatest compliment a person can say about his or her work is, "I'd do this for nothing" or "I can't believe they pay me to do this." This reveals, of course, that this person's job is not work. It is a primary source of their joy.

The same can be said of you: You're going to find an area that is the most fun for you to play with. It won't necessarily be what you already know how to do. For example, many people know how to cook, but only a certain percentage enjoy

Teens' Views on Creativity and Play

Question 7: "How do you think creativity relates to play?"

"Both allow a relief of stress."—Ashley, 17, California

"When I was a kid, I would act out stories on the playground. Just going outside and exploring a playground or the woods gets your mind flowing with ideas."—Kyle, 19, Florida

"What you're doing might be work, but you're enjoying it."—Chandler, 13, Florida

"It can be considered play."—Cameron, 16, California

"I think it relates to play by using your imagination."—Analyse, 16, California

"Creativity is fun. Play is fun. Creativity is play."—Justice, 17, California

"What you do in your play time generally stems from what makes you creative."—Glennon, 17, California

"It's fun. Creative people don't feel like they're working. It's a source of pleasure for them."—Gregory, 18, Florida

"Creativity is play. It's a tool, it's a game, it's ourselves."—Hannah, 18, New York[9]

cooking. If cooking is something you know how to do, but you don't cook for enjoyment (only because you have to make meals for yourself or others), obviously keep looking for what makes you feel joyful. If your most playful area may not have surfaced yet, this is good news. You can continue to play around in a variety of "sandboxes." And if it takes you longer to discover what your creative niche is, you'll still be able to use what you learned in those other sandboxes in the niche or niches you eventually choose.

The best way to get creative is to have fun. Not to *make* yourself have fun. Simply go out and have *fun*.

"We do not stop playing because we grow old. We grow old because we stop playing."—attributed to George Bernard Shaw (1856–1950), author, playwright, wit, co-founder of London School of Economics[h]

Silliness

Have you ever noticed how the silliest things can be fun? Like you start playing around with a project—assigned or not—and then you find yourself organizing all your paper clips by size. Or changing the order of your playlist by organizing it by season or song length?

Maybe you do silly walks like Jim Carrey?

Or back to cooking, if you are following a recipe, you start adding items not on the ingredient list—really odd ones, just to see what you'll end up with. Some of the dishes may not be edible and maybe no one will enjoy the final dish. Yet you had fun (and so did everyone else as long as you cleaned up and kept the household calm). Truly, this is all that counts.

The point is, you were *playing*. Did you notice how you felt? (Remember, at least one scientist calls "play" an emotion.) Joyful, silly, and mischievous are all possibilities, but almost certainly you felt relaxed. If you were feeling any or all of those you also weren't being critical of yourself while playing. You probably didn't realize how much time had passed, either. How would you like to continue playing like this? Maybe you'd like to schedule a play date.

A Creativity "Play Date"

You've probably grown up going on play dates, so the idea of setting aside time for play may not be so foreign to you. This date will be a different kind of fun, however, and you will, at least at first, have to go on it alone. (Hey, at least there's no scheduling hassles.)

"Humanity has advanced, when it has advanced, not because it has been sober, responsible, and cautious, but because it has been playful, rebellious, and immature."—Tom Robbins (1936–), U.S. novelist[i]

Julia Cameron, the woman who designed this exercise, called them "artist dates."[18] Because you already know that all people are artists, we'll call this the creativity "play" date.

This date is designed for you to spend two hours a week alone doing something fun. You may want to be with a friend or friends on these dates, and eventually, you can have creative fun with other people, but not in the beginning. This date is not for you to *figure out* what gives you the most joy, but for you to explore so you discover it yourself. Figuring out means you're thinking about the activity. Exploring means you're involved in the activity, that you're directly experiencing what you feel during it. You get to choose what you think is fun, and you have to tell the truth about what that is. It might be that you think you're *supposed* to like the music your friends do, but what you really like is music from another era. So, listen to it. (Are you understanding now why at first you need to have a creative date by yourself?) If you had a friend along on your date and you chose music your friend didn't like, you would hear about it!

At this point, you're a little baby—choose your favorite baby animal—coming forth to explore this big, creative, *playful* world. As this baby animal, you're vulnerable. Obviously, you don't want your friend's (or anyone else's) criticism or judgment about what you choose for fun. What you are doing, as Julia Cameron puts it, is "filling the well"—your creative well with whatever you wish.[19]

Maybe the image of putting money in an account works better for you. Just like you can't withdraw money from an empty account, you can't withdraw cre-

Suggestions for Your Creativity Play Date

Listen to music *you* like. Dance (who's gonna see?). Sing if you feel like it. Paint your face. Paint your toes. Paint your face to match your toes. Go somewhere you've always wanted to go: an art or national history museum? The circus? A new hairdresser? A hobby or craft store? (Get anything you want for $10. If you enjoy challenges, spend only $5. Or $1. See how much fun you can have.) Write a poem. Draw a picture. Paint. Walk. Knit. Do cartwheels. Crochet. Fly a kite. Rake leaves and jump in. Make snowballs. Climb a tree. If you like clothes, design some. Ditto for any sort of design—cars, houses, pet clothes, video games, backpacks. Watch the sky. Daydream. Swing. Slide. Make up a language. Are you starting to get ideas?[i]

ative ideas or energy from an empty account either. *You are filling your account* by having fun. This exercise has two outcomes. You get to have fun for two whole hours, and later, when you have a project that calls for creative ideas and energy, you'll have something to draw from.

During the time you are filling your account, you simply need to play. You also need, as best you can, to stay clear of judging yourself. There's no need to produce anything during these hours. You can make something if you wish, but you need to not *try* to make something (unless it's totally fun and you *want to*—but then you're not trying; it's just happening).

There are a few ground rules to creativity dates, solely to maximize your fun and minimize any risk: (1) You don't need to leave your room or your home. You don't need to stay there either. (2) You don't need to spend money. You can spend money. (3) Be honest about the places you want to go or activities you want to do. If you've had a secret desire and can feasibly do it, indulge. If you're afraid to try something but it also tempts you, try it. (Not if you're *really* afraid, only if you're equally attracted and hesitating.) Make these hours be out of the ordinary. (4) If you leave, let someone who cares about you know where you are. Give him or her a time you'll return. (5) Except for number 4, make this a social-media-free date. If you're tweeting, texting, IMing, Facebooking, and so on, you're not exploring your creativity. You can connect with your friends in two hours. (If you know that you won't be able to resist texting, etc., don't take your phone. Borrow someone else's, maybe an emergency-only phone. Put your cell on vibrate and leave it. All your messages will be waiting.)

Three Viewpoints of Play

"The supreme accomplishment is to blur the line between work and play."—Arnold Toynbee (1889–1975), historian, best known for his twelve-volume *A Study of History*

"Realize that almost every sphere of human society can be seen as a game."—Martha Beck (1962–), sociologist, life coach, author

"Play is the exultation of the possible."—Martin Buber (1878–1965), Austrian-born Israeli Jewish philosopher, Nobel-nominated author[k]

When you're done, see how you feel. You don't need to tell anyone or write a report or show anyone what you made. Just notice your response. If you like it, set aside time for another play date. If you can do one a week, that's ideal.

Play Therapy

We've talked about play in the chapter, so let's explore what it's like when play is combined with therapy.[20] You probably have an idea of what therapy is, and some of you have had at least one therapeutic experience. Therapy is *not* the same as counseling. In counseling you get information, often some guidance, maybe even a plan. Therapy is different because it provides both confrontation and healing. Confrontation sounds scary, huh? Like someone in your face. Actually, the word *confrontation* comes from the Latin meaning "to face" (you were sorta right).[21] However, the negative in-your-face confrontations you see on reality TV shows are not therapy. Any "facing" has to be done by you. Someone may tell you something about yourself, positive or negative, but until *you* face it, it's not therapeutic confrontation. After you do face it, however, you are now in the position to make the choice to heal. Actually, choosing to heal is not all *conscious*. The truth is, we're unconsciously "wired" to heal. Once you've faced a situation, "the odds are ever in your favor"[22] that healing will begin.

If you've experienced some therapy, you know it mainly consists of a therapist asking you questions and you responding . . . or not. If you weren't open to answering the questions, or it was too painful, or for whatever reason, you might not have talked much. The point is, traditional therapy involves lots of talking. This type of therapy, like all therapies with teens, relies on "a radical trust in adolescents' ability to find their feet when supported."[23]

There are other therapies, however, that do not rely on talk as much, and some not at all. They are as effective, and in many cases, *more* effective, than talk therapies. Many of these fall under a category called *play therapy*. "Play therapy is the use of toys to take the place of words in telling the child's story and expressing the child's emotions."[24]

Originally used with small children because they could not articulate their emotions, play therapy has become a popular and successful healing method for adults and teens.[25] Even though you as a teen can articulate your emotions much better than when you were a child, you may not want to. Choosing to attend play therapy sessions may be advantageous for you.

How do you go about getting into play therapy? Contact a psychologist, counselor, school counselor, social worker, psychiatrist—any mental health professional (MHP)—about your interest. Of course you can surf the web. Usually you will not enter immediately into play therapy. After some talk sessions with a

MHP, you will be referred to a registered play therapist (unless, of course, your MHP is trained in play therapy).

Available play therapies are art therapy, sandtray therapy, music therapy, dance therapy, and drama therapy. They sound pretty basic, don't they? They are, as far as your involvement, but MHPs must have the required training to work with teens in any of these areas. This is not simply play. It is therapy that *incorporates* play. As in all therapy, you must feel safe, you must be with someone who is competent and understanding, and your process must be kept confidential.[26]

It's not possible to describe the various techniques of play therapy for teens in much detail, but you can learn enough to get a layperson's understanding (i.e., not as a MHP, but as client) and a sense of whether you'd like to try some of these activities to help you with a problem.

Art Therapy

This is the most common of the play therapies, probably because it is the easiest to manage in terms of materials and maybe because there are lots of artists in the world who want be involved in healing. Or it could be there are many healers who love art. Most likely, it's both!

In art therapy, you start by talking a little about your problem and then you draw, paint, sculpt, make collages, or take photos in order "to help yourself grow, rehabilitate and heal, [which] comes from the actual making of art."[27] How well you do any of these is not a concern. (This is the main difference between art therapy and art class. In art therapy, you're *not* producing; you're expressing.) The room you're in will be stocked with various types and sizes of paper, all kinds of drawing materials, sculptor's clay (not kids' clay or silly putty), and, often, collage materials. Your MHP may let you draw (with crayon or pencil, chalk or charcoal) freely, with no instructions, for as long as you feel you need to. Or he or she may "direct" your drawing to a particular aspect of your problem; for instance, "Draw how you feel about your baby kangaroo jumping out of his cage" (or your parents' divorce or whatever's concerning you).[28] The room may also contain paints, which provide another depth to art therapy. Paints are wet and can be messy, so they're helpful when you want to express messy emotions and/or chaotic experiences.

The MHP could not care one whit about your artistic abilities; you can use stick figures to express yourself if that's most comfortable for you. You can pile up blobs of clay or mix paint colors in unusual combinations and put them on the paper any way you want.

After you've drawn, painted, or sculpted, at some point, the MHP will ask you to talk about what you've made. Whatever you say is fine because whatever you've expressed is in your own language. Don't be concerned if your picture doesn't match accepted symbolism. Just because you drew a kangaroo jumping out of its cage doesn't mean that's what it means to you. That kangaroo might be your way of describing how you want to leave a confined situation. It could mean you're playing or exploring out of bounds. Or it could mean you want to get out of Australia! The play therapist has been trained *not to interpret your art*. In fact, what you've made is not actually art; it's an *expression* of you at the current time. No one is permitted to judge such an expression in a therapeutic setting. Your art and your words describing it are the most important factors in this form of therapy.[29]

Why enter art therapy? For sure, it's often way more fun, especially if you are a teen who is less talkative or is currently dealing with heavy emotions. Drawing, painting, and sculpting clay help you to *directly* access what you're feeling. It's also more private; you don't have to verbalize unless you want to. As a teen trying to establish your identity and struggling with independence from your "old self," making your own art provides you with the experience that you are original, you are authentic, and you are in control. Art therapy has been especially effective with teen clients diagnosed with trauma due to sexual abuse, terminal illness, anorexia, bulimia, and body image issues, as well as with adolescents in crisis.[30]

Sandtray Therapy

Most teens enjoy sandtray therapy, which is defined as "imaginative activity in the sand."[31] Like art therapy, it is an adjunct to talk therapy.[32] Some art therapy rooms also contain materials for sandtrays, which are shallow trays, usually plastic and rectangular, sometimes round, that contain the fine sand that's used in sandboxes. The room will also contain shelves of miniatures, ranging from domestic to wild animals; sea creatures; transportation; soldiers; small dolls of all sizes and ethnicities; fantasy creatures like witches, fairies, and dragons; buildings; doll furniture; tiny trees; plants; food; geometric shapes; modern and ancient weapons; and musical instruments. Also available are stones, marbles, and plastic shapes for fences, roads, and bridges. Every sandtray room is unique; if a therapist has been practicing sandtray therapy for years, there may be thousands of miniatures.[33]

Your task is to select a sandtray (if there's more than one) and select from the shelves any miniatures you wish. Your MHP will advise you to "feel" which ones attract you.[34] It's not necessary to know why you're drawn to particular miniatures. Simply pay attention to what feeling—positive or negative—an object may bring up in you. Consider choosing it, even if it makes no sense. Take your chosen objects to your tray and arrange them any way you choose.[35] You can return for more miniatures, you can remove some from your tray, and you can move them around as much as you like.[36] This isn't a race. It's your life and the problem you're currently dealing with, and you can express it in the sand with tiny objects. The therapist is trained to actively observe you from a compassionate stance and not to suggest any miniatures nor comment on your choices or placement.[37]

Sometimes clients only want to play with the sand; this is perfectly acceptable. Sand has a sensual feel, and running your hands and fingers through it may be what you want to experience on that day. There is no wrong way to have a sandtray experience.

When you feel complete with your tray, your therapist will ask you to describe your experience.[38] You don't have to talk, but usually people are ready to. The therapist may ask permission to photograph your tray for files. If you agree, your tray will not display your name or other identification. These photos are treated the same as your client file; they are completely confidential. You may take a photo of your tray if you wish. At the end, you will be free to leave without putting your miniatures away.[39]

Music Therapy

Music therapy is a form of play therapy that can be guided by a play therapist or by a certified music therapist.[40] Either one can explore your favorite music with you, or discuss songs that are personally meaningful to you. You are also free to sing, play an instrument, or write a song.[41] You are not performing, so you are not being judged on your performance. The goal is to connect to your psyche through music. Music therapists, who play at least two instruments and sing, will have more repertoire and experience in evoking moods that will assist your healing. It will be no surprise to you that music therapy has been particularly effective with teens.[42]

Dance Therapy

Whether you're comfortable with physical movement or not, dance therapy can help you explore "radical changes in body image and awareness."[43] Dance therapists are trained in putting their clients through certain movements. Dance can loosen you up and help you express your feelings in ways other than words. If you are confused or angry, you can express your feelings in a safe environment; these feelings, and especially trauma, are locked into muscles and the tissues surrounding the muscles.[44] Releasing feelings and trauma through movement is a more direct and dynamic healing process. Other movement exercises are deep breathing, muscle relaxation, centering, and body boundary. The latter is especially effective with teens who may suffer from anorexia.[45] Dance therapists are trained to assist you to express deep-seated emotions in a safe and compassionate environment.

Drama Therapy

Of course, you can expect to speak in drama therapy, although some drama therapy exercises do not include speech. If you've been willing to reveal a problem in a therapeutic group setting, you may have already participated in a form of drama therapy. One of the most effective therapies is psychodrama,[46] which allows you to "act out" a problem, either by playing all aspects of the issue yourself or by playing all the people involved. Or others may act out parts of your trauma. Because you are role playing, it is often safer for you to experience painful, even long-buried feelings. You also have the group to support and witness your healing. All play therapists are trained in drama therapy; of course, some specialize in this form. Sometimes drama therapy involves watching films to raise self-esteem, or "highlight values and decision making." This is called cinematherapy.[47]

Confidentiality

Be very sure that everything you draw, paint, sculpt, photograph, create in sand, sing, write, or act out is as confidential as any words you might speak in a traditional therapy session. *You* may choose to show your drawing, painting, or photo of your sandtray, or talk about your song or psychodrama to whomever you wish, but the therapist can*not* do so without your written permission.[48] Even if your parents are paying for your session and the therapist reports to them, he or she will talk about your progress in general terms and not describe your specific experiences. Of course, as in all therapy, if a therapist gets the sense that you may harm yourself or others, he or she will take appropriate action.

HOW TO CRUSH YOUR CREATIVITY

Actually, a better title would be "How to Kill Creativity," but that's already been used on a paper by Dr. Teresa M. Amabile that looked at the "creative climate" (how creativity is supported) at an organization.[1]

OK, here are the rules for destroying creativity:

1. Expose yourself to criticism at every opportunity.[2]
2. Make sure a good part of that criticism is self-inflicted.[3]
3. Never acknowledge anyone's contributions.[4]
4. Make darn sure never to acknowledge your own contributions.[5]
5. Always be in a rush. That way you can ignore all the sensory input around you.[6]
6. Never allow enough time to work out problems.[7]
7. Make a competition, like a Jeopardy game, to reward producing creative ideas.[8] (Make sure to keep precise count of the points each person or team scores.)
8. Reward creativity with more money or prizes (movie tickets, cruises, iPads).[9]
9. Always, always, *always* punish anyone who makes mistakes.[10]
10. Punish yourself worse for your mistakes.[11]

There are more ways to crush creativity, but you don't need to be concerned about those. These ten will work just fine; they'll guarantee that any creativity from you or anyone around you will be crushed savagely and thoroughly.

Were you surprised by the creativity crushers in numbers 7 and 8? How could rewarding people for their creative output possibly be a negative influence? That seems crazy. Games shows reward winners all the time and they are ecstatic.

Agreed, it does sound odd. Don't people like getting rewards? Yes, they do, but in the case of creativity, the system of rewards has to be structured differently than for tasks at jobs or school.[12]

Actually, there is no "system" of rewards that works with creativity. That's because to be consistently creative you must be motivated by yourself, and for yourself, not from some outside force.[13] You need to *want* to write a poem, design a website, learn how to make rubber-band bracelets, figure out an end-run play for your team, learn a song, practice a speech, plan a party, run a campaign because you like doing it. (By the way, what does work for creativity is to give people a bonus *after* they've created.[14])

The truth is, if you want to keep cultivating your creativity, you need to do the preceding tasks because you want to. Repeat: you need to do all those activities because you want to. This is called "intrinsic motivation."[15] (Being intrinsically motivated eventually leads to getting paid for what you love doing.)

Want to test this yourself? Try giving prizes. Make people vie with each other. It won't work, unless there is a spirit of fun in the game. This is not conjecture; this has been proven in experiments on creativity.[16]

Another quality that kills creativity is competition.[17] Creativity is not like games, where at best, the whole point is for one group to win and the other one to lose. You can imagine that if you need to keep self-criticism out of your personal creative life, it's even more important to keep it out of your public creative life.[18] Now does this mean that you can never enter your art or music in an exhibition with the work of other artists or musicians? That you can never be in a dramatic contest? That you can never enter your invention in a science fair? Of course not. What it means is that it works best for you to create without the "umbrella" of competition—to write, draw, play music, invent on your own, freely, without judgment, worry, or time pressure. By doing this, you'll develop a portfolio of poems or stories, drawings or paintings, or songs. Then when a competition arises, you can select the work you feel is your best and enter that.

There have been studies to verify that competition among creative people (and remember, you're *all* creative) damps down creativity.[19] Even some professional artists have admitted that when they have been given a commission—to make art for pay—they feel they are not as creative as when they simply make the art for its own sake. They feel that pressure to "perform" and it works against them.[20]

Wanting to get simple clear-cut answers, quickly, and trying to rush the creative process will crush creativity.[21] You need to get comfy with ambiguity, complexity, and the process of incubation.

In the business world, according to Lee Silber, an artist, musician, workshop leader, and author of three books for creative people, "speed kills creativity" and "mass production kills art and uniqueness in favor of commercialism and uniformity."[22]

So now you know—criticism is the "very big, bad C." It is the cancer of creativity, destroying it like cancer destroys cells.

Teens' Views on What Stops Their Creativity

Question 2 (Part 2): "What stops you from being creative?"

"It's sometimes hard to be creative when really upset; also when life is normal."—Skye, 18, California

"A teacher once commented on a short story of mine. 'Is that logical? That really can't happen.' I feel that really stops creativity."—Kyle, 19, Florida

"I feel relaxed at times, but only if I'm personally choosing to be creative. School and other requirements stop me from being creative."—Ashley, 17, California

"Strict guidelines."—Dakota, 17, California

"What stops me from being creative is fear of what others think."—Alicia, 16, California

"My own logic can stop me from being creative."—Sam, 16, California

"The only thing that stops me from being creative is laziness, or no enthusiasm."—A.J., 16, California

"I haven't yet found what stops me from being creative. There are times when I am less creative due to school or exhaustion or other commitments, but I find that I'm still contemplating and using my creativity to think up things I can do down the road."—Darius, 16, Florida

"Hesitation and second guessing myself is what stops me."—Arianna, 18, California

"My own doubt and fear of failure."—Glennon, 17, California

"Standards stop creativity."—Max, 16, California[a]

Alex Osborn, the inventor of creative problem solving, knew all about the effects of criticism on creativity. That's why when his advertising creative group met to develop ads for its clients, Osborn's *number one rule* for brainstorming was that *any* idea was valid.[23] *No one* was allowed to criticize *any*one else's ideas, no matter how crazy or inappropriate they seemed. Osborn introduced this rule because he'd noticed that when someone on his creative group verbalized an idea and someone responded, "Oh, we've tried that before" or "That'll never work" or "It's too much like what we did last time," or the worst comment of all, "That's the dumbest idea I've ever heard!" the flow of ideas slowed down, trickled, and finally dried up.

If you ever get a chance to participate in a Creative Problem Solving (CPS) group session led by a CPS-trained facilitator, pay attention to the second stage, Generating Ideas (also known as brainstorming). You'll probably hear someone say about somebody else's idea, "That isn't very good." At this point, the facilitator's job is to point out that *all* ideas are acceptable. When I facilitated CPS sessions and heard someone say his *own* idea wasn't any good, I always commented, "Every idea is good. Write it down."

Unfortunately, humans are very imaginative at manufacturing all kinds of criticism. Of course you recognize the obvious comment "That sucks" and you don't have to figure out how those words feel. If you feel strong enough, however, you can reply to that comment by responding, "Did I ask your opinion?" Or more politely, you can say, "Thank you for sharing." This response doesn't mean you accept the comment, only that you're acknowledging that this person said it. "Thank you for sharing" often stops the person from making more comments because you're not angry or upset and you have listened to what she or he has said. This can confuse critics.

Here's a different scenario: How do you feel if someone says, "Well, it's not *too* bad." You still feel hurt, right? But you might be confused because you aren't sure if the comment is actually a criticism. How about this one: "Are you sure you want to do it that way?" How do you feel when you hear that? How can/do you respond to it? First, you need to recognize that these questions are not genuine questions. They're covert criticism. *All of these statements or questions are covert criticism.*

Even if the person says, "I think you ought to try . . . ," "Why don't you do it this way?" or "Don't you think you should . . . ?" it's important for you to recognize that these kinds of questions and statements *are* criticism. If you don't recognize them for what they are, you might notice that you feel bad, but you won't realize why you don't feel like creating. Eventually you *will stop* creating and you'll wonder why. These covert comments are the reason. Julia Cameron, who wrote *The Artist's Way*, calls these "useless comments."[24]

Here's the *big* takeaway about comments regarding anything you create: *if you didn't ask for feedback*, and someone makes a comment that is *anything* but posi-

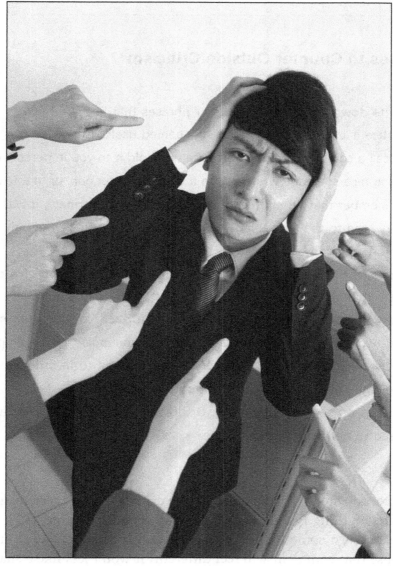

This is how criticism feels in your body.

tive about what you're doing, it's *criticism*. It's as simple as that. If you're practicing a song, drawing a picture, working on your dance moves, writing a poem, working on your lay-up shots, or experimenting with makeup, and someone gives you negative feedback *that you didn't ask for, be sure to recognize it as criticism.* (This doesn't mean you fight back. It means that if you feel bad, there's a reason.)

Parents, teachers, siblings, even friends, are going to say stuff that hurts.

So when you create something and you aren't in a brainstorming session where it's safe to express any idea, how will you deal with others' comments? You need to know what to do because your creations are going to receive criticism. See page 82 for some suggestions.

Exercises to Counter Outside Criticism

1. Write down any specific words or phrases that bothered you.
2. Notice if anything in the criticism seemed useful to you.
3. Recall a compliment, from someone who told it to you in person, or something nice someone wrote you in a card, on Facebook, or in a text.
4. Remember that no matter what you made (or performed), it was a necessary step to the next thing you'll do. (You've got to be the ugly duckling before you can be the swan.)
5. Examine the criticism once again. It probably reminds you of a past criticism that shamed you.
6. Now write a letter to the person who criticized you. *You are* not *going to send this letter, via Facebook, text, or snail mail!!!* You're simply going to write this letter and say everything you need to in order to get your feelings out and help you feel strong again.
7. Plan to do something creative. Or do something creative right away. You need to get back on your horse.[b]

One important step is to look again at the criticism you received and ask yourself, "Is there anything I could learn from this person's comment?"

If you can learn something, this is a "useful comment." You can tell if it's useful because that comment will feel different; it won't feel like a snarky remark or an out-and-out word bashing. A useful comment will feel *true*. It will point you in a positive direction, toward improvement.[25]

This is the last step in the plan to counter others' criticism because it's hard to hear any useful comments when you're smarting from the critical remarks.

By the way, you'll also hear *useful* comments in unasked-for *and* asked-for feedback.

Another method for handling your bad feelings that come from criticism is to go *do something you love*. Do something that puts you in the "flow." (Don't know what *flow* means? Check out chapter 8, "Creativity and Happiness.")

In *The Once and Future King* by T. H. White[26] (which was turned into the movie *The Sword in the Stone*),[27] Merlin asks young Arthur what's the best thing to do when Arthur is hurting. Arthur (who obviously knew the answer from many sessions with Merlin) replied, "Learn something." If you change Arthur's words to "Do something you love," you'll soften the hit and be building your creative skills at the same time. Actually, your being involved in creativity is what softens the "hit."

> "Creativity is the only cure for criticism."—Julia Cameron (1948–), teacher, playwright, journalist, filmmaker, composer, author of *The Artist's Way* and sequels[c]

"Friending" Creativity

So what does this mean? Are you always going to be so sensitive that you'll never ask for feedback? Of course not. However, the truth is, you are probably vulnerable right now. You need to construct an environment with the most favorable conditions for getting feedback on your creations. First is timing. You must ask for feedback *only* when *you're* ready. The timetable is your choice. You are the only one who can decide when you feel comfortable enough to ask for someone's feedback on your project, your song, your dance moves, your poem, your fashion sketches. (The only exception is if you're performing for an audience or displaying your project or art in public. In that case, it's understood that you're open to feedback you didn't specifically ask for. But if your creations are displayed for the public, you made the choice.)

Now there's a problem with this feedback timetable. Because you are a teen, your friends' opinions of you and what you do are vital. As discussed in chapter 2, your relationships with friends are helping you establish an identity separate from your parents and family. Interaction with your friends is a huge part of your life. Your friends (and unfortunately, your non-friends) *are* going to make unsolicited negative comments. You aren't going to be able to choose when you want that feedback, but you don't want to alienate your friends either. You could ask them to tell you only the good stuff—for now—because you're vulnerable. You can promise that later you'll ask for tips on improving your creative project.

HOW TO CULTIVATE YOUR CREATIVITY

The Big Picture

This will be a really short chapter because you can learn to cultivate creativity in three steps (one more step than on a shampoo bottle):

1. Read the ten rules for crushing creativity in the last chapter.
2. Do the exact opposite.
3. Repeat.

This chapter really could end right here. Although there's more explanation on how to cultivate your creativity, truthfully, it won't be any clearer than the instructions just given. If you want to cultivate your creativity, all you really have to do is the opposite of whatever it takes to crush it.

The Larger Scene

Now that you've finished reading almost half of this book, here's a little experiment. Ready? It's simple. Go out and be creative. Go ahead, pick something and go do it. Take your time.

Oh, you're done so soon? How did it go? What did you create?

What . . . you *didn't* do anything creative? Why not? What happened? What's *wrong* with you?

> ! **Major Creativity Takeaway**
>
> ⊙ If you take only one lesson from this book, make it this one: You will create an acceptance of yourself, your ideas, your projects. You will not try to create in a critical atmosphere.[a]

That worked well, right? What do you think happened? Oh, sure, you didn't like being told what to do. (No one really does.) Your reaction to the command, "Be creative" might have been, "Are you *kidding*?" or "Get real!" (Maybe you said some nasty words that can't be printed in this book.) If you reacted in any of these ways—or *any* way that expressed what you truly felt—your response was absolutely correct. You didn't create anything *and* you were resistant to an order to create. You were perfect subjects for demonstrating that is not how creativity works. On some level you knew this; your resistance was appropriate.

Or maybe your response was confusion or disgust. Those are also normal reactions. At any rate, somehow you knew that commands and creativity don't mix. You're not a dog; it is trained to respond to commands. It doesn't *create*. However, even a dog that doesn't understand any words will respond to its master's mood and tone of voice. Dogs respond to vocal tone because they are *sensitive* to their masters' moods. They may only have the understanding of a four-year old child; however, four-year-olds are very aware of their parents' moods.

So why bring up the subject of dogs in a book about creativity? Because your creativity, like a dog with its four-year-old mind, is also sensitive to your moods. Unlike a dog, however, creativity will *not* respond to commands. Any order to you to "be creative" is ridiculous and counterproductive. It puts pressure on you to perform. (Note: Some of you *might* have responded well to that pressure, but that's due to your psychological makeup. You consider pressure and competition challenging. However, the only reason your creativity responds to challenges is because you *choose* them.)

Most of you, however, when you read the words "be creative" didn't stop reading and pick up a paintbrush or mold clay, invent something, or do *anything* creative. Whether you got mad, disgusted, or confused, whether you stopped reading or kept on the page, you weren't able nor willing to follow such an order. Instinctively, you knew that commands and creativity are adversaries.

Creativity *won't* work on command—it never has and it never will.[1] The bare, basic, blinding truth is that you can't be creative while trying to control the outcome, which is what a command is designed to do. You also can't be *critical* at the same time that you're creating.[2] The exclusion principle in quantum mechanics states that two objects can't occupy the same space at the same time.[3] This principle also applies to creativity. Stated simply, *criticism and control cancel out creativity.* (It's easy to remember this truism because it's alliterative—all the key words start with *c*.)

This might be your new mantra: "Criticism and control cancel out creativity."

The fantastic on-the-other-side news is that being in an environment that is nurturing and freeing works very well for creativity.[4]

Another strategy for you in nurturing is to ask someone who cares about you *and who you know will be kind.* At this point, you are vulnerable and fragile—you need only positive comments. You can't trust anyone who might not give you those. In fact, what you do is set up the conditions so that positive comments are *all* this person is allowed to give you. For example, pretend you wrote a poem. You want to know how your poem sounds to others, so you go to that kind person and say, "I came to you because I can trust you to be kind. Please listen to my poem and tell me what you *liked* about it. And please, that's *all* I want you to tell me. I'm not ready to hear anything negative yet. Thank you."

If you don't trust someone to give you positive feedback, do *not* ask him or her. At this point, you are vulnerable and fragile—you need only upbeat comments. You can't trust anyone who might not give you those.

The reason you need to ask for this feedback approach is because you have already had way, *way* too much negative feedback in your life. You have loads of memories of negative comments (yes, many are your own comments, but you learned them from negative sources). At this point, in order to open up your creative capability, you need to start building a "bank account" of positive feedback. The positive comments you are going to get from the kind person are going to build up points in your positive bank account.[5]

Dr. John Gottman, a couples counselor and researcher for over thirty-five years, noticed that whenever one partner in a couple made a negative comment to the other partner, the first partner needed to give *five* positive comments to offset the negative *one.* If the two partners kept to this ratio on a regular basis, they could restore equilibrium and have a healthy relationship. Interesting stuff

Steps for Appreciation

1. Start small, appreciating one of your accomplishments, one of your personality traits, or one aspect of how you look.
2. Write each one down so it is more real.
3. Offset each negative self-comment with *five* positive comments. (One to five is the necessary ratio to counteract negative comments.)[b]
4. Accept yourself when you are critical. Accept your self-criticism—not that it's OK to criticize yourself, but that it's OK to slip up and then forgive yourself.[c]

about couples, you say, but how does this information apply to you? Because this strategy doesn't just apply to couples, it applies to *all* relationships.[6]

Friending Yourself

By now most of you aren't using Facebook much (Instagram and IMing are your online social media), but applying Facebook's concept of "friending" to yourself is a twenty-first-century update for being "your own best friend." When you criticize your *own* ideas, your *own* creative projects, you need to "friend" yourself instead. When you judge your projects so harshly you wouldn't dream of asking anyone else's opinion, you need to friend yourself. Although others' comments hurt and hinder you, self-criticism is the worst part of the big *C*. You know why. If other people are criticizing you, you can walk away, you can tell them off, you can go to your room, you can shut off your phone or leave a nasty IM. But how do you walk away from yourself? How do you shut off your own thoughts? You've probably noticed that it's really, *really* hard to shut down the critical, mean voice in your own head.

To be honest, getting yourself to stop your inner critic is going to be the hardest part of the creativity process for you. (It is for most people.) That's because we as humans actually have a built-in tendency to accentuate the negative.[7] This tendency makes sense. In order for our species to survive, our ancestors *had* to notice what might be dangerous in their environment. They *had* to pay attention to what might be a threat in order to prepare for it and to protect themselves. We still have this tendency to notice what's wrong embedded in our brains; in fact, it's located in the amygdala (pronounced "uh-mig-duh-luh"), sometimes called "reptile brain," which controls fear and aggression.[8]

In order to unconditionally accept ideas you generate, you have to override your amygdala, which is suspicious of anything new. You also have to be aware of your tendency to be sarcastic or contemptuous. Sarcasm and contempt are both forms of verbal aggression, which will shut down your creativity very effectively.

Three-Step Plan for Overriding Self-Criticism

1. Phase out obvious, deliberate self-criticism.
2. Be aware of sarcasm, disrespect, and disregard.
3. If you criticize *you*, notice and forgive yourself.[d]

One way to handle your critical voice is to learn to meditate. Mindful practice will help you help handle it well.[9] The suggestions on page 88 are helpful when you can recall them. But in many situations, you can't. You're too upset to think of meditation practices (other than deep breathing). Here's another method for soothing yourself that is *easy* to remember: COAL. This means curiosity, openness, acceptance, love. Apply these qualities to yourself when feeling self-critical.[10]

Here's how it works: You hear a critical voice in your head. Of course, you're going to try not to listen to it. However, *don't try to stop it.* (You've probably tried to shut this voice up many, many times. Have you noticed that hardly ever worked?) What you do instead is appreciate some aspect of yourself, and you must be very specific. You have to say more than, "I'm a nice person."

At first it may feel really odd appreciating yourself. You may even wonder if you're being egotistical. Not at all. The truth is *you've been criticizing yourself* and *you've accepted that behavior as normal.* Now it's time to train yourself in the idea that *appreciating yourself is normal.* Because this may be such a new concept, you will need to start small. However, there's another method for handling your unkind thoughts. *Simply* appreciate yourself.

Why? The truth is, there is scientific research on love that has shown how love affects us. The energy from the heart energy can be measured. You've heard of electrocardiograms (EKGs), which test the heart's rhythm, as well as MRIs, X-rays, and ultrasound, all of which determine how the different parts of the body are functioning. Since the 1970s doctors have been able to differentiate between certain heart energy fields, and they are care, nonjudgment, compassion, forgiveness, and appreciation. The field that measures the most heart energy is appreciation.

I'm sure many of you have heard of gratitude exercises and gratitude journals. Gratitude is similar to appreciation; however, as one of my students once said, gratitude speaks more about the past, while appreciation is more involved with the present.

In fact, start with *the smallest appreciative remark about yourself that you can handle.* If the one you've chosen makes you uncomfortable, you've started too big. You have to begin with a compliment about your toes or your eyebrows because anything more might make you feel uncomfortable. That's fine. (For instance, you can notice that your socks match.) You don't have to come up with a top ten appreciation list. If you really want to speed this process along, write down the

---

! Appreciation Is the Highest Form of Love

So appreciating yourself and your creativity is the greatest love you can give yourself.°

This is your face on a creativity high.

comments on notes that you can see every day. Seeing them in your handwriting on paper will make your appreciative thoughts more real.

What will also reinforce this new thinking is that *you must appreciate yourself for appreciating yourself*. Carol Dweck explains that a person's mindset, *which is the way a person talks to him- or herself*, changes the meaning of failure, success, and the meaning of effort. We now know that intelligence and talent are not static entities; they can be improved. Dr. Dweck calls this a "growth mindset."[11] With this mindset, there is nothing to prove, there is only growth to be achieved.

Book: *Mindset: The New Psychology of Success*

Dr. Carol S. Dweck. New York: Random House, 2007, 288 pages. Dr. Dweck described mindset as the way a person talks to him or herself. She observed that people were either in a "fixed mindset," which meant they believed their qualities were "carved in stone," or they had a "growth mindset," which meant they believed that they could cultivate their basic qualities through their own efforts in order to grow.[f]

You have to defer judgment when you're creating, which means you have to give your creations a chance to breathe before you start giving them pointers. The time to give those will come.

At first, your creativity—your music, your dance, your experiments, your writing, your fashion designs, your songs you write or sing, your leadership ideas—is a like newborn baby. You know how you have to treat new babies. You can't just toss them around or neglect them. What's different about creativity, however, is that you're able to have *a lot* of newborns, because ideas come along more often—they don't take as long to germinate as babies. Plus you don't need to protect all your ideas as if there will never be another one coming along. You don't have to hoard them jealously.

Mainly, what you have to do is be kind to yourself. Really, really be kind to yourself, because you are the one the creativity comes through. *You're* the precious resource, not the ideas, not the dance steps, or the drawings, or the science explorations, or the leadership platform, or the songs you write, or the roles you play—any of that. That can't continue without you.

So how do you do that? How do you cherish yourself? One way is to clean out your emotional closet. Keep a journal every day—and it doesn't have only words in it. Put down all your thoughts, yes, but also go ahead and draw. If you like music and it won't distract you, play it and draw to the rhythm. Imagine yourself doing what it is you like doing. Write about what's bugging you and what you really hate. To keep yourself from stopping, write as fast as you can and don't worry about spelling, grammar, how silly or stupid it might sound. Definitely defer judgment on this journal![12]

Another practice you can do is take yourself on little excursions. You don't necessarily have to go places; you can do some of this at home. But if there are places you've never explored and you've wanted to, those are perfect to go to if you can get a ride to them or can drive yourself. These are called "creative dates" (a variation of "artist dates").[13] Only we're labeling them "creative dates" so we can include the creative people in the world, not only artists.

You don't need to make these more than two hours, and there are some rules. You do something that is nurturing to you—whatever that is. This is not a time to do your homework or be on the phone. You need to do this time alone. You do this by yourself. That's because you need not to be swayed by your friends' ideas of what to do. And you also have to pay attention to what you're feeling as you go on these "dates." That's much harder to do when you're with another person.

Three Components of Creativity

Look at the creative components below. You already have the first one. Domain or expertise skills refer to the ones you have in the area you like. You may not be an expert yet, but if you keep playing Buddhist basketball or Goth guitar, or even an activity that *seems* as passive as reading, you'll become one.

Here's a question: Why are you practicing Sith skateboarding or making caramel castles? This is a no brainer—because you want to! It is that simple, but because psychologists like to give fancy names to simple concepts, they call the desire to do something for its own sake "intrinsic motivation." Intrinsic motivation comes from *within* a person, compared to "extrinsic motivation," which comes from an outside source. Obviously if you're involved in your particular activity for no other reason than you love it, this is very powerful. Because you've often done what you loved for no money, no recognition, and through frustration, you've invested many hours in it. You'll continue investing time and because of your commitment, this activity will be the source of your greatest creativity. That's the reason intrinsic motivation is the second creativity component.

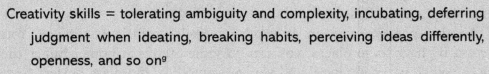

Three Components of Creativity

Domain/expertise skills = your choice!

Intrinsic motivation = what you love!

Creativity skills = tolerating ambiguity and complexity, incubating, deferring judgment when ideating, breaking habits, perceiving ideas differently, openness, and so on[g]

The three components of creativity. Drawing by Neil Battiste

The last component, creativity skills, includes the three described in chapter 1: tolerance of ambiguity (keeping options open for as long as possible); tolerance of complexity (appreciating that most situations are not simple); and incubation (being willing to let ideas rest). Other creative skills include suspending (deferring) judgment when ideating (a synonym for thinking up ideas); breaking out of well-worn habits; and perceiving ideas in a new way.

All the points in this chapter will help you cultivate your creativity. But if you forget them, you can always return to the list in "How to Crush Your Creativity" and do the opposite!

CREATIVITY AND HAPPINESS

There's a song with lyrics that claim, "Happiness is anything and anyone that's loved by you."[1] Do you agree? Do you know what makes you happy? Can you give a definition of what happiness would be for you?

Did you answer something like having a girlfriend or boyfriend? Or having a nicer or cooler one? Being popular? Getting your parents to get off your case? Owning the coolest clothes, electronics, car? Getting asked to the prom? Getting into the school you want? Moving out of the house? Finding a job you like?

Whatever you answered, what does your definition of happiness have to do with creativity? There is a definite link, but first, let's explore what the psychologists have discovered about what really makes people happy.

In the 1970s, a Chicago psychologist, Mihaly Csikszentmihalyi (me-hy cheek-SENT-me-hy-ee), began studying what made people happy.[2] (What would make me happy right now is not to type Dr. C's name again. You'd probably be happier not reading it too, so let's keep calling him "Dr. C.") So, Dr. C and his research team handed out pagers (no cell phones then) to participants in the study. At random intervals throughout the day, Dr. C's researchers paged participants. The participants then filled out a questionnaire that described what they were doing when paged and how they felt while doing it. (This paging/questionnaire technique became known as the Experience Sampling Method [ESM].)[3] Dr. C and team selected descriptions at random and began compiling data. (Dr. C's team was not the only collector of such data. Researchers around the world spent months and years using the ESM to amass similar reports.)[4]

As the responses accumulated, Dr. C's research team noticed that unlike the way people usually respond when asked what will make them happy (more money or fancier possessions, a better job or a nicer boss, no hassles at home, or the classic response—living carefree on a tropical island), these participants reported they felt happiest when engrossed in an activity. They felt energized and alert, and were concentrating so strongly on what they were doing that they not only lost track of time, they also shut out any critical thoughts about their performance.[5]

Thumbnail Biography of Mihaly Csikszentmihalyi

Dr. Mihaly Csikszentmihalyi (1934–), a Hungary native, is the former head of the psychology department at the University of Chicago. Since 1999 he has been at Claremont Graduate University in California. Dr. C. is noted for his research into happiness and creativity. He coined the term *flow* to describe the effortless state people achieve when engaged in personally meaningful tasks. His writings include *Flow: The Psychology of Optimal Experience* (1990); *Finding Flow: The Psychology of Engagement with Everyday Life* (1998); and *Creativity: Flow and the Psychology of Discovery and Invention* (1996).[a]

You're probably wondering what activity could be this engrossing. (You thought it was sex, right?) The truth is the activity was *any*thing the participants enjoyed doing.[6] They might have been "singing in a choir, programming a computer, dancing, playing bridge [cards], reading a good book."[7] Some participants reported that they felt happiest during leisure activities (playing or watching sports, viewing movies, listening to music, reading, dining out).[8] Or it "may occur in a social interaction as when good friends talk with each other."[9] What really startled researchers, however, was that regardless of the participants' ethnicity, gender, socioeconomic status, education, sexual orientation, geography, or age, they described their happiest moments using almost identical words. Dr. C observed, "The psychological conditions that make [flow] possible seem to be the same the world over."[10]

Dr. C described this happy state of being as "flow." "Flow tends to occur when a person's skills are fully involved in overcoming a challenge that is just about manageable."[11]

To basketball players, flow is the same as "in the zone"; for musicians, it's playing "in the groove."

Teens' Feelings about Their Creativity

Question 2 (Part 1): "How do you feel when you are being creative?"

"I feel as if I'm having an out-of-body experience, life's daily worries and emotions, fears, deadlines, fade away and I'm left with an open canvas to create whatever I want. There is no limit and it feels like anything is possible."—Darius, 16, Florida

"I feel consumed, like nothing else is around me."—Sofia, 17, Minnesota

"I feel like I'm in a whole new world creating characters and worlds by my rules."—Kyle, 19, Florida

"I feel good because I have just created something that hasn't been created before."—James, 15, California

"I feel energized when I am being creative."—Glennon, 17, California

"Full of energy, working on adrenalin, and nothing stops me."—Chandler, 13, Florida

"When I feel creative I feel a rush of energy racing through my mind and I have visions that I can see an invention."—Thomas, 13, Virginia

"Free. At peace. Excited. Centered."—Skye, 18, California

"I feel liberated, with a touch of euphoria."—Dakota, 17, California

"I feel relaxed. It is as though I am at peace. Like I have reached total Nirvana."—Arianna, 18, California

"Uplifted, in a relaxed, focused way."—Gregory, 18, Florida

"I feel confident and powerful. Nothing can stop me from being creative because there are no limits."—Shai, 16, California

"I feel excited, rebellious, and passionate."—Nina, 15, New York

"I feel like myself."—Anne Marie, 16, California

"When I'm creative, I feel happy mostly."—Klarissa, 16, California[b]

Did you notice any similarity between Dr. C's definition of flow and these teen's feelings about being creative? Don't their descriptions match the following definition of *flow*, which is defined as "exceptional moments" when what we think, what we want, and what we feel come together.[12] "The metaphor of 'flow' is one that many people have used to describe the sense of effortless action they feel in moments that stand out as the best in their lives."[13]

When Darius states, "I'm left with an open canvas to create whatever I want. There is no limit and it feels like anything is possible," and Sofia says, "I feel consumed, like nothing else is around me," don't they sound like they are experiencing "a loss of a self separate from the world around [which] is sometimes accompanied by a feeling of union with the environment"?[14]

Or look at Kyle's words, "I feel like I'm in a whole new world creating characters and worlds by my rules." Do you think his experience in creating characters (for books, films, or video games) matches this description: "When high challenges are matched with high skills, then the deep involvement that sets flow apart from ordinary life is likely to occur"?[15]

Notice the word *balance* in the description of flow. Skye, Dakota, Adrianna, and Gregory imply that sense of balance when they described how they felt when creative.

Were their words similar to "dynamic equilibrium"?[16]

When Darius mentioned "deadlines fall away," isn't that close to "time seems to disappear"?[17]

Three teens, Glennon, Chandler, and Thomas, mentioned a feeling of energy while creating. Although the description of flow does not include the word *energy*, it is impossible to imagine being in flow without an increase in energy.

As you hear how closely these teens' descriptions of their creative moments match Dr. C's descriptions of flow, it's easy to see a connection between happiness and creativity. Let's do a tiny bit of algebra with the transitive property of equality. This states that if A = B and B = C, then A = C. If you substitute flow for A, happiness for B, and creativity for C, then flow equals happiness, happiness equals creativity, and *flow* equals *creativity*. As sixteen-year-old Klarissa from California wrote, "When I'm creative, I feel happy mostly."

So if flow is the happy conduit to creativity, the next step for you is to discover the activity that will give you as much flow as possible. Your "flow activity" has to be something you enjoy and have skill in. Because you enjoy it, you're motivated to improve your skills so you'll be willing to challenge yourself.[18] However, you must have the appropriate level of challenge. To illustrate this, pretend you enjoy playing tennis. During a game of tennis, if you're playing against an opponent who is much better than you, most likely you're going to feel discouraged. If you play against someone whose skill level is much lower than yours, you'll probably get bored. If you and your opponent are evenly matched—in other words, you have the appropriate level of challenge—at some point while playing, you're going to achieve flow.[19]

You have to choose what Daniel Pink calls "Goldilocks"—the choice that's neither too hard nor too soft—the "chair" that's in the middle.[20] (Buddha called this "the middle way."[21]) It's also called the "happy medium." In fact, the term *happy medium* is a perfect description of you—you are halfway between confidence and challenge in an activity you enjoy spending time in.[22]

Really, truly enjoying that activity is crucial. If you don't enjoy the activity for its own sake, you'll have no intrinsic motivation to engage in it; you'll have no "love of the game." Actually, the term *love of the game* applies to areas outside of sports. You must find a "game" you love. Now you understand why, in Dr. C's happiness studies, people were engaged in a very wide range of activities when they experienced flow. Like you, every one of those pager-carrying participants had an intrinsic motivation for spending time in his or her particular activity.[23] When you spend time on what you love, the time you invest increases your skill. (Michael Jordan had "love of the game" written in his contract, as well as the right to play pick-up games whenever he chose.[24])

By the way, our founding fathers recognized the power of intrinsic motivation, which is why the Declaration of Independence includes the phrase "pursuit of happiness." At that time, the word *pursuit* meant "livelihood" or what we would call "career." The declaration stated people had a *right* to pursue that in any way they wanted. This was a radical idea because at that time most people did not have the freedom to do work that suited their abilities or interests. People were born into a certain class (what we call a socioeconomic status) and either inherited titles, money, and land or carried on the family occupation. The men who founded the United States realized that citizens would enjoy more security, prosperity, and happiness if they were permitted to spend time and energy on activities they chose. The founders also recognized that people must be responsible for choosing those activities. Including the phrase "pursuit of happiness" in the Declaration of Independence acknowledged that happiness was balanced between freedom and responsibility.

Finding Your Flow

It could be you're not sure what activity makes you happy. Or you may be very clear and remember times you felt happy doing it, but wonder how you can keep that happiness flowing.

To get insight into your "flow activity," remember the last time you recall being happy. When was it? Where were you? What were you doing? (If it's relevant to what you were doing, who was with you at the time?) How long did that happy time last? Did you recall feeling confident in what you were doing and at the same time, feeling pleasantly challenged? Can you recall other times when you felt as happy?

It could be that you recall being happy while involved in more than one activity, but the activities don't seem to be related. Maybe you recall being happy while singing, cooking, and riding a motorcycle. You could conclude that you like all three and become the first singing, motorcycle-riding chef, or maybe there's a common factor in these activities. (You can have flow in more than one area of your life; in fact, that's ideal.)

It could be that all those activities brought happiness because you were by yourself. Or you were performing for others. You need to discover the common factor. Did these activities occur outdoors? Were you solving problems? Did you get to be a leader? Then maybe it's nature you love. Or maybe the common factor is performing, problem solving, or leading. As long as that particular factor is present, you can be happy doing many activities.

Discovering Your Strengths

If you already know what your strengths are, you can skip this section. If you don't know, there are other ways—some simple, like questions, and some more formal, like assessments—to help you discover your strengths. If you still have

Myths and Truths about Strengths

Myths about Strengths

1. Each person can learn to be competent in almost anything.
2. Each person's greatest room for growth is in his or her areas of greatest weakness.

The *Truth* about Strengths

1. Each person's talents are enduring and unique.
2. Each person's greatest room for growth is in the areas of his or her greatest strength.[c]

questions about your favorite activity, you can take assessments. StrengthsQuest will give you an accurate inventory of your strengths. The Myers-Briggs Type Indicator, True Colors, and the Enneagram can provide more clues. If you're willing to go low-tech, ask your friends and family when they've noticed you're happiest. Finally, you could turn to chapter 13, "Creativity Catchall," and experiment with the Talent Map, the Value Tree, and/or the Value Grid.[25]

As you know from reading about StrengthsQuest in chapter 4, working on your weaknesses is like trying to write with your nondominant hand.

You've also learned that one of the three components of creativity is intrinsic motivation, which comes from *within* yourself.[26]

Because you are intrinsically motivated to spend time in your chosen activity, you can choose to re-create the conditions for flow rather than waiting for flow to "just happen."[27]

Now let's explore how to stay in flow as much as possible. Even if you know what you love doing, you can't do it all the time. What you want to do, however, is engineer your life so you can be in flow as much as possible. Assuming you know what you love, work on accumulating those 10,000 hours. Maximizing these times in your life is important to you now, of course, but it will be essential for the rest of your life. That's because people don't feel differently about what they loved as kids or as teens. By putting hours into what you love, you will be more likely to turn what you love into a career.

When you have finished high school, find a way to get more training in your chosen activity, either at college or at a trade or arts school. While you're still in middle or high school, explore careers that utilize the skills you've learned.[28] When you're able to earn a living involved in this activity you love, you'll be spending much of your time in flow.

In the meantime, being in flow will increase your creativity. While in flow you aren't criticizing what you're doing.[29] Flow equals a lack of self-criticism. A "no-criticism zone" is the ideal environment for creativity. Your critical voice crushes creativity. ("What critical voice?" you ask. The one that just asked you, "What critical voice?" and probably added, "I don't hear a critical voice.") Being in flow shuts it up.

Appreciation

The opposite of criticism is appreciation. The opposite of self-criticism is self-appreciation. When you appreciate yourself you are doing more than building your creative muscles, more than strengthening your creative immunity. What you are actually doing is *creating yourself*. (Remember what George Bernard Shaw said . . .)

She's in flow with her cell-o.

Some day you will get so used to appreciating yourself that when you lapse into self-criticism, you'll be able to give yourself five appreciative comments for every negative comment, which will return you to equilibrium.[30]

If negative self-talk has such a damaging impact, then it's logical that positive self-talk must have an empowering influence. It does. Researchers have shown that simply smiling will make you feel better when you don't actually feel happy. Part of the reason is because it takes a lot fewer muscles to smile than to frown. What's the other reason? If you're walking around smiling, other people are smiling back. Those smiles add to your happiness.

The same goes for thinking good thoughts about yourself. That doesn't mean you have to think *perfect* thoughts. If you didn't perform your best in the school play, it's fine to say that. It's absolutely crucial, however, that you appreciate yourself for getting on stage. Whether you try something new or try something old in a new way, you *must* appreciate yourself.

You know why appreciation works? Because the critical part of yourself *needs* to be offset, to be rewarded instead of hurt by words. Words are powerful, both in the ways they hurt and heal. Try to remember to say appreciative words to yourself.

Self-Esteem and Creativity

Let's explore the topic of self-esteem for a while.

You could also say, as the psychologist William James did over a century ago, that self-esteem depends on the ratio of your expectations to your successes.[31] This means the less you expect, the happier you'll be. (If you are in despair or depressed, however, expecting less is not healthy.)

By now you may be wondering how all these "self" definitions connect to creativity. Self-esteem, self-worth, self-image, self-concept, and self-confidence all relate to having respect for, being worthy of, having regard for, having strength in, having ideas about, and finding power in oneself. And they all appear to be boosted—positively affected—by creativity.

When I taught courses on creativity, usually based on books by Julia Cameron or Martha Beck (a nationally recognized life coach), I observed that any student

Definitions of Self

Self-esteem: a realistic respect for *or* favorable impression of oneself.

Self-worth: the sense of one's own value or worth as a person.

Self-image: the idea, conception, or mental image one has of oneself.

Self-concept: the idea or mental image one has of oneself and one's strengths, weaknesses, status, and so on.

Self-confidence: realistic confidence in one's own judgment, ability, power, and so on.[d]

who completed a course demonstrated a noticeable increase in self-esteem. I didn't design this goal into the courses; I wasn't trying to make my students' self-esteem improve. They weren't consciously trying to increase theirs either. What occurred was that from the start of any particular course to the end (eight, ten, or twelve weeks), not only did students report that they had unlocked much of their creativity, but they all declared that they felt much better about themselves. "Feeling better about yourself" may not be a scientific measurement, yet those words certainly indicate increased self-esteem.

There weren't enough students in these classes to be statistically significant and I'm not aware of any scientific studies that link increased self-esteem to people's creative efforts. I suspect, however, that there is more connection between creativity and self-esteem than is currently known. There are several possibilities why this may be so: one reason is that when you're in flow, you're nonjudgmental. The other reason is what you produce while creative is meaningful and unique— at least to you.

Mstkes, Mistaks, Mistkes

Those misspellings were intentional. Got your attention, didn't they? The third, and maybe most important, reason for involving yourself in the trial-and-error component of creativity is accepting that mistakes are not only part of the process; they are its most vital component.

This Is Your Brain on Mistakes

Dr. Antoine Bechara, psychologist and professor at the University of Southern California (USC), studies complex behaviors, including how our brains make decisions (decision neuroscience). Bechara isolated two equal-sized centers in the prefrontal cortex of the brain (behind your forehead), which he claims are responsible for our fear of failure (risk) and our desire for success (reward). "We always knew people could learn from their mistakes, but now we're finding out exactly how and where this happens. Basically, it all comes down to survival. In a normally functioning brain, failure is welcomed as an opportunity for learning and strengthening the species."[e]

The creative process thrives on mistakes.

We fear risk and yearn for reward, and we must constantly choose one or the other. That act of choosing between them occurs between these two centers. If you think of the centers as the "devil (risk/failure) and angel (reward/success) on your shoulders," those areas are the ones that interact in the brain during your decision-making process.[32]

The concept of failure is key to creativity. Failure, making mistakes, and trial and error aren't *part* of the process of creation. Making mistakes *is* the process! *Trial and error is the only way we know how to operate in the creative process.* Now that you know a little about how decisions are made in our brains, this makes sense.

By the way, the bigger the project you're working on, the more mistakes you'll make. One of the cofounders of Twitter, Biz Stone, agrees. In the first months after Twitter launched, its servers kept crashing. Of course, Stone and other Twitter executives got complaints! Finally, after weeks of server crashes, Stone sent an e-mail to Twitter customers apologizing and letting them know how hard the company was working on the problem. Amazingly, Twitter customers sent understanding e-mails in support of the techs who were trying to fix the servers. Stone also posted an animated cartoon of flying birds carrying a whale. Naturally, the birds weren't able to hold the whale up for long, so everyone began calling it "the Fail Whale." Whenever Twitter had server problems, the Fail Whale appeared, reminding customers that Twitter was a new system and failures were bound to occur.[33]

Contrast how people responded to the 2013 launch of the Affordable Care Act (ACA) national website. Its servers also crashed and ACA got thousands of complaints. The story of the website failure made national news for weeks. There was no explanatory e-mail or an ACA version of the Fail Whale to mollify customers. Regardless, it was unrealistic and ridiculous to expect a national website, which is basically a massive creative project, to launch without sizable glitches. Back in the low-tech 1930s and 1960s, when the Social Security and Medicare programs were introduced, people were equally unhappy with their bureaucratic chaos.[34]

Since it's doubtful your mistakes will take place on a national stage, you can begin to get comfortable making them. (Bonus: It isn't a far reach from getting comfortable with mistake-making in creativity to having this comfort filter into the rest of your life. When you make mistakes in areas outside creative projects, you start to become a little more understanding of yourself, less judgmental, less harsh. In other words, what you experience in creating carries over to you feeling better when you're *not* creating.)

Being in a creative process, feeling good about it, then feeling good about yourself channels you back to the creative process. Yes, this is a circle. You could call it a "luscious circle"—the opposite of a "vicious circle." Or you could call it a "creative circle," a continuous feedback loop that builds up your creativity, your creative output, and your radical acceptance of yourself.

> "In order to create good art, you must give yourself permission to make bad art."
>
> —Julia Cameron (1948–), teacher, playwright, journalist, filmmaker, composer, author of *The Artist's Way* and sequels[f]

So, like bookends, creativity holds up in both directions. You're creative when you allow yourself to make mistakes *and* you're creative as you get more and more comfortable with mistake-making. As you get comfortable with the whole concept of mistakes, you begin to relax with your own mistakes. You want to be more creative because you're actually enjoying the *process* of experimenting—which is really what mistake-making is: experimentation.

People seem to forget this. They certainly forget that they didn't learn to walk in a week or two. When you first began walking, you stood on someone's lap—many times. Then you stood in your crib or playpen, holding onto the rail. At some point you got out of your "jail" (crib) and you held onto a table or a chair or something that would hold you up and not let you fall over. But you still fell down. Then you got back up. You kept getting back up. One day you took a step. You probably fell down right afterward.

Did you get frustrated? You bet. You probably *cried* in frustration many, many times. Hopefully, some people saw you stand and take a step and cheered you on. And then you felt happy. But you kept getting frustrated too. But you kept taking steps, one at a time.

You know what you *didn't* do when you were learning to walk? You didn't say, "This is too hard. I can't do this. I'm no good at walking. Everyone else walks better than I do. Look at her. She walks really well. Look at him. He walked three months sooner than I did. Forget it. I'll never get this right. I give up."

Kinda silly, huh? Hopefully, you'll soon realize it's as silly (and sad) to beat yourself up for your current mistakes as it would have been to criticize yourself when learning to walk. You were a toddler then, and as you practice your chosen activity, you're a toddler now. Or, if you prefer, you could borrow the term that Buddhists use to describe this inexperienced state—"beginner's mind."[35] From your beginner's mind you can move to "building" yourself a new "heart."

Build Your Own Heart

You know when you're faced with a difficult situation, people will advise you to "have heart"? Or to "take heart"? This advice refers to courage. (Courage is the English translation of the Italian word *corragio*, which means to "have heart." In olden days, people believed that courage originated in the heart.)

When you're born you're issued one heart. "Build your own heart" refers to the process of you creating your own *emotional* heart. You can it build it with whatever materials you want; however, you might want to consider the following components, which have been of use to other teens: *Safety, Identity, Power, Strength, Abundance, Appreciation, Possibility,* and *Self-Protection.* (These are the components of Build Your Own Heart program.)[36]

Since your main focus as a teen is to establish your unique identity, you might want to start with the *Identity* component. Next, you might want to establish a sense of *Safety.* To do this, you must go back to what you learned about suspending criticism of yourself, embracing errors as a part of the creativity process, and having compassion for yourself. These criteria are essential for you to experience yourself being safe.[37]

Power refers to your personal power. You've already explored *strength. Abundance* refers to more than money; it means having what you want in life, including loving relationships, meaningful work, and joyful experiences. In chapter 7, you explored the benefits of *Appreciation. Possibility,* of course, refers to your goals and your future. While the significance of *Self-Protection* may seem obscure, it means that you need to shield yourself from all criticism, including your own.[38]

As much as possible, allow yourself to be so immersed in your creative projects that they carry you into flow. In that state you'll be able to quell your critical voice and feel the energy and satisfaction that is closest to happiness.

DIVERGENT AND CONVERGENT TOOLS FOR CREATIVE PROBLEM SOLVING

"There is always a well-known solution to every human problem—
neat, plausible, and wrong."—H. L. Mencken (1880–1956),
Prejudices: Second Series, 1920, U.S. author and editor[1]

Mr. Mencken may have known something about creative problem solving long before it was developed by Alex Osborn. (Rarely is there a neat solution to a problem, especially a complex one.) As mentioned in chapter 6, Creative Problem Solving (CPS) is the method Osborn formulated in the early 1950s to help creative teams at his ad agency generate ideas for products. You might recall the most famous method Osborn developed was called "brainstorming."[2]

Since that time, many people in business and at universities have produced more ways to assist people with generating ideas and helping to sort through those ideas. The tools that assist in idea generation are called "divergent thinking" tools. The sorting types are "convergent thinking" tools.[3] Many of these tools have acronyms, often with three letters. (CPS people love acronyms!)

Check out the teens' views on solving problems on page 110. Do your ideas about problem solving reflect any of theirs? Did you notice any references that point to divergent or convergent thinking? You have time to think about your answers. In the meantime, here are some excellent divergent thinking tools (with links, if available):

Teens' Views on Problem-Solving

Question 5: "How do you think creativity can help solve problems?"

"Creativity can lead to unorthodox solutions."—Sam, 16, California

"Everything is like a puzzle, and creativity is the way of solving the puzzle."—Klarissa, 16, California

"Creativity combined with practicality and necessity solves problems."—Max, 16, California

"Problem solving requires good ideas because sometimes things are difficult to solve, which means you need creativity."—Heather, 16, Illinois

"Creativity allows new and imaginative ideas to approach and fix issues."—Angela, 18, Florida

"Once I heard something along the lines of, when you lose your keys you start searching in all the logical places you may have misplaced them. Pocket in your coat, kitchen table, car, office. After you look in all the obvious places and find nothing we start searching in our fridge, sock drawer, oven. Often times when we think we are hunting for what we were in search of we find things we didn't know were missing."—Hannah, 18, New York

"Sometimes the solution to a problem is an idea that no one thinks of, and you need to think outside the box to find it."—Nina, 15, New York

"You could think of new, original ways to solve problems that other people may not be thinking of."—Justin, 12, Florida[a]

Creative Problem Solving: Then and Now

Alex Osborn, founder of the Creative Problems Solving (CPS) process, called the three phases of CPS by different names in his 1953 book, *Applied Imagination*. Fact Finding morphed into the first phase, Exploring the Problem; Idea Finding changed to Generating Ideas (not a big semantic leap); and the third and final phase, Solution Finding, became Planning for Action. The CPS process, however, remains essentially the same as Osborn described it in his book.[b]

Divergent Thinking Tools

First, a recap of the definition of divergent thinking: this is when you—creativity cliché alert—"think outside the box." You readjust your perspective on your problem and include novelty.

CPS has been researched since its inception in the 1950s and it continues to be the most well-known and effective process used in education and business. (CPS will be described further in chapters 10 and 11.)[4]

As you may recall from chapter 3 ("Creativity's Roots and Branches"), while working with creative teams at his advertising agency, Osborn developed a repertoire of techniques to stimulate their creativity. One of those techniques is part of the Generating Ideas phase, and truthfully, you are already familiar with it.[5]

In *How to Think Up*, Osborn described the key technique of his creative model—the most famous creative technique in the world: brainstorming.[6]

Rules for genuine brainstorming are listed on page 113. The reason this is "genuine" brainstorming is because of these rules. You might have dabbled in generating ideas before; however, if you didn't follow these four rules, it wasn't the brainstorming technique that Osborn developed. Chances are the rule that you or those in your group have violated the most is Rule 1. That's because it's a job for a superhero to get that critical, judging voice to shut up.

So here is what you do: If you're brainstorming by yourself, you need to write down *every* idea that comes into your head, no matter how stupid or silly it seems, and no matter if it sounds almost identical to one you've already written. One tip: The faster you write (ignore your messy handwriting and forget about spelling),

Diverging: going for novelty!

the easier to shut out that voice. In minutes you'll have a hefty batch of ideas, some of them original and on target for solving your problem. That's the whole reason for "storming" your brain. (If you're in a group brainstorming session, you really need a qualified facilitator. Without one, it's nearly impossible for a group to monitor the "critical voice syndrome" while trying to generate ideas.)

There is one form of brainstorming, however, that you *can* use in a group that will help reduce both those inner and outer critical voices. No wonder it works —it's a cousin to brainstorming. It's called *brainwriting* and it is a simple and very effective group technique.[7] (In brainwriting, the Client is the person who brings a problem to a CPS session, the Resource Group are people who help solve the

The *Genuine* Brainstorming Technique

(Accept no substitutes! Really, don't.)

Follow these rules and you'll become an expert brainstormer. When it's necessary to think divergently (also known as brainstorming), you must *always*

1. Defer judgment.
2. Go for *quantity*, not quality.
3. Go for wild ideas.
4. Build on other ideas.[c]

Client's problem, and the Facilitator is the person who makes sure everyone uses the CPS process correctly.)

1. Before the session, gather five to seven sheets of printer paper (the number depends on the number of people in the Resource Group). Leave enough space at the top of each paper (you can draw two lines at top if you like) in order to write the problem. Below the lines, place square unlined sticky notes in three rows of three.
2. When the Client determines the problem, write it on the top lines. (It's OK for others to write the problem in as well as the Facilitator, but the wording must be identical on all papers.)
3. Remind each person about the rules for brainstorming. (It'd be even more effective if you ask *them* to repeat them to you!)
4. Pass out one paper with sticky notes to each group member. Instruct each person to write an idea on each sticky note on the top row *only*. (Suggest that the members write quickly to help gag their critical voices.)
5. As soon as someone has finished writing a row, pass the sticky note paper to someone else to fill out the second row. (Make sure the group knows it can build on other ideas.)
6. When the third row of sticky notes is filled in, collect the papers. Put the sticky notes on a blank page on a pad on an easel or a wall so everyone can view them. Your group will have a slew of ideas for solving the problem.

Vision Quest: The Mouse and the Eagle

This is a non-CPS technique for adjusting your perspective on a problem. What you do is look at the problem from two angles. First, drop to the vantage point of a mouse—focusing intently on whatever is directly in front of you. Then scout out your big picture from the height of a soaring eagle. Keep alternating these views until you achieve another way (or ways) of dealing with your problem.[d]

SCAMPER[8]

Sounds energetic, doesn't it? Actually it is energetic, for your mind. Developed in 1971 by Robert F. Eberle, SCAMPER is an anagram for Substitute, Combine, Adapt, Modify, Put to other uses, Eliminate, Rearrange. SCAMPER is designed to help you "mix it up" when you're trying to generate ideas.

Under each of the seven categories in SCAMPER are lists of questions to stimulate idea generation. For instance, the questions listed under *Substitute* include "What else can you use instead?" and "What other group can be included?" Under *Combine*, there's "How can you combine parts?"[9] and "How about a blend?" *Rearrange* asks "What other layout might work?" and "What if you reversed it?" You can find additional questions for all the categories at litemind. com/scamper/. They will help you look at your problem in as many ways as possible. By employing unusual perspectives, you'll find solutions.

Forced Connections[10]

Before you do this exercise, refresh your memory with the rules for brainstorming. Now, keeping those rules in mind, point to an object in the room or a picture that is *totally unrelated* to your problem. Ask yourself, "What ideas do I get from this object or picture that might help me solve my problem?" Next, "force" a connection between the object/picture and the problem that will help you generate more ideas. Repeat this step as often as you need or want to.

To make this exercise more effective, you might begin collecting photos of animals, scenery, food, buildings, patterns, or any picture that reveals only a portion of an object. Make sure the photos you collect are as generic as possible—without ads, people, signs, or writing of any kind. The more generic they are, the more useful they'll be in generating ideas. (Note: Every month *Reader's Digest* presents two photos in the feature "See the World . . . Differently." The first photo is intentionally difficult to identify; this is exactly the one you might want to clip or scan. The second, often startling photo, reveals the mystery.)[11] You can put these photos in clear plastic sheets in a three-ring binder and label it "Forced Connections."

To understand how this process works, say you are trying to come up with a fresh approach for your club's next fund-raiser. You've gotten some ideas, only they weren't original, and by this time you can't even think of any ideas, much less anything novel. So you locate your Forced Connections binder. Perusing photos that are *totally unrelated* to your problem allows your brain to make unusual connections to it and generate novel ideas. Soon you will have your own collection of photos you can use to force connections when your brainstorming abilities have gone stale. (You could keep the photos in a Forced Connections file on your laptop or phone.)

This chapter contains only five of the scores of other divergent thinking tools. To find more, Google "divergent thinking" or "divergent CPS tools" on the Internet. You'll most likely find some favorites. (Some are even featured in YouTube videos.)

Convergent Thinking Tools

These tools and techniques are used when you already have a lot of ideas and you need to shake them out to find the best ones for the situation you're in. Many of these tools are very simple and you may already be familiar with some of them. (You might not have known they were creative tools, however!)

Remember the brainstorming and/or brainwriting you did? Did you know what to do with all those sticky notes once you put them on the easel? Probably not, so here is a convergent tool you'll find useful in sorting them. (This tool is also used in CPS sessions.)

Highlighting[12]

1. Hits: Review the ideas on the sticky notes and pay attention to those that intrigue you. Using a dot marker, colored dots, or stars, mark those sticky notes. Make sure to include some novel ideas. (You'll know you've got a "hit" if the idea feels right, is clear, on target, "sparkles," is going in the right direction, is relevant or workable, and of course, if it solves the problem.)

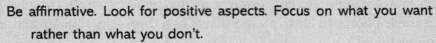

Rules for Convergent Thinking

Be affirmative. Look for positive aspects. Focus on what you want rather than what you don't.

Be deliberate. Give yourself time and be aware of your own assumptions and prejudices.

Check your objectives. Remember the original goal and let it guide you to appropriate choices.

Improve ideas. Not all ideas are workable. Be disciplined to strengthen ideas.

Consider novelty. Take a risk and be open to original ideas. Reflect on ways to adapt them.[e]

2. Cluster: Next, group similar ideas together by moving the sticky notes into clusters.

3. Restate: Finally, write a statement about each cluster. You can do this if you capture the essence of each one. Eventually, you'll be able to take all the cluster statements and formulate a single statement, which is actually a statement of the problem.

PPCO (or Praise First)

This is an extremely powerful and effective tool that helps you determine the excellence of any product, project, or presentation you or another has designed. PPCO can also determine the viability of a group-made plan. If you are ever asked to be a judge of a project (art, a paper, play), you'll be grateful to know this technique. It's a wonderful way to give people genuinely honest feedback without damaging egos. Another plus: it's easy to remember![13]

PPCO (also known as Praise First)[14] stands for

P: Plusses—What is good, positive, a *plus* about this idea, project, product, presentation?

P: Potential—What are the potentials of this idea, project, product, or presentation?

Converging: agreeing on ideas!

C: Concerns—What are the concerns (weaknesses, limitations, shortcomings) about this idea, project, product, presentation?

O: Overcoming Concerns—What are ways to overcome the concerns (weaknesses, limitations, shortcomings) about this idea, project, product, or presentation?[15]

Card Sort[16]

This tool is designed to help you prioritize up to fifteen options. It is useful with groups or an individual, and it is low-tech, which is part of its charm. (If you adapt it to high tech, let me know.) Here's how it works—and yes, you'll need 3 x 5 inch index cards.[17]

1. Write down each option you're considering on a separate card and arrange the cards in a row.
2. Count the cards. (This is permissible in this exercise.)
3. Identify your *least* favorite option and on it, write the number of total cards you have (i.e., if you have seven cards, write "7" on this one). Put the card aside.

4. Identify the option you like *best* and write "1" on it. Put it aside, too.
5. Identify your next least favorite option and write on that card the total number *minus one*. For example, if you had seven cards, mark this one "6."
6. Identify your second favorite option and write "2" on the card.
7. Continue the process, switching from least favorite to favorite until all the cards have been marked. (Marking cards is also OK here.)
8. Arrange the cards you have in numerical order. Now you can look at how you've ranked your options.

For you visual types, there's also an excellent YouTube video from the International Center for Studies in Creativity at Buffalo State College, which shows how to use Card Sort.[18]

You will be able to use these diverging and converging thinking tools to assist you when you need to make a decision in a problem that affects you alone, with a partner, or in a group. Some of these tools are also used in CPS sessions.

CREATIVE PROBLEM SOLVING SESSION

The Big Picture

As you learned in chapter 3, Alex Osborn developed the original creative problem solving process, including his famous brainstorming technique. Osborn described the original steps of Creative Problem Solving (CPS) in his book *Applied Imagination*.[1]

There are three phases in a CPS session: Exploring the Problem (Phase 1), Generating Ideas (Phase 2), and Planning for Action (Phase 3).[2]

There are several "players" in a CPS session. First, there is the Client, a person (or an organization) who has a problem and has agreed to participate in a CPS session in order to solve it. Second, there is the Facilitator, who is trained in the CPS process.

The third human component of CPS is the Resource Group, the members of which may or may not be familiar with the Client *or* the problem. The Resource Group does not need any training prior to the CPS session; the Facilitator will provide the necessary guidance.[3]

The success of CPS is largely based on the fact that CPS describes a natural process. We all naturally want to solve our problems, we're all looking for solutions, and when we've arrived at our solutions, we want a plan for acting on them.[4] CPS is effective because it is both structured *and* flexible.[5] The structure depends on the three phases of the CPS process. The flexibility stems from the ideas generated (brainstormed), as well as how the Facilitator "steers" the session. No two CPS sessions are exactly alike, so the Facilitator knows how to modify aspects of the CPS process so that the Client's needs are met.

Since the advent of CPS in the 1950s, many researchers, inaugurated by Dr. Sidney Parnes, have clarified and developed the CPS phases so that anyone can understand and utilize them.[6] Other CPS proponents have applied the process to problems in businesses, organizations (such as nonprofits and schools), and communities around the world.[7] These CPS practitioners, including Osborn himself, learned how to make the CPS process as effective as possible for solving real-world problems. Thus CPS has benefitted from being honed and polished by both academia and the marketplace. Practitioners in both arenas will continue to study and streamline the three-phase process of CPS, making it as dynamic and effective as Osborn intended.

The term *Creative Problem Solving* is trademarked; however, the process itself is open and available to all who want to use creativity to solve problems.

The Larger Scene

The easiest way for you to understand how CPS works in a group is to describe it in an imaginary session. (Yes, I could continue describing a CPS session in generic form. In fact, that was how I wrote my first draft; however, when I read it over, the bore factor was mega-million plus. Describing a CPS session that way isn't fair to you or to CPS itself. Being a part of a CPS session, whether as a Client, a member of a Resource Group, or a Facilitator, is truly a dynamic experience. In the next section, you can watch an imaginary CPS session on display. The information on CPS in the sidebars, however, is genuine.)

Imaginary CPS Session

Let's pretend that a group of teens decide they'd like to start a creativity club at their high school. The school has guidelines for how to start up and run a club. They've decided to call theirs the Creativity Club. The teens explain the problem (how to attract club members from the entire school) to their art teacher, who becomes the club adviser.

The adviser suggests Creative Problem Solving, or CPS, to help solve their problem. They meet with a CPS process expert, known as a Facilitator, who explains that CPS participants consist of a Client, who "owns" the problem; a Facilitator; and a Resource Group that provides ideas, energy, and insight and perspective on the Client's problem. CPS sessions take two and a half to four hours.[8]

A few days before the session, the Facilitator asks the teens questions to determine the scope of the problem. Certain problems are not appropriate for a CPS group session. Those would be emergencies or any situation that must be dealt with immediately; when there's not complete "buy-in" from all the people involved in the problem; when the Client is not willing to be held accountable for the problem; or when the problem does not belong to the Client.[9]

The ideal number of people for a Resource Group is five to seven. (Four or fewer means the group has to work harder to generate ideas and may not

Sample Questions for Clients to Answer *before* the CPS Session

Who is the decision maker?

How long have you had this problem?

Who will be taking action on this problem?

Who does this problem belong to?

Who else is involved?

What's worked in the past?

What successes have been achieved so far?

What have been some of the obstacles?

Where have you gotten help?

Who has helped you?

Who would gain if this problem were solved?

How are your feelings affecting the problem?

What other data is relevant or important to this situation?

When would you like to see action taken on this problem?

What is your ideal outcome?

The Facilitator needs to determine (1) the Client has ownership and accountability to solve the problem; (2) the Client really *wants* to solve the problem; (3) the Client needs new ideas.[a]

generate enough new ones. Eight or more is too large a group to manage.) The generating ideas process also works better if people of different ages, careers, and life experiences are included. At least one person should attend who has no knowledge of the problem because he or she will bring a fresh perspective to solving it.[10]

After the Resource Group is formed, the Facilitator lists the materials needed for the session: colored markers with narrow tips, sticky notes in two colors, nickel-size multicolored sticky dots, an easel and a large pad of paper, chairs, and two tables.[11]

On the session day, the Facilitator arrives with a laptop and a binder. A Process Buddy handles logistical tasks so the session runs smoothly. The Facilitator explains the CPS process consists of three parts: exploring the problem, getting ideas to solve it, and making a plan.[12]

Phase 1: Exploring the Problem

The Facilitator points to the pre-session questions and the answers the teens gave and informs everyone that the exploring the problem phase of CPS has begun. The teens and the Facilitator alternate reading the Q&As, then the Facilitator asks if anyone has anything to add.

The Facilitator asks, "Which part of the problem do you want to work on?" The teens reply that the problem is convincing people that the Creativity Club is not just for artistic people.

The Facilitator informs the Resource Group that before it begins working on the teens' problem, it'll be participating in a warm-up exercise involving brainstorming. An example of a warm-up exercise: A men's shoe factory accidentally made over 1,000 extra left shoes before the machine was shut off. The CFO doesn't want to take these shoes as a loss. So he needs some help from you. How many uses can you find for these left shoes?

The Facilitator flips the page on the large pad on the easel to reveal the four rules for brainstorming: (1) Defer judgment. (2) Go for quantity, not quality. (3) Go for wild ideas. (4) Build on other ideas.[13]

The Facilitator then instructs people to write one idea per sticky note that will be posted on an easel. Some ideas for using the extra shoes are "Plant flowers in them," "String a bunch together and add Christmas lights," "Spray with plastic

Why Include Warm-Ups in CPS?

Research has shown that brainstorming warm-up exercises are essential for the success of CPS sessions. By generating ideas for a simple, even silly problem, the exercise helps the Resource Group relax and have fun. This, in turns, helps the Resource Group generate more and more original ideas for the Client's problem. When the warm-up has been omitted, fewer and less novel ideas are produced.[b]

coating, mount on poles, and use for bird feeders," and "Marry a right shoe." The Facilitator explains that all ideas are valid, that none should be criticized. By generating many ideas and accepting all of them, the atmosphere will lead to generating original and useful ideas.

After a warm-up exercise, the Resource Group works on the problem, which is how to convince non-artistic students to enroll in a Creativity Club. In this phase, the Resource Group must write its ideas in the form of questions, each one beginning with a Statement Starter.[14]

The Facilitator instructs the Resource Group to write each idea as a question using a Statement Starter.

CPS Statement Starters

Statement Starters are acronyms for phrases that begin problem statements *or* describe a Client's goals. Some of the most commonly used are listed here.

> Statement Starters for Phase 1, Exploring the Problem:
> > How to = H2
> > How might = HM
> > In which ways might = IWWM
> > What might be all the = WMBAT
> Statement Starters for Phase 3, Plan for Action:
> > I wish = IW
> > It would be great if = IWBGI
> > What I would like is = WIWLI
> > What I see myself as doing = WISMD
> > What I *now* see myself doing = WI*N*SMD

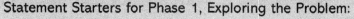

Statement Starters were not part of the original CPS process. They have evolved over the years in many CPS sessions when Facilitators observed that such starters streamlined the process of exploring the Client's problem or assisted in framing the Client's goals.[c]

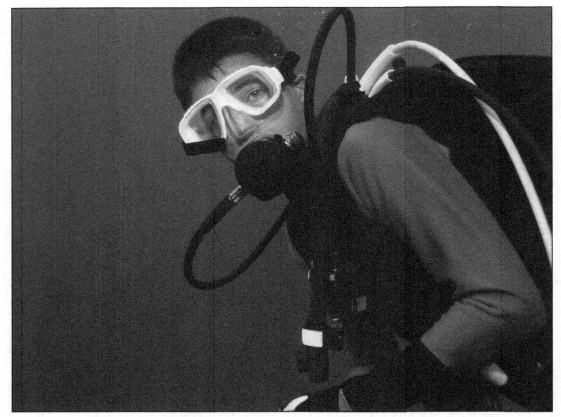

Diving deeply into the problem.

The Facilitator displays a binder called Forced Connections. The binder contains colored photographs, whose purpose is to help generate ideas. Thinking about a problem and looking at the photos "forces a connection" between them. The Process Buddy projects photos from a laptop onto a screen. The Facilitator explains that sometimes larger pictures work better for some people.[15]

Once the easel is full of sticky notes, the Facilitator reads some: "HM the Creativity Club (CC) advertise itself?" "H2 find a different hook?" "WMBAT nonartistic ways to reach everyone?" "HM the CC put on a nonartistic demonstration?" The questions point the Client in the direction to solve a problem.

The Facilitator asks the Client to mark the sticky notes they like the best with colored dot labels. The Facilitator says this is a convergent thinking technique called "highlighting." She asks the Clients to put highlighted ideas that have similar themes into groups. These groups can be any size, and it's acceptable to place one idea in its own group or "cluster." When the Clients are finished, the Facilitator asks them to label each cluster. The Clients label some clusters "Getting the word out," "How to interest the whole school," and "Recruiting ideas." The Facilitator asks the Clients to choose the cluster they like best.[16]

Why Exploring the Problem in Depth Is Crucial

Research has shown that the biggest impediment to problem solving is that people are not clear about the problem they need to solve. This is why the first phase of CPS takes the longest. Einstein agreed. He once was asked what he would do if imminent disaster threatened the earth. He replied that he would take fifty-five minutes to explore the problem and five minutes to solve it.[d]

They decide on "How to interest the entire school." The Facilitator directs them to state this solution with a Statement Starter like "It would be great if . . . [IWBGI]" or "What we would like is . . . [WWWLI]."[17] The Facilitator informs the Clients that this is the problem they will be working on.

Phase 2: Generating Ideas

The Resource Group next deals with the problem statement. "H2 recruit students from the entire school into the CC" is written on the easel pad. The Facilitator reminds the Resource Group of the brainstorming guidelines and instructs them to generate ideas as statements, not questions.

The Facilitator asks the Clients to highlight and cluster the new ideas and select one of the groups. The Clients choose "How to explain the Creativity Club."

The Facilitator asks the Clients to examine the statement "How to explain the Creativity Club?" with a convergent thinking tool—PPCO. This tool will help evaluate the Pluses, Potentials, Concerns, and Overcoming Concerns of the Clients' choice. As the Clients and the Resource Group discuss each of these, the Process Buddy makes lists under the headings.

The Facilitator explains that if instead of one idea, the Clients have many to choose from, they would use other convergent thinking tools to help evaluate them.

The Facilitator asks the Clients to create a statement about the problem, beginning with a Statement Starter such as "I wish . . . [IW]," "It would be great if . . . [IWBGI]," "What we would like is . . . [WWWLI]," "What I now see myself doing . . . [WINSMD]" or "What we now see ourselves doing . . . [WWNSOD]."[18] The Clients write, "IWBGI we could explain the Creativity Club to the student body so they understood it was for everyone (not just artists) so all would join."

The Facilitator explains that this is the new goal, the one the Clients will be putting into action. To do this, the Clients need a plan. The new goal is written across the top of a new page.

Phase 3: Planning for Action

Underneath the goal, the Facilitator writes the words *What, Who, By When,* and *Who Helps* with extra space between the words *What* and *Who*.[19]

Then the Facilitator asks the Clients to think about the steps they'll need to take to reach this goal. They must determine how long each step will take, in short-term, middle-term, and long-term time frames.

Then, with the help of the Facilitator and the Resource Group, the Clients write all the steps needed to take in order to reach the goals, such as who will do them, by when, and who'll be their supporters.

The Facilitator informs the Clients that the papers on the walls are theirs and that she will send them an e-mail with the Plan for Action. The CPS session is over.

Analyzing the Session

Did the preceding scenario give you a taste of how a CPS session might proceed?

Although a key part of the Facilitator's job is to make sure all phases of the process are included, the Facilitator must also "go with the flow" and allow the Client flexibility when he or she wants to focus on a particular aspect of the problem or wants to zero in on a solution. The Facilitator is trained to be unattached about the outcome of the process. If the Client is satisfied with the solution(s) for her or his problem, then the Facilitator has "steered" the CPS process correctly.

The Resource Group's task is to suggest solutions that the Client has not explored; the members of the Group must also refrain from influencing which solutions the Client chooses. Again, it is always the Client's choice to make the final decision about the solutions.

You may have noticed that the role of the Process Buddy was not described in the introduction before the fictional CPS session. Truthfully, the Process Buddy role was not part of the original CPS process. Over the years, however, Facilitators learned that having an assistant—a Process Buddy—who could take care of many of the logistical details in the session was extremely helpful. Because the Process Buddy set up tables, handed out materials, and generally managed the physical space, the Facilitator could focus on the Client's needs and direct the Resource Group.[20]

What is unique about the CPS process is how it focuses on a clear definition of the problem (which is why the first phase is the longest). This makes the planning phase (on how to use the solutions generated) much more effective.

CREATIVITY AND LEARNING

The Big Notebook

J. P. Guilford, in a 1950 speech to the American Psychological Association, lamented "education's appalling neglect of creativity."[1]

Listen to how Sir Ken Robinson, the education expert who has studied the lack of creativity in schools, explains this neglect: "Employers everywhere say, for example, that they need people who are creative, who can work in groups, who can collaborate and innovate. Our current systems of education do almost exactly the opposite . . . the creative capacities of generations of people have been sacrificed needlessly to an academic illusion."[2]

Not only will ignoring the importance of creativity affect business and the job market, it will handicap us in developing solutions for increasingly stalemated world problems.

What's ironic is that the meaning of the words *educate* and *create* are not that far apart. *Educate* stems from the Latin word *educare* (ed-ju-cahr-A), meaning "to draw out that which lies within." In the dictionary, the first definition of *create* is "to cause to come into being."[3] Don't those sound pretty similar? So how did most of you get stuck in an educational system that seems dedicated to pouring facts into your brains so you'll memorize them, spew them back on standardized tests, and be considered educated? Gilbert K. Chesterton (1874–1936), an English author and mystery novelist, claimed that "education is simply the soul of a society as it passes from one generation to another."[4] Frankly, the souls of many societies appear to be damaged because the current system of education in *most countries* has devolved about as far as it can from its true purpose. Robinson's research reveals that "every education system on earth has the same hierarchy of subjects: . . . at the top are mathematics and languages, then the humanities, and at the bottom are the arts."[5] This ranking concerns him because "creativity is not solely to do with the arts or about being an artist. . . . I believe profoundly that we don't grow *into* creativity, we grow *out* of it. Often we are educated out of it."[6]

Thumbnail Biography of Sir Kenneth Robinson

Sir Kenneth (Ken) Robinson (1950–) educator, author, speaker, international adviser on the arts and creativity in education, believes that schools must foster diversity, curiosity, and awaken creativity, in addition to encouraging students to discover their natural aptitudes. His books include *All Our Futures: Creativity, Culture, and Education* (The Robinson Report, 1998), *Out of Our Minds: Learning to Be Creative* (2001), and *Finding Your Element: How to Discover Your Talents and Passions and Transform Your Life* (with Lou Aronica, 2013). His presentation "Do Schools Kill Creativity?" was the most-watched TED talk in its history.[a]

Do you remember that list from "How to Crush Creativity"? It's regrettable, but truthfully, you could add to it "Attend a typical school."

Of course, the lack of creativity in your classes is not new to you—unless you happen to be fortunate enough to attend a school that focuses on, or at least encourages, creativity. If not, you may feel uninspired, even stuck, but you have some insight about what would support your creativity.

Part of the problem with education is that much of the information has been categorized. It's actually very artificial and counterproductive to divide learning into subjects or categories. The brain is not designed to learn that way.[7] Even when you're trying to separate knowledge into subjects, you can't help learning a little math when you're checking out a country's history. You can't help picking up some new vocabulary when studying chemistry. It's kind of like a teacher saying, "OK, for this hour, you get to use your eyes, but not your ears. Take these earplugs and plug 'em up."

Although all these students have answers about how creativity could be included in school, so what? How can their ideas—and yours—make any impact on what you experience in school every day? First off, try to not to think of education as something you "receive" or "get." Learning is natural. (On occasion, students would defiantly tell me that they weren't going to learn anything. I always laughed and replied, "Too late. You can't *help* learning—it might not be about this subject, but you're always learning about *something*.") You, whether you realize it or not, *are your own best teacher*. Most school administrators—and many teachers—do not recognize this fact. As Peter Gray explains, "Self-directed learning is a marvelous sight to behold. . . . Self-directed education has never been easier. It has also never been more essential to success. Our rapidly changing economy puts a premium on self-motivation, innovation, and the continued, life-long ability to acquire new skills and evaluate new ideas."[8]

Teens' Views on the Role of Education in Creativity

Question 6: "How do you think creativity could be included in education?"

"More opportunities for real world outlets (internships, performance opportunities)."—Skye, 18, California

"Many schools encourage knowledge but aren't very famous for encouraging creativity. Because of this they should add a mandatory class that allows kids to make ideas and show others that."—Thomas, 13, Virginia

"With looser instructions, and more freedom to solve problems."—Dakota, 17, California

"I think creativity could be included [in] education in assignments so an individual can show their original, unique, creative ideas."—Alicia, 16, California

"Creativity comes from individuality so in school they could teach you how to think for yourself instead of being a drone."—Chandler, 13, Florida

"Hands on projects can boost creativity. Free response essays and projects that you have to make up yourself."—Meagan, 16, California

"As a high school student in a theatre arts school, creativity is greatly infused into my schooling. We are taught how to be creative in designing our characters on stage but also to be able to think of creative ways on the spot instantaneously in case something goes wrong."—Darius, 16, Florida

"It already is. It's called art, and other projects."—Melanie, 14, California

"We could have school festivals where sports, health, and art all make booths and can show what they know or can do. Even some plays or shows. It is also a great way for the school to get closer to each other and the community."—Arianna, 18, California

"Through the reduction of standards and introduction of issues requiring critical thinking."—Max, 16, California

"Through giving students the option to have no boundaries on their project without a rubric."—Shai, 16, California

"By teaching in different ways, lectures and own work mixed. When children are young you can paint, play music etc. but without grading this."—Sofia, 17, Minnesota

"More real-world, cross-referencing work. Anything that leads to solutions rather than teaching them. Multi-subject work."—Gregory, 18, Florida

"Less testing with only one answer, more having the kids ask questions rather than answering them. Drawing, writing (more)."—Nina, 15, New York[b]

One of the reasons we love to learn is because our brain is hard-wired both to absorb facts *and* to organize them into stories. Here's how it works:

You may have heard that the left side of the brain is the analytical side and the right side is conceptual. The truth is the left brain *leads* certain processes, and the right brain *leads* others.[9] In speech, for example, your left-led brain determines *what* you say and your right-led brain determines *how* you say it.[10] When looking at artwork, your left brain registers the details, the right brain looks at the "whole picture"—in this case, the actual whole picture![11] The left-led brain excels in the *analysis* of the details—or the "trees," while the right-led brain specializes in *synthesis*—the entire "forest."[12]

You've probably already figured out that most of your education is geared toward your left-led brain strengths. Chances are you are not given opportunities to increase your right-led brain conceptual skills, where stories—and creativity—begin.

Think about it: When children are read to, and later learn to read for themselves, no one reads from—or gives them—a long list of words. They're given *stories*. Having students memorize a bunch of facts and repeat them on tests only satisfies how *half* the brain absorbs and retains knowledge. Ignoring the other half of the brain's function is unnatural and bound to be painful. You know from experience that this is true. So what would it look like to be able to combine these functions and direct your own learning?

The View from the Inside

Read what a high school student at Sudbury Valley School in Framington, Massachusetts, has to say about student-directed learning:

> I didn't understand the idea of having to artificially "get" an education . . . you got smarter because every day you were learning . . . one day you were talking to someone about one subject and another day you were talking to someone about another . . . eventually you would get around to all of them. We don't do classes. . . . There are no classrooms. . . . We were learning in a much more organic manner . . . bits and pieces . . . adding up to much bigger pictures. [When] you were done learning . . . information was coming from so many different sources . . . books and . . . people . . . and from a long drawn out experience . . . you had no idea how you learned it.[c]

Even though the student just quoted is designated as a "high school student," that was only a descriptive title. At Sudbury, students learn with no classrooms, with no teachers, and as you might expect, with no grades. The student body ranges from four to nineteen years old; however, students are not divided into elementary, middle, and high school. Students of *any* age may participate in *any* learning experience. (This practice is based on research proving that students learn better when *not* segregated by age.)[13]

As the Sudbury Valley School website states, "Students . . . develop traits that are key to achieving success: They are comfortable learning new things; confident enough to rely on their own judgment; and capable of pursuing their passions to a high level of competence. [They] are adaptable to rapid change, open to innovation and creative in solving new problems. Beyond that, they grow to be trustworthy and responsible individuals, and function as contributing members of a free society."[14]

So now you see the sort of learning environment Robinson and Gray are talking about—one that encourages autonomy, exploring passions, problem solving, and creativity. You may be envious that not only has this school eliminated standardized tests and grades; it has also disposed of classes.

"So what?" you're thinking. "I still have to go to a school with classes that are divided into separate subjects. I have to memorize stuff and take tests, especially

---

Thumbnail Biography of Peter Gray

Dr. Peter Gray (1944–), psychologist and research professor at Boston College and a proponent of self-directed learning, is the author of *Free to Learn: Why Unleashing the Instinct to Play Will Make Our Children Happier, More Self Reliant, and Better Prepared for Life* (New York: Basic Books, 2013), 288 pages. Gray writes the blog *Freedom to Learn* for *Psychology Today* as well as academic articles on natural ways of learning. He co-launched www.alternativestoschool. com, designed to assist parents and students toward self-directed learning.[d]

---

standardized ones. And I have *tons* of homework! Although I want to be creative, I don't have time!"

You could try to get into a more open school, but that's problematic. There aren't many of these schools, they aren't free (although Sudbury schools are, surprisingly, much cheaper than other private schools), and your parents might not trust those schools to give you an education that will, as they will say, "get you into college and be successful in life."[15]

Remember the part about you being your "own best teacher"? You are already doing a lot of what you need to do to encourage your own creativity and take the lead in your own learning.

The truth is, you're probably deep into a curriculum you didn't know you already created *and* you got there because of intrinsic motivation. Chances are, you're hitting on the Wikipedia site several times a week, if not several times a day. You're looking up information on all kinds of other sites. You're reading e-books (this might be one). You're certainly shopping, looking at YouTube videos, and playing games. You're probably e-mailing people in countries around the world. You might be e-dating. You might be part of international organizations or movements. If you didn't know it before, know it now—*all* these activities are learning.

Yep, even shopping e-tail provides you with knowledge about pricing, marketing, what's valuable, what's bogus, and how to make a deal. You learn strategies in war games, spelling and word usage in Scrabble or Words with Friends, and what constitutes a culture and a society in avatar worlds. You learn what film techniques work—and don't work—by watching exciting, funny, or achingly boring YouTube videos. You learn about current events in news stories and world cultures from your contacts outside the United States. You learn all kinds of information on Wikipedia. (You must check out your topic on other sites because Wiki isn't 100 percent accurate.) You learn about human rights, policies and politics, and unfortunately about war on news sites and from being a member of international organizations. You even learn how to gather money from sites such as Kickstarter. (And do I need to mention you also learn about sex? Make sure you're safe, though, and maybe ask someone you trust if some of that stuff is real—especially if you plan to spend money.)

You probably don't have free access to the Internet—in other words, *parental-free* access. Because you don't, you're learning how to negotiate with your parents for what you need and want from the Internet. You have all these learning opportunities without spending an hour in school (which might lead some of you to tell your parents you don't need to go to your current school). The point is you have an international classroom just beyond your keyboard.

Learning creative skills with your friends.

Five Ways to Transcend the School Mindset

1. Divergent thinking
2. Full body learning
3. Utilizing the "Goldilocks" effect
4. Diminish the focus on instruction
5. Recognize free play as learning

—Laura Grace Weldon, poet, homeschool mom, author of *Free Range Learning: How Homeschooling Changes Everything* (Prescott, AZ: Hohm Press, 2010), 312 pages.[e]

You have not been abandoned by all educators. Ken Robinson, Peter Gray, and thousands of teachers (myself included) are aware that the current educational system doesn't work. Or as the photographer and environmentalist Ansel Adams (1902–1984) put it, "Education without either meaning or excitement is impossible."[16] Many parents are aware, too, and some of them have decided to homeschool their children or to place them in alternative schools that develop their individuality and creativity.

Laura Grace Weldon is one of these parents. Look above at her list of ways to transcend the school mindset. Isn't it interesting that divergent thinking and playing freely were listed? By now you might be including both of them in your daily practice. You read about divergent thinking techniques in the two chapters on Creative Problem Solving. You learned that play is "important because it's about time and freedom. You get to be aimless. You get to forget any agendas" (chapter 5). You learned why play is useful for creativity. Now you know that aimless—or free—play is an essential avenue to learning.

Full body learning might have been a novel concept for you, although you heard Logan LaPlante in his TEDx talk video share that he assigns himself one day in nature every week.[17] You might also recall from the discussion on incubation (chapters 1 *and* 4) that besides sleep, other ways to incubate include using the entire body: walking, running, swimming, or engaging in any physical activity that frees your mind. Full body learning, however, also refers to movement that "allows sensory input to stimulate the brain as it absorbs a flood of information. This is the way the brain builds new neural pathways, locking learning into memory."[18] Ken Robinson claims that most formal education seems to stop at the neck. In other words, we focus on the brain and forget the body. He once said, "I think maths is very important, but so is dance."[19] (Note: "Maths" is the British word for "math.")

While you may not have recognized the term *Goldilocks effect*, you know it well in another context. The Goldilocks effect is how flow operates—balanced between your level of skill and an appropriate challenge,[20] which includes embracing your mistakes.

The fourth method for transcending the school mindset is to "diminish the focus on instruction." In other words, learn by yourself. You are fortunate; due to the Internet, you have access to more information than any previous generation in the history of the world. With this access you can actually create your own outside-the-class curriculum.

Granted, you're not going to learn equally in all subjects. That's due to two reasons: (1) Even if you could learn the *exact same amount* in every subject area, you would never have time to cover them all. (Besides, how would you determine what's equal learning across subjects? Would learning one algebraic formula be equivalent to learning one poem in English literature? Would learning one law of physics equal learning about one era in American history?) (2) You are not *interested* in learning much in some areas. In fact, there are some subjects you want to skip learning altogether!

That's because you were born with certain strengths that lead you to want to learn more in areas related to them. (If you took the StrengthsQuest assessment, you know what your strengths are.) People who are born with a good voice or a sense of rhythm—or both—are curious about music. People who are good at running and jumping want to learn how to go faster and leap higher. People who are good at words like learning where words come from, and later on, they like putting their ideas into written words. People who are—you get the drift.

Years ago, people (teachers, parents) believed that other people (kids, teens) were skilled in only two areas: either you had a knack with words (verbal) or you were good at math and science (logical). Most curriculums were designed around

Thumbnail Biography of Howard Gardner

Howard Gardner (1943–), a developmental psychologist who studied people's aptitudes, observed that people had innate abilities in areas other than words or logic. He determined that these abilities were just as important, just as *valuable* as the verbal and logical skills that monopolized academics. Since verbal and logical abilities were considered "intelligent," Gardner named these other abilities "intelligences."[f]

these two skills, and how well you did in these areas is how you were measured as a student. So what happened if you weren't good in either verbal or logical skills? Basically, too bad for you. You had to get past your feelings of failure when you tried hard to perfect these skills and didn't succeed. Not to mention that the strengths you did have were often ignored.

If you weren't very verbal or mathematical you didn't fit in and *couldn't ever fit in.* If you were lucky and you had athletic abilities or you could draw or sing, you might have gotten encouragement to join a team, get some art lessons, or get a little voice coaching. Maybe you'd gather some kudos along the way, but you still didn't fit into mainstream education. (Have you noticed which courses get cut first in schools? It's always art, music, theater, and dance.) Those course cuts made orphans of many students with intelligences in the arts. Educating students who had strengths in those intelligences (if they were even *considered* to be intelligent) was considered unimportant. Being an artist, an actor, dancer, or musician was considered frivolous and "not a real job." (I was told more than once when I mentioned I'd majored in theater in college that I hadn't trained for "real work." Many of my musician, theater, and art friends were told the same.)

What about other teens, who weren't even strong in the arts? What about those who were sensitive to others' feelings or to nature? How about teens who thought about life's big ideas? We didn't value these teens' aptitudes as much. We really had no room for *them.*

Today, however, people recognize that teens (and everyone) can be smart in nonverbal and nonmathematical ways. Developmental psychologist Howard Gard-

Multiple Intelligences

Intelligence Name	Ability	You Can Call Yourself
Linguistic	verbal	word smart
Logical-Mathematical	reasoning	number/reasoning smart
Spatial	artistic	visually smart
Musical	rhythmic-harmonic	musically smart
Bodily-Kinesthetic	athletic-mechanical	body (and object) smart
Interpersonal	social skills	people smart
Intrapersonal	introspection	self-smart
Naturalist	ecology	nature smart
Existential	philosophical-spiritual	deep thinking smart[g]

ner called these abilities "intelligences" (see page 138 for a complete list). While you *could* take an assessment to determine which of these are your "intelligences," you already know in what you excel. (Plus you darn well know what you *don't* excel at!) Chances are, though, that you have more than one area of strength (intelligence). Knowing your strengths or intelligences is vital to continue developing creatively. Basically, you need to "go with the flow"; or more accurately, to go with *your* flow. Not only will you produce more and better in your intelligences, but it'll be much easier and more fun because you're in your own mainstream.

It's highly likely that your intelligences align with the career(s) that you desire. The only issue you may have to deal with is the way people—particularly adults (yes, talking about parents here) view achievement and your "not reaching your potential."

Marcus Buckingham, a career coach and proponent of the StrengthsQuest assessment, asks, "What do parents usually do when they see all A's and one F on their kid's report card? You can guess. They rarely spend much time commending their child for all those A's. Instead, they go all nuts on their kid and say, 'Get that "F" up to a "C" or a "B"!'" Buckingham says that those parents—and most of us—have it backward. We need to stop wasting time fixing our own and our children's weaknesses and focus on what we do *well naturally*. Strengthen *that*.[21]

One of the best models for learning, ironically, has come about unintentionally from a nonprofessional arena—homeschooling. Over the years, parents have developed—or more likely, stumbled upon—the method of asking the student (their child) to select a topic to explore holistically. This was a smart move for two reasons: first, because it gives the student buy-in, in other words, a choice in the direction of his or her education; and second, the student can examine a chosen topic from every angle. She or he can explore whether it has a history or possibly a political background. She or he can see how it might relate to mathematics or any of the hard sciences (physics, chemistry, biology, or geology). Maybe it's more aligned with the soft sciences (psychology, sociology, anthropology). Does it have a geography or its own language? Does the topic express itself in different varieties? Are there artistic facets to the topic, whether visual, musical, dramatic? Even if artistic aspects are not obvious, the student will have the opportunity to create something artistic based on her or his topic.

The easy access to the Internet has led to learning online or as Logan LaPlante calls it, "hackschooling."[22] Teens and preteens developed this way of learning themselves. While educational institutions have offered teens classes and access to materials online, in the twenty-first century teens themselves realized that through the Internet, they can do more than design their own education; they can carve out a viable and satisfying future for themselves. By investigating topics that are personally meaningful (thereby having intrinsic motivation to study them), teens explore fields in depth. Teens will require some adult feedback, of course, but they will insist that any supervision must expand rather than restrict their learning.

Let's use an example. Say you are interested in the topic of butterflies. First, of course, you'll be looking at butterflies from the biological standpoint. You'll examine the structure of butterflies' anatomy and their life cycle. You'll be able to catalog many butterfly varieties and their habitats. You might learn the Latin names for some of these varieties and even what these names signify. You can use math to calculate the sizes, wingspans, and routes of butterfly migration. You might wonder what the relationship of butterflies is to other winged insects and go find out.

You can research how different cultures used butterflies as symbols, maybe on flags or for political movements, in war and peace. You might speculate about the most unusual uses for butterflies. You might ask, "Have they influenced food, clothing, décor, or architecture?" How have butterflies inspired music, song, or drama? You can learn how to say the word *butterfly* in many languages, of course, but you can also research how butterflies have impacted language, in literal and symbolic ways. You will have the opportunity to see how butterflies have affected both visual and performing artists.

You may want to visit a butterfly garden. After you return, you might be inspired to plan one and create your own garden. You might go to a museum or talk to a butterfly expert (a person who studies butterflies, or "lepidoptera," is a lepidopterist) and ask what they eat, how they adapt to their environment and survive in it, and what their defenses are against predators. You may want to raise some caterpillars and watch them turn into butterflies.

So you can see how studying a subject in this depth, from these many angles, gives you a complete picture. It teaches you how to make connections *within* the topic, and it shows you how the topic links to *other* topics. (You get both a micro and a macro view.) This approach to learning about a subject may help you pinpoint which branch of knowledge you enjoy most, and/or for which you have the most ability.

When you're encouraged to learn in this manner, you not only accumulate an incredible amount of information, you also train yourself to pay attention to connections, to see the world holistically, to explore in depth, which is extremely satisfactory to right-brain-led processes. Since you are directing the research, you are in control and can be resourceful and creative in how you design your results and presentations.

Directing your own learning leads to a joy of learning that will last far beyond school. (By the way, we know that students who are homeschooled or enrolled in other free-learning schools are able to accumulate 10,000 hours of learning in the subjects they like best by the time they reach their mid-teens. So surfing the web, reading what you want, and choosing your own projects takes the focus off instruction and aims it toward *learning*.)[23]

By taking learning into your own hands you are developing means to finding a passion, determining your own direction, learning how to make choices, organizing what you've learned and *how to learn* it into the next steps, following through, and communicating the results. Taking responsibility for your own learning requires you to call on curiosity (remember it is the number one creative quality), it draws on your intrinsic motivation, and of course, it requires you to *use* your creativity. You are actually training yourself to be a creative adult. You, like Mark Twain (1835–1910), are not allowing "schooling to interfere with [your] education."[24]

One feature about learning a topic holistically is that it will require all kinds of learning skills. You will be reading about your topic, of course, and at some point you'll be writing about it. You'll also be listening to music. You may watch movies or YouTube videos or TED (technology, education, and design) or TEDx talks. You may visit museums or gardens, or you may deliver a talk about butterflies. If you buddy up with someone else who is also curious about butterflies and you decide to construct a group project, you'll be learning collaborative skills as well.

Of course, all the effort you have put into this in-depth, holistic project can't possibly be judged by a standardized test. It wouldn't be fair to you and it wouldn't give your teachers an accurate evaluation of your learning. You've done more than memorize some facts so you can darken little bubbles on a Scantron. Besides, the skills needed to pass those tests are limited (mainly how to do rote work and give the "right" answer, both of which take you in the opposite direction from creativity). Instead, you've learned to research your topic the way a college student does, maybe even how a graduate student researches.

Not only do you, as a teen, *want* to learn this way, you *need* to learn and practice creativity skills until you become comfortable with them. This knowledge and practice will be utterly essential after you graduate from high school, college, or technical school and enter the world of work, which in this century, is demanding creative competence.

Setting the Tone

While you are teaching yourself to learn holistically, it is important to understand the best conditions in which you, personally and individually, learn. Some of those conditions may be the way you sense the world. You may have heard of VARK, which assesses the sense you rely on most in order to learn: visual (V), auditory (A), read-write (R), or kinesthetic (K).[25] Knowing your "learning style" can help you do better in school because you'll know *how* you learn. While it is not always possible to learn in your ideal style, you can at least design as much of your learning around it. (Note: There has been some research that shows that

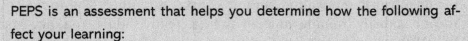

Productivity Environmental Preferences Survey

PEPS is an assessment that helps you determine how the following affect your learning:

- Immediate environment (sound, heat, light, and design)
- Emotionality (motivation, responsibility, persistence, and structure)
- Sociological needs (self-oriented, peer-oriented, adult-oriented, or combined ways)
- Physical needs (perceptual preference[s], time of day, food intake, and mobility)[h]

humans don't learn in distinct styles, but until VARK is disproven, go ahead and take the assessment if you wish.)[26]

It's also useful for you to be aware of your best learning environment. The Productivity Environmental Preferences Survey (PEPS) contains a series of questions, such as how warm or cold you like your room, the lighting you prefer, what time of day is best for you to study, your preferred noise level, whether you like to be alone or with a partner or group, and so on.

Your PEPS profile might inform you that you work/learn best in bright daylight, with music or the TV on, sitting at a desk with the option to get up often, with plenty of snacks, with lots of structure, with many people around . . . you get the idea. Not only is this how you learn/study best, it is also a major part of *your* "creative climate"! Think about it. How well can you do on a project if the room you're sitting in is too cold or hot? Or if it's too noisy? Or if you're hungry or sleepy? Or if people are all around and you need quiet? Or maybe you work better in a group. You need to have the opportunity to custom design a supportive environment for yourself. Sure, you *might* be able to read or think with the TV or music on, but is that the best environment for you?

PEPS will help you determine the best environmental conditions so you can get the most out of your learning. There are FAQs (frequently asked questions) on the website, and you can check out other research on PEPS. The following link provides a *free two-week pass* to take the PEPS Learning Style Inventory. You can also ask for a quote on the cost beyond the two weeks: www.humanesources.com/organizations/program/peps-lsi/.

The Human eSources site also offers a more complete look at what PEPS offers, as well as a list of the environmental conditions that affect learning: humane sources.com/site/PEPS-learning-style-preferences/.

I-education

From accessing PEPS on the Internet, you've discovered the best environment for you to learn. Also on the Internet are online courses and programs, which will continue multiplying. Obviously, many of those programs are structured for certification and degrees, but remember more informal i-education options also exist, such as YouTube "how-to" videos. More digital learning options include apps for iPhones, smartphones, iPads, and tablets. Of course, apps (and prices) change constantly; however, languages, computer programming, speed reading, math, and skill learning (such as cooking and musicianship) are constantly in demand.[27] The Internet and digital options may not be creative in themselves, but their existence can help you design education—or learning—that will be uniquely creative for you.

Three More for the Road

Educators have determined that students will need three skills after they leave school. Actually, the first you already have: whatever skill you have in your interest—your "domain skills," or its synonym, "hard skills." These refer to whatever you need to do in order to do your job: fix computers, fly a plane, run a business, be an EMT (or a nurse or doctor), do people's taxes. You get it.

You'll also need "soft skills," which you can probably guess will apply to many situations, in and out of work. Soft skills incorporate sales skills and communication skills—not only speaking and writing, but nonverbal communication; lots of people forget about those. How about getting-along-with-other-people skills? Those are "emotional" intelligences we all need. (Softening our negative impact on people is at least as important as leaving a small footprint on the environment.)

The third category is "attitude, values, and dispositions." Of course you know how your attitude affects your success and enjoyment of life and others' enjoyment and trust of you. "Values" and "dispositions" are harder to define, yet examples of them are everywhere. They aren't tied to your career or education; instead, they help promote a healthy and happy society. These qualities might include having an appreciation of the arts, a dedication to community service, or a commitment to live a healthy lifestyle.[28]

While it won't be possible for you to ignore the impact of your learning on your future, you can relate to what Ken Robinson says: "Thinking of education as a preparation for something that happens later can overlook the fact that the first sixteen or eighteen years of a person's life are not a rehearsal. Young people are living their lives now."[29]

CREATIVITY AND CHANGE LEADERSHIP

Before we look at the link between creativity and leadership, let's look at the common definitions of leadership. One is "the position or function of a leader, one who guides or directs a group."[1] It has also been defined as "a process of social influence in which one person can enlist the aid and support of others in the accomplishment of a common task." Or "the ability to motivate a group of people toward a common goal."[2] There are many other definitions of leadership as well, some from people who have studied the leadership field, many others from those who have had a lot of experience being led, and finally, from those who have experience as leaders.

As one of Gen Wii, the oldest of you are now twenty years old. You are out of high school and you're either in college or tech school, working, or both. Others

 Teens' Views on Creativity and Leadership

Question 8: "How do you think creativity could be useful for leaders?"

"I think it would be useful for leaders for creative, original, unique mindset and ideas."—Alicia, 16, California

"I think it [creativity] can be useful to leaders because if one way's not working [or another] and it's a traditional way to do something you can create a way that everyone understands."—Analyse, 16, California

"Creativity can create the engaging factor that leaders may need to get people to listen and help."—Sam, 16, California

"It would be very useful for leaders because it would allow them to think outside the box and use creativity to propel their country or company forward."—Darius, 16, Florida

"Leaders need to have creativity to form their own state of mind, or else they're followers."—Sylvana, 16, California

"Creative solutions for global problems are necessary for good leaders."—Justice, 17, California

"Allows to inspire new ideas. Imagine different viewpoints."—Glennon, 17, California

"With changing circumstances, creativity allows for leaders to be innovative and succeed."—Max, 16, California

"It is useful for leaders because it shows they are flexible."—Shai, 16, California

"Leaders often help a larger group of people solve problems. If the leader is creative, he or she can come up with different solutions."—Sofia, 17, Minnesota

"Leading by problem solving. Helping followers."—Aspen, 16, Florida

"It allows them to find new ways around old blocks. Leaders are also given positions to inspire others."—Gregory, 18, Florida

"Creativity engages followers and keeps them."—Angela, 18, Florida

"Most of the problems we have are recurring, so if a leader is creative, it might help those same problems from occurring by choosing a different path."—Nina, 15, New York

"Being creative in your approach to solve problems can mean being creative in your resolution. Someone in a place of power, a leader, who's thoughtful and using their mind to create change and solve issues is the best example to inspire others to do the same."—Hannah, 18, New York[a]

of you are still in middle or high school. Wherever you are on this generation's timeline, you're "on deck" to be the next leaders in American society. Since this is true, it's vital for you to have your personal definition of leadership.

The Link between Creativity and Leadership

Teens perceive that creativity has a role in leadership, but why exactly is this true?

At first, there doesn't seem to *be* a link between creativity and leadership. What could possibly be the connection between the two? One answer stems from the four Ps, which you may recall from chapter 1. For those who don't, they are person, process, product, and press. Some creativity researchers, however, have added a fifth *P* to the list—persuasion.[3] This makes sense. Wouldn't the ability to persuade be a valuable asset for a leader? What is a leader except a person who *persuades* others—either by words or example, and often both? Of course, there are many styles of persuasion. In history, there have been leaders who have used coercion and punishment as "persuasion." Nowadays, however, we have a higher vision for leadership than as a form of tyranny.

So that's settled—persuasion is a vital attribute of leadership. What else connects creativity and leadership? To answer that question, let's look at a basic psychological construct of human beings for a moment. Aren't we, as a species, resistant to change? Like a slogan on a T-shirt says, "I welcome change as long as nothing is altered or different." That sentence sums up most people's attitudes toward change. This is understandable, because much of the time change is out of our control, and that scares us. Change also involves loss. Even if we didn't much value our former situation or an object or person, we still don't like feeling we lost it, especially since often it wasn't our choice.

When we decide we want some change in our lives we want to be able to control it. We want to take our time buying new shirts and shoes. We don't want to have to buy them in another city because the airline lost our luggage! We want to make a new friend in our own time. We don't want to have to make one because our best friend moves away. If conditions are basically fine in our lives, we want to keep them that way. If they are not that fine, we want to be able to make the changes we want—how and when and where and even who—come into or leave our lives. We absolutely do not want to give up the control that change usually takes from us!

As you know, though, most change happens without our consent, much less our control. You certainly didn't know that when you reached puberty, so many changes were going to occur in your brain and body and even in your environment in the ways they have (and still are). If you had been given control of those monumental changes, you might have slowed some down (growth spurts), sped some up (getting your driver's license), and eliminated some completely (zits)!

Since people don't like change (unless they are in control of it), they have to be persuaded to accept, even welcome, it. Being persuasive is a leadership quality. Often, in order to be persuasive, the leader must use creativity. Consider the following scenario. What if you had to transfer to a new school? (For many of you this isn't/wasn't a hypothetical situation.) You're apprehensive—who's going to talk to you, show you around, do homework with you, sit with you at lunch, be your new friends? While you're contemplating the transfer—or even worse, while you're in the middle of it—if someone tells you to "suck it up" or "deal with it," those words are neither persuasive nor creative (nor kind).

Now imagine a new factor enters this situation: What if you know (or meet) someone (let's say "she") who persuades you that students at the new school are less snobby than at your old school (that'd be cool). Or she informs you that the school has an excellent college prep program (terrific). Or the basketball team is winning this season (you love b-ball games). Or she says you'll have a brand new audience for your "class clown antics" (you love attention). Or the drama club's going to stage *Grease* next semester (you know all the songs by heart). Now, how do you feel about transferring to the new school? You gotta feel more enthusiasm than before you talked, right? Maybe now you're even a little excited.

Didn't this someone use creative persuasion to give you hope? It wasn't vague or cliché hope, like what you usually get. ("Maybe the kids will be nicer" and "Don't worry, you'll fit in.") Instead, she got your attention by pointing out *specific* aspects about the school that would appeal to *you*: sports, advanced courses, a chance to show off your funny side, and possibly be part of a musical. This persuader drew a very detailed, *creative* picture to inspire you about changing schools.

The truth is, if nothing ever changed, people would have no need of leaders, either in their personal lives, workplaces, communities, or governments. With no change, unknown situations would not surface; therefore, solutions—much less creative ones—would not be necessary. As we know, change "happens," so we need leaders to guide us through it. We need creativity to help craft useful solutions for accommodating change. Change is the reason for leadership and the need for creativity. Change is the bond between the two.[4]

Change leadership is necessary when people either *want* or *need* change to happen. In this case, people are choosing change. They need a leader's guidance and creativity to make change as smooth and effective as possible. Thus, change leadership is "the process of positively influencing people, contexts, and outcomes through a deliberate creative approach aimed at identifying opportunities and resolving predicaments."[5]

The other reason people need leaders is because there are problems. Of course, change brings about problems, too. Yet sometimes the problem is that necessary changes aren't happening. As you know, solving problems almost always involves developing creative solutions. Alex Osborn claimed that "the quality of leadership depends on creative power."[6]

It's no surprise that the "notion that creativity drives leadership is why [Creative Problem Solving] has become a process that can promote real change in any organization through a group of empowered individuals."[7]

By using creative skills (and Creative Problem Solving when appropriate) in leadership roles, you will be more in touch with where you are leading—in the school council or club, at drama presentations, in community groups (Kiwanis, Elks, Lions), or in the political arena, and will be open to more innovative solutions that might result in successful change.

You've all had experience with leadership, mostly from the point of view of being led, either alone or as a member of a group. Maybe you've had the opportunity to be a leader. Maybe you've led a sports group, a marching band or a cheerleading squad, a Boy Scout or Girl Scout group, a fund-raising drive at school, a school club, a Sunday school class, or a small group in class.

If so far you've only been a member of a group headed by a designated leader, what do you recall about the experience? What was your impression of the leader? Was he or she organized (which included being on time, in the right place, and having appropriate materials)? Did the leader facilitate the group choosing its goals and developing methods for achieving them? *Did* the group achieve the goals? Did the group work well together? What was your emotional experience of being in this group?

If you've been a leader, how was the experience for you? Were you aware of the tasks you did well? Did you notice other areas in which you could do better? Because the function of a leader is to ensure that the group fulfills its purpose (which usually includes a goal or goals), did you achieve this?

> "The most dangerous leadership myth is that leaders are born—that there is a genetic factor to leadership. This myth asserts that people simply either have certain charismatic qualities or not. That's nonsense; in fact, the opposite is true. Leaders are made rather than born."—Warren G. Bennis, (1925–), U.S. founding chairman, the Leadership Institute, University of Southern California[b]

Did you enjoy being the leader? Would you want to be one again?

These questions are provided so you can reflect on your experience. Whether you were in the group or led the group, you have a point of view about your role.

It's possible you liked leading one type of group and not another type, or one bunch of people and not another (teachers have this experience all the time). Whichever role you played, it's crucial for you to understand that you don't need to have "natural leadership talent" to lead. (There was no "leadership intelligence" on Gardner's multiple intelligence list in chapter 11.) Just as you can develop creativity skills, you can develop leadership skills.

Leadership Styles

Leaders can lead in many styles: autocratic (the leader makes the decisions and gives orders, which the group follows); facilitative (the leader makes suggestions using a process, then allows group members to choose their roles); cooperative (the leader ensures that people experience a sense of community); and laissez-faire (the leader is almost completely hands-off, which effectively forces groups to make decisions—in therapy groups, this style is called "mutual aid"). Now that you've looked a little bit at what leadership is, and given your own definition, how do you think creativity can affect leadership? Does it seem like there is any connection?

Since it is often difficult to match descriptions of concepts to real-life situations, let's try an example here. Pretend there is a group that needs to raise money for a community project. Now, the leader could simply tell everyone how to raise the money. (This would be an autocratic style and might come from a leader who believes that he knows best because he *thinks* he is a born leader with certain inborn leadership traits.) Let's say another group has to raise money too, but this leader asks for input from the group: "How should we do this? Who has got experience raising money? Who do we contact?" This democratic leader seems to trust the participants' input in leading themselves.

A leader who looked at what the group needed to do—raise money—would see this as a contingency and would examine the variables in the environment (some variables: Is this a wealthy or poor community? Do people care about this project enough to give money?). Plus a leader using a situational theory would look at the members of the group itself. (Are they able to ask people for money? Do they themselves have money to give? Are they able to plan an event to raise money? Are they willing to plan one?)

A leader following a management theory would set up a system of rewards for those who raise the most money and punishment for those who don't (the punishment might be as simple as derision from the achievers, but it's still a penalty).

Change leaders are open to new ideas.

Many jobs are designed around the management theory, an approach to leadership, which contrasts significantly with change leadership.

Let's compare the functions of managers and change leaders: (1) Managers focus on tasks that need to be done immediately; they are often "putting out fires." Change leaders take a personal attitude toward goals. (2) Managers are reactive and focus on solving problems. Change leaders are proactive and shape ideas. (3) Managers make sure day-to-day business is carried out. Change leaders look for potential future opportunities. (4) Managers want order and control. Change leaders are willing to be unstructured and allow for complexity. (5) Managers want to keep the situation the same (status quo). Change leaders look for opportunities to encourage change. (6) Managers can tolerate mundane, practical work. Change leaders are energetic, inspiring their subordinates in the creative process. (7) Managers limit choices and try to coordinate opposing views to get solutions accepted. Change leaders are open to new ideas on issues, develop fresh approaches for enduring problems, and avoid settling for "quick and easy" solutions. Finally, (8) managers believe "If it ain't broke, *don't* fix it." Change leaders have the motto "When it ain't broke may be the only time you *can* fix it."[8] (This contrast/comparison exercise isn't meant to imply that change leaders are *better* than managers. Businesses, organizations, communities, and governments need both.)

Leadership Styles

You might start realizing that being a leader who can move between styles could be a *creative leader*. This person—let's pretend it's you—would be willing to make mistakes and allow the group to make them as well in order to reach his or her goals. As a change leader, you would be the type of leader who would encourage creative thinking in the group, which spans exploring the problem to generating ideas to making an effective, workable action plan. (You may recognize these as the phases of Creative Problem Solving.) You would be the type of leader who would promote curiosity, innovative ideas, and novel ways for group members to relate to each other in service of the group's goal.

You as a creative leader *could* be democratic in style, but more likely you'd adopt a laissez-faire approach, allowing the group to make its own decisions. You would never lose sight of the relationships between the group members and the possibility of their transformation. You would facilitate the group sticking to the group goal, not by coercion or intimidation, but through suggestion and gentle guidance. You would constantly acknowledge instances when the group introduced novel ideas designed to achieve the goal.

You would be open to the group's suggestions and genuinely ask for and take in feedback—not simply pretend you wanted it. You would exude sincerity and concern for the group as a whole and for the individual members in it. All of these actions would make you a creative leader.

Leverage for Leaders

Let's face it: People like to be leaders for a number of reasons. One of the most common reasons is that they get to have power. What exactly is power and why is it so attractive? Let's look at dictionaries again: power is (1) "the ability to do or

Five Ws and an H

When looking at a situation, ask

Who: Who's involved? Who's the main decision maker? Who's everyone affected by this situation?

What: What's the situation's history? What's the ideal result? What's been tried already?

When: When did this start? When would you like to take action? When would you like a resolution?

Where: Where's this happening? Give a description of the physical and psychological factors of this situation. Where have there been successful solutions for this situation? Where were they managed? Where are situations similar to these? Where are they different?

Why: Why is this important? Why is it occurring? Why are you, or others, involved in *this* situation?

How: How else can the five Ws be elaborated on?[c]

act; the capability to do or accomplish something."[9] OK, but don't all people have that capability (even if they don't think they do)? If this is true, what's the big deal about being a leader? Let's look at some other definitions about power: "the possession or control of command over others; authority; ascendancy."[10] That definition makes more sense of why leadership is so coveted—at least by certain people.

So are some people just born leaders and others aren't? Actually, no, although we used to think so. We believed in the myths of "the great man" and the "trait" theories of leadership.[11] Now we know that anyone can learn to be a leader. No doubt there are people who are more *attracted* to the idea of having power or control over others, whereas some may simply want to achieve an essential end. Then there are those who feel so passionate about a project that they will supervise its completion. People also differ in the *manner* they lead. The approach can—and does—vary greatly with each individual. It is untrue that you need to be commanding or bossy to be a leader. (That works against you, as you might imagine.) You can learn to be a leader, but that knowledge doesn't—and shouldn't—change who you are.

Just as there are many styles of leadership, there are many types of power as well. Some forms will be familiar to you, such as reward power, which is based on

Four Simples Step to Leading and Inspiring Change

1. Accept change: It's happening and it's needed. Help others to accept change. (Hint: Identify what will be the consequences if change does not occur.)
2. Envision new change: Have reason for change, but more importantly, have a vision for how change will affect the future.
3. Communicate change: Let others involved in the change know the vision, and show the vision through your actions. *Walk the talk.*
4. Implement change: This will go through phases and these take time. Knowing this alleviates frustration. Don't skip steps. Set short-term goals and reward yourself and/or others when they're reached.[d]

a leader's ability to give rewards and positive consequences, and referent power, based on a leader's likeability. You certainly recognize legitimate power, which is based on a leader who is in an authoritative position, such as teachers, police, politicians, and coaches. Leaders who have access to and control of information have (duh) information power. Experts, with their skill and knowledge, boast expert power. People who have strong relationships with people (powerful or not) have connection power. The last form of power, the one we all know, is based on a leader's ability to invoke fear in others, which is called coercive power.[12]

So, which of these forms of power most sounds like you? Or maybe there's one or two powers you would like to have? (For example, you may like the idea of being an expert and having its resultant power.) Knowing the type of power that suits you is important because it will be reflected in your leadership style. Or is that the other way around? Your leadership style will show others what kind of power you think suits you best. Now, be aware that others may not agree with you!

Remember, change is the reason people need leaders and why people take on leadership roles. To be a change leader, you need to incorporate your style, your approach, with how people need to be approached when they are experiencing stress about change.

When you're deciding on what ideas to choose, consider how the ideas "come at you."

Unusual Points of View on Leadership

Leadership is an open mind and an open heart.

Leadership is your heart speaking to the hearts of others.

Leadership is the integration of heart, head, and soul.

Leadership is the capacity to care, and in caring, to liberate the ideas, energy, and capacities of others.—John C. Maxwell (1947–), American author, speaker, pastor[e]

When looking at solutions, ask yourself these questions: Which of them . . . jump out at me immediately? Stand head and shoulders above the rest? Sparkle? Tickle my fancy? Make me laugh? Are intriguing? Are unique? Fill the bill? Are "right on target"? Are clear winners?[13]

Add your own . . . and you will add your "own" to your leadership.

CREATIVITY CATCHALL

The Big Picture

Basically, this chapter adds some ideas and exercises, including one that relates to creativity assessment (chapter 4), before looking into how creativity will affect your future.

Personality Strengths Survey

Remember taking the survey in "Creativity Guidelines and Assessment" (chapter 4)? This chapter has the explanation for the sections of the assessment. Look at the sections on your paper: upper left (UL), upper right (UR,) lower left (LL), and lower right (LR) to see which category each corresponds to in the explanation that follows.

Personal Strengths Survey: Explanation

Count up the number of strengths you have in *each* section (UL, UR, LL, LR). *Don't* add the sections all together! The category with your highest score indicates your primary strengths; your second highest score are your secondary strengths. It is also possible to have a fairly even number of strengths in three or four categories, but most people's scores gravitate around two categories.

UL (upper left): Lion

1. Lions are born leaders.
2. Lions like to accomplish things with immediate results.
3. Lions' time frame is now!
4. Lions are decisive.
5. Lions want *Reader's Digest*–length communication.
6. Lions often feel threatened by questions.
7. Lions are not afraid of pressure or confrontation.

UR (upper right): Otter

1. Otters just want to have fun.
2. Otters are great at motivating others into action.
3. Otters avoid the fine print.
4. Otters focus on the future.
5. Otters avoid confrontation at all costs.
6. Otters are tremendous networkers.
7. Otters are very susceptible to peer pressure.

LL (lower left): Golden Retriever

1. Golden retrievers are loyal.
2. Golden retrievers have a strong need for close relationships.
3. Golden retrievers have a deep need to please others.
4. Golden retrievers have hearts full of compassion.
5. Golden retrievers define the word *adaptable*.
6. Golden retrievers often react to sudden changes.
7. Golden retrievers hold stubbornly to what they feel is right.

LR (lower right): Beaver

1. Beavers keep a close watch on their emotions.
2. Beavers actually read instruction books.
3. Beavers like to make careful decisions.
4. Beavers like using their critical skills to solve problems.
5. Beavers live by the motto, "Let's do it right!"
6. Beavers often turn anger inward.
7. Beavers tend to focus on the past.

In practical terms, lions and beavers are hard on the problem *and* hard on people. They have no problem with confrontation but they can often lack compassion. Otters and golden retrievers are soft on people *and* soft on the problem. They do not like confrontation, and they are very compassionate, especially golden retrievers. As Gary Smalley and Dr. John Trent (the authors of the survey) explain, lions and beavers represent the hard side of love, otters and golden retrievers the soft side.

(Note: Smalley and Trent, both psychologists, designed this survey after examining over thirty other psychological assessments.[1] Another psychologist introduced this survey to me fifteen years ago. Since then I have given it to my family, friends, and people in creativity groups. It is simple to take and easy to understand, and people are amazed how accurately their "animals" describe their personalities. I highly recommend reading *The Two Sides of Love* for stories about these personality types. [Some of the stories are hilarious!] The book is easy, fun to read, and provides many insights.)

Discussion of Personality Strengths Survey

The downside of each category:

- Lions are often bossy and lack empathy.
- Otters need to work on responsibility, especially time management.
- Golden retrievers take care of everyone else and put themselves last.
- Beavers can get lost in the details and can also be critical.

Now that you've taken the survey and discovered your top two categories (or for a few of you, a balance among three or four), you can see what your strengths and weaknesses are. You can also see what motivates you as an individual. This knowledge not only benefits you as an individual, but it is invaluable in discovering how best to operate in groups.

Say you're a lion and you have a group project. You meet the other three or four people in the group, and after a while you notice that everyone in the group is

It takes all kinds to make a great team.

ready to get the job done. Everyone's decisive and no one wants to procrastinate. This is great news. However, it soon becomes clear that no one can agree much on what needs to be done. Even if there is some agreement on the goal, everyone wants to do it his or her way, so nothing actually gets done. You now have an idea of how a pride of male lions would function. (Why do you think Congress is so dysfunctional? Way too many of them are lions!)

Say you're an otter. You meet up with other playful, fun people for your group project. You're all having so much fun, however, that you keep brainstorming and it's not until the last minute that you put everything together. The project turns out pretty slapdash, plus you probably missed the deadline. This is an otter team at its playful best and working worst.

What if you're a golden retriever? If you end up with others of your breed, it'll be a wonderfully nurturing and stress-free environment. You all will feel heard and validated, and most likely will also get very little done.

If you're a beaver and you latch onto a bunch of other beavers for a group project, you'll all make sure you're doing it right. Only problem is, chances are your group will spend too much time on the ground rules. You all will still be gathering details on the project till it's too late, so it won't get done either!

Notice that as individuals, you all have strengths. However, everyone having the same strengths in a group has the same result: an unfinished project (and because they are goal-oriented, a lot of frustration for lions and beavers). The otters and golden retrievers will regret their grades (if it's a class project), but not the fun they had nor the connections they made.

The optimum goal would be to have equal numbers of lions, otters, golden retrievers, and beavers on a team. That's not going to happen too often, but if you can trade off with other groups so there are at least three types in your group, you'll get the project done, generally on time, with a lot less frustration.

In Student Life Skills classes, designed to assist freshmen students succeed at academics and careers, the personality type that was the least represented was the beaver. (It makes sense; beavers are very organized people. They know how to manage their notes, homework, and time, so they rarely need an entry class like Student Life Skills.) Each class would usually have one or two beavers, no more. Of course, every group wanted one! I always remarked to the beavers, "You've probably never been so in popular in your lives." Then I'd recommend that groups scout for classmates who had beaver qualities as their *second* strength. These people helped balance the teams.

Teams need to mix it up—have lions for leadership, otters to come up with new ideas and make it fun, golden retrievers to make sure everyone's opinions are heard and validated, and beavers to remind everyone about the details, as well as manage many of them.

In no time, you may find yourself calling yourself and everyone who's taken this survey a lion, beaver, otter, or golden retriever.

Other Group Assessments

If you took the FourSight measure (chapter 4) online, you discovered your main approach(es) for creative problem solving. (You'll see a parallel to the results of this survey.) FourSight is also extremely useful for forming teams.

If you've ever been on a team, you know the problem usually isn't the goal—it's how to achieve it. That's because the people in the group have many viewpoints. Those viewpoints are sometimes based on people's experiences from reaching past goals, but more often they're a result of personalities (or styles, which are a reflection of personality). People with different personalities have different expectations. Varied expectations lead to poor communication, and ultimately, the strong possibility that the group will not work well together. The team either accomplishes its goal under great stress (and with far less creativity) or it falls apart without ever attaining the goal. This history of group failure might make you wonder, "Wouldn't it be better to have a homogenous team?"

With the benefit of FourSight, however, you'll understand that it isn't necessary—nor desirable—for groups to consist of people with the same personality. All you really need to know is how to apportion tasks based on those personalities. People will perform best when given assignments that match their interests and abilities—another example of the effectiveness of intrinsic motivation. For fun, compare your FourSight results to your animal types; they'll correlate. (After you've taken a few personality assessments, you'll see a pattern in what they reveal about you.)

If you get the opportunity to take the Kirton Adaption-Innovation Inventory, you'll see a similar pattern. Ditto with True Colors (you don't want to blanket a project in one hue) and the Ennegram (too many of the same type will sideline a successful outcome).

You'll also need the *hard skills, soft skills,* and *attitudes, values, and dispositions* discussed in chapter 11. These are all necessary to work well on a team.

Formula for Creativity

Don't get excited—this formula does *not* contradict what you learned about creativity skills in chapter 1. There is no formula for producing creative products. There has, however, been a formula, to explain creativity itself. Dr. Ruth Noller, a mathematician (one of the few women in the field of creative studies at that time who, by the way, worked on the early mainframe computers), suggested $C = F_a$ (K, I, E), which means creativity is a function (F_a) of knowledge (K), imagination (I), and evaluation (E).[2] As already noted, this is *not* a formula for making something creative; it's only a formula for the *process* of creativity itself. Of course, this formula includes one other *P—person* (no *product* or *press*). Just thought you'd like to know that creativity has a little bit of algorithm to it—leave it to a creative mathematician!

A Few (Fun) Creative Activities

OK, here are a few creative activities that are of general interest.

Chindogu

Design a chindogu, or useless invention, as described in chapter 1. The rules for chindogu design can be found at www.chindogu.com/tenets.html. Submit your original chindogu at uselessinvention@designboom.com (If yours makes it online, post me a note on my website: www.stateofyourheart.com.)

Body Art

Buy some washable tattoo markers and draw some art on your body. Zig-zag, squiggle, polka dot, doodle, plaid, and funny face your way to a new you. You can add towns and roads up and down your arms and legs. How about adding solar systems and aliens? Draw the animals you love. Include your fingertips and, of course, the classic, ink mustaches on your face. Make sure to check with your parents and let them know the ink's washable![3]

Vision Boarding

This exercise requires simply choosing images (photos mostly) that represent your goals. When you've accumulated all you want, *either*

1. Put them on a poster *or*
2. Put them into a computer file that you look at every day *or*
3. Put them into a desktop photo slide show. This is a terrifically effective idea because you'll be able to see your goals many times every day.

Make sure to

1. Include "selfies" of you in the scenes that represent your goals.
2. Add any new images to the poster, file, or slide show that represents your goals.
3. Include photos that appeal to you, even if they *don't seem to* represent your goals. You don't know why you're attracted to those, but don't concern yourself about the reason. Simply *choose them*. On some inner level, you want or need what's in the photos.[4]

Talent Map

To make a talent map, look at your life when you were young. Put your talents on a visual timeline or a map when you were four, seven, ten, thirteen, and every three years until the age you are now. Use photos (selfies are perfect), drawings, and key words to represent each phase or age and your talents at that time. (Note: Your talents can be singing or dancing or they could be climbing trees or making fudge.)[5]

Value Tree

To make a value tree, draw a picture of a tree trunk and draw the branches in all directions. In the trunk, write your biggest belief about yourself. Add your key abiding value. On the branches, write your other values such as *creativity, respect, family*. Underneath each value, draw a piece of fruit and write in words such as *painting, honesty,* and your parents' names.

Value Grid

Eliminate the values you can do without. Cross them off or write down the ones you'll keep.

Children	Power	Loyalty	Health
Career	Prestige	Integrity	Fitness
Freedom	Inner peace	Spirituality	Respect
Recognition	Order	Trust	Fame
Financial security	Education	Excellence	Balance
Friendships	Family	Helping others	Travel
Adventure	True love	Kindness	Job security
Challenge	Fun	Independence	Home

Creativity	Hobbies	Profit	Awards
Integrity	Free time	Position	Tranquility
Joy	Happiness	Wealth	Other_____

Go through the list again and cross off as many values as you can. Now, get tough and get the list to your top ten values. Go away and incubate for two days. When you return, narrow your list to five values. Check your last five with the career you want and make sure there's no conflict. If there is, rethink what kind of work you should be doing.[6]

What If?

What if a famous, successful, innovative person (whom you admire and know something about) were to help you plan your career? What would this person suggest? Think the way that person would think.

Storyboarding

This is a drawing exercise for goal setting in which you can use stick figures—artistic talent doesn't count! The idea is to work toward your goal—backward. Get a large piece of paper and divide it into two rows of three boxes each. These are your cartoon panels.

1. In the *first* upper left panel (UL), draw your goal as it stands today.
2. In the *last* panel on the lower right (LR), draw you reaching your goal. Put in as much detail as you wish.
3. In the lower middle (LM) panel, draw a step that is three months *before* your goal.
4. In the lower left (LL) panel, draw a step that is *six* months before your goal.
5. In the upper right (UR) panel, draw a step *a year* from your goal.
6. In the upper middle (UM) panel, draw a step that is eighteen months from your goal. (You can change the dates on the panels if your goal will take longer or shorter to achieve.)
7. You can add more panels to the storyboard if you wish.[7]

Pour Art Project

The purpose of this project is to loosen you up regarding painting. There's really no wrong way to do this, so pour and enjoy!

You will need

- Several colors of latex (water-based) paints in portable containers. (Collect paint mistakes from hardware stores or leftovers from friends and garage sales.) *Use a lot of black and white.*
- A wood, metal, or other slick surface as a "canvas." (Note: it will be easier to contain the paint if your canvas is at least 24" in both width and height.)
- Drop cloths.
- Rags.
- Gloves (optional).

Instructions:

1. Make sure to prep the floor and area where you are painting with drop cloths. Have rags nearby and wear gloves if desired.
2. If desired, prep your "canvas" surface with white paint up to the edges.
3. Pour paint in *your own style* and at *your own pace*. To create a "canvas wrap" design, allow paint to fall off the edges.[8]

Questions from State of Your Heart Site

The following are two questions from people who visited my website (www .stateofyourheart.com). The first questioner needs some guidance. The second questioner wants to explore a philosophical aspect about creativity. The answers are ones I actually posted on my site.

When Should You Ditch Something That's Creative That Isn't Working Anymore?

It sounds like you're stuck. If you've been stuck for a while, ask yourself some questions. One of the first ones is "Am I still enjoying working with this? Am I sticking with it because I have to (for a class project, for work)? How can I make this less serious and more play?" Depending on the answers, you'll have an idea what your next step is. If you've only been stuck for a short time, try some divergent thinking exercises found at www.humorthatworks.com/how-to/20 -problem-solving-activities-to-improve-creativity/; some excursions at www .ideastogo.com/lateral-thinking; and many Creative Problem Solving (CPS) tools at creativeproblemsolving.com/tools/index.htm. (Or Google "Creative Problem Solving" and "Creative Problem Solving tools" to find others. The Internet is full of them!) Another way to get unstuck: *try a new form of creativity.*

One of the best ways you can help yourself when you are stuck is to take yourself in another direction creatively. Find some other kind of play or creative activity. For instance, if you're writing, and you're really stuck, don't keep writing. Go bake something. (Julia Cameron makes soups and pies when she's stuck on her writing.)[9] If you're composing, go make origami—only if you know how to make it already. If you're sculpting, do something non-hands-on—write a poem, for instance. And no matter what art you're involved in, a classic ploy is to go out and look at nature. If you can, walk in it.

If It's Creative, Can Something Ever Be Considered Evil?

Look at the most accepted definition of creativity: "novelty that's useful." If you're a very creative bomb maker, and you're using your skill to blow holes in mountains to build tunnels for highways, that's destructive and useful. If you're building bombs to blow people up, that can't be considered ultimately useful, no matter your reasons for doing it. A horrible case in point: Germans in World War II were extremely clever in exterminating people in concentration camps. This cleverness would be considered useless and evil and definitely *not* creative.

It's also a matter of time—not historical time, but how long the creative process *appears* to be destructive. For example, when you're working on an art project, you might have paints and brushes and paper and canvas lying all over, and splotches of paint on the easel and floor and all over you, too. An even better example is cooking—some of the best cooks are the messiest! A creative mess is temporary, however, *and* it can be cleaned up. No rooms were (ultimately) harmed during these creative processes!

That's an important point: the process could be creative and the product evil. However, there are also evil processes that lead to both bad and benign results, such as the Tuskegee syphilis experiment. This was a forty-year (1932–1972) medical experiment sanctioned by the U.S. government that involved 600 African American sharecroppers in Tuskegee, Alabama. Of these men, 399 already had syphilis; 201 were inoculated with the syphilis bacteria; and none of them were told they had the disease. The men were fed, paid, given health care and burial insurance; however, not only were they unaware they had syphilis, they were not given penicillin, even after it was discovered in the 1940s to be an effective treatment for the disease. Once the unethical and callous nature of this experiment was revealed, public outrage led to establishing ethical treatment of human subjects in the United States. No one denies that this experiment was a blot and a shame on public health history, yet from its evil existence benign research methods emerged.[10]

My view: Creativity can be (and very often is) messy, but a product can't ultimately be destructive to be considered creative. That logic applied to the atomic bomb. Once atomic bombs were used for atomic energy, their function evolved from destructive to creative (for the most part).

Art and Writing Tools

So while creative tools are not a recipe, they do provide a heuristic model, a guideline, to generating more of your creative energies.

Here are two: one for painting, one for writing.

Life, Paint, and Passion: Just Play

"Painting is a simple gesture, a little red, a trace of blue, a line, an image, a dot, a step by step going toward oneself, listening to the inner voice."[11]

For you painters, try this for *fun.* Say/ask these statements/questions to yourself when painting:

"This is a free stroke—I won't do it if it isn't free."
"I won't be caught up in the aesthetic (beauty), so I will paint what seems ugly here."
"If I paint this way, it will be too consistent, so I won't do it."
"If I am caught in the meaning, I have to do something absurd."
"In other words, I won't make it important. I'll simply *play.*"
"If I were five years old, what would I paint?"
"If I paint instead of plan, what would I paint if it didn't have to fit?"
"I will paint for the joy of freedom itself."

How did it feel to paint while saying or asking these compared to other times when you had other (probably negative) thoughts in your head?

Writing the Natural Way: Mapping

This tool is not only very helpful when you need to write something, but when you need to generate *any* ideas on a topic. Sure, you can start with Wikipedia and get an overview. But then try mapping, or as it's sometimes called, "mind mapping," because it assists you in exploring a topic. It's really a form of brainstorming; however, instead of writing a list (or if you're in a group, using sticky notes), draw a circle in the center of a blank sheet of paper and write your topic in the middle of the circle. Then draw some lines out from the main circle, each with its own circle at the end. Leave lots of room to draw more lines and circles around the second group. Now, fill in the first bunch of circles with the first ideas that pop into your mind about your topic. Remember not to censor any ideas that come to your mind. It's not important that these are not brilliant ideas nor your best, but they will start you off. Now if an idea springs from one of the circles you have already filled in, then draw a line and a circle from there. (By the way, these circles are going to look more like lopsided ovals than real circles. Let them go—don't go for perfection!)

Another important element of this technique is to *write as quickly as possible*. It's not designed as a speed race, but to keep your head from censoring the ideas you come up with. Speedy writing tends to block out critical thoughts.

OK, now you're done with your mind map. Examine it. What do you see? What patterns do you find? Do any thoughts seem like they don't fit in with the others? Pay extra attention to these. These are your novel ideas, what sociologists call "outliers." They are the ideas that tend to take you in a direction you hadn't planned on, which is exactly what you want. This is where your creativity surfaces. (Julia Cameron says that instead of thinking things "up," which is hard, you are actually taking things "down"—a much easier direction to go. It's almost like you are taking dictation from both your conscious and unconscious brain.)

H2 (How to) Use Creativity to Make Excellent Presentations

Honestly, you already know how to do a lot of this. If you've added "bling" to a poster or cool graphics to a PowerPoint slide show, you've already used your creativity in a presentation. Years ago, however, Dr. E. Paul Torrance, often called the "Father of Creativity," designed the Torrance Incubation Model (TIM) to include specific tools for creating excellent presentations. Torrance's purpose was to help audiences really "get" and remember important points from presentations, and this was difficult if presentations were uninteresting. (This was before PowerPoint and other computer graphics.) Even when presentations have these, they can still be boring. So maybe TIM isn't as outdated as you might think.

You're doing—or you have done—a lot of work on your presentation, whether it's a solo or a group project. TIM will add appeal to a science project, a model for social studies, or a presentation in language class.

TIM is comprised of three stages—Stage 1: Heightening Anticipation; Stage 2: Deepening Expectations; and Stage 3: Keeping It Going. (Torrance included the word *incubation* in the title because it occurs *after* these three stages.)[12]

She's using the Torrance Incubation Model in her talk.

As an example of how to include a component in your presentation, look at "Make It Swing, Make It Ring." This technique means that you need to add rhythm and sound to your presentation. This is effective because people learn naturally to rhythm so your presentation will be memorable.

In fact, any creative elements you add to your presentations will make what you're trying to say more memorable, and if you're lucky, *you* may be memorable

Torrance Incubation Model

E. Paul Torrance designated these techniques to enliven presentations:

* Find the Problem * Produce and Consider Many Alternatives * Be Flexible * Be Original * Highlight the Essence * Elaborate, but Not Excessively * Keep Open * Be Aware of Emotions * Put Ideas in Context * Combine and Synthesize * Visualize Richly and Colorfully * Enjoy and Use Fantasy * Make It Swing, Make It Ring * Look at It Another Way * Visualize the Inside * Breakthrough: Extend the Boundaries * Let Humor Flow and Use It * Get Glimpses of the Future[a]

as well. Additionally, this model is one of the best ways to teach, so many teachers use the TIM in their classrooms. [13]

Here is a more complete explanation of the TIM techniques:

Find the Problem is simply Torrance's term for Exploring the Problem, the first stage of CPS (chapter 10).

Produce and Consider Many Alternatives is renaming CPS's second stage, Generating Ideas. You'll be using both divergent and convergent thinking.

Be Flexible means that during presentation, unforeseen events occur. As the Boy Scouts say, "Be prepared." To be flexible you can utilize the TIM tool "Look at it another way." This'll help you see possibilities for handling surprises.

Be Original. Obviously, this tool is prodding you to do something even a little bit different. Actually, if you include any of the following—Make It Swing, Make It Ring, Visualize the Inside, Visualize Richly and Colorfully, Enjoy and Use Fantasy, or Let Humor Flow and Use It—these will automatically make your presentation original.

Highlight the Essence. Let people know the purpose behind your presentation. If people walk away from your talk *with one main point*, you've done a *good job*. If they walk *with two points*, you've done an *excellent job*. If they leave *with three*, you have performed *superbly*. Make sure you *highlight your main point*. Figure out what your next two main points are and highlight them, too.

Elaborate, but Not Excessively. You need to give people enough information so they won't walk away scratching their heads, wondering what you meant, but you don't want to provide so much detail that they'll get bored or worse, fall asleep. (Consider elaborating on your three main points.)

Keep Open. This one is a partner to Be Flexible. If you're open, you'll be flexible. If you're flexible, you'll be open to new approaches.

Be Aware of Emotions. Is this an emotional topic for you? If so, you must be aware of your feelings and have a strategy for how to handle yourself if you feel angry or sad. Even showing too much enthusiasm can put people off; they might think you're making a sales pitch. Or the topic might be an emotional, even a controversial one. If so, be aware that you might receive passionate feedback from your audience, even before you finish. If you prepare for this contingency, you'll be more able to deal with unexpected comments. (Stand-up comics know this well. They train themselves to handle hecklers, especially ones "under the influence"—that is, drunk.)

Put Ideas in Context. Make sure your ideas fit into a framework and that people can see clearly how they connect. One way is to make your topic relevant to your audience. (For example, if your topic is the Asian tiger, tell your audience that it and the tiger have something in common, but withhold the details of what that commonality is. Your audience will be motivated to watch and listen to locate the commonality. People love solving mysteries.)

Combine and Synthesize. This may be the most commonly used tool in creativity. Many inventions have resulted from people combining items that appeared completely unrelated. Examples include sporks, flying boats, sweet and sour sauce.

Visualize Richly and Colorfully. This is probably the technique you are most familiar with because you're comfortable with images. If not, add drawings and photos! Add YouTube links! Add color! Make your presentation capture people's attention. (No one wants to look at a boring presentation. Would you?) There are thousands of images and clip art on the Internet and in many computer programs. Use them. If you have friends who are artists, use their images. Ditto if you are an artist.

Enjoy and Use Fantasy. Make your presentation a story. Borrow plots from fairy tales, comic books, anime, well-known movies and cartoons, and add your own ideas. (Research shows that if people need to recall facts, an excellent technique is to put the facts into a story. Example: You want your class to remember the table of elements. After showing them the chart, have each student concoct a story or possibly several stories using the names.)[14]

Make It Swing, Make It Ring. To repeat: Add a musical component, even if it's only a beat. Experiment with including your main point in a song or in a poem with a strong beat. At the end of your talk, you might hand out simple percussive instruments and ask your audience to repeat your main points to a beat. (They'll most likely be successful because, as mentioned earlier, our memories respond to rhythm and music.)

Look at It Another Way. How would your topic look to someone standing on her head? How would it look from a hawk's point of view? From a bug's? Through a microscope? How would you interest someone who hated this topic? Or someone who was blind?

Visualize the Inside. It's easy to see the outside of something, but how would your topic look from the inside? (For example, a banana's outside and its inside look very different. Or you could pretend you woke up *inside* your topic.)

Breakthrough: Extend the Boundaries. This is the best way to see how your topic relates to other topics. For example, if your topic is about antelopes, instead of focusing only on them, include predators as part of your presentation. Or add the antelope's genetic ancestors or its influence on nearby humans.

Let Humor Flow and Use It. Find some appropriate jokes or cartoons on your topic (often available on the Internet). Be careful that you match jokes or cartoons to the audience level and to the points you're making. Make sure *not* to overdo the humor. (Test it out; if your friends don't laugh, skip those jokes.)

Get Glimpses of the Future. Leave your audience with an idea of what might happen with your topic in the future. Is more research planned? Will new inventions result? Will your topic change law, medicine, business? Will it change how people live? Will it be a positive or negative influence? (You can use drawings or a map to show these possible influences.)

H2 to Make Bad Creative Projects

What does this mean—how to make bad creative projects? Maybe you consider that you already know how to make those just fine on your own. You don't need advice on how to make them worse. Actually, that is not what this method means.

If you used the earlier technique for writing, you now have all kinds of ideas to incorporate in your essay, story, poem, or report. Not only do you have lots of ideas, some of them will take your writing into an original, unusual direction, which is exactly what you want, right?

If you used this technique to gather ideas for a project—either an individual or group one—you now have lots of those, too. Again, some of your ideas will be fresh and take your project in unexpected directions, so those are the ones you want to concentrate on.

So here you are, you need to produce something, anything—a history project, a poster, a presentation, a float for the homecoming parade, an art project, an invention for the science fair—and everything you're doing for that project seems stupid, uninteresting, absolutely boring. You feel that there's no originality to what you're doing. You're tired before you begin, or you're in the middle and mystified why you ever started. At any rate, you want to give up at some point long before the project's finished.

The first thing you do is what? Think back on what you learned in chapter 7 on friending yourself. Now you are going to be *friending creativity*. What is the one thing *not* to do? That's right, don't get critical about yourself. Everyone runs out of gas, runs out of ideas. No one, not even da Vinci or Edison or any creative person you can think of, had great ideas *all* the time. Your account does get empty. How long has it been since you filled it? (Remember your "creativity date.") If it's been recently, then maybe you're tired, sleepy, hungry, or have other more important things on your mind.

But still . . . even if your creativity account is empty, you simply don't have time to take yourself on a creativity date now. You have to do this project.

So what you do is make a bad one—absolutely make every mistake you can. For instance, if you have to make a history project, make it completely lame. Maybe you can get the dates all wrong, put it in the wrong era, have the historical figures wearing the wrong clothes, driving vehicles that weren't invented when they were alive, saying words they never heard, eating food that they never knew. Or if you have to make an art project, draw whatever your subject is as sloppily as you can. Don't try to make it look good. Make it bad. Make baby scrawls or slashes across the paper. For drawing materials, use a crayon—a broken one, or an old lipstick, some medium you know would never be acceptable. Instead of art paper, which is nice stuff, draw on newspaper, paper bags, old pizza boxes, or on the back of your old term papers (you probably have them saved in your hard drive anyway).

If you have to make a model, make a really lousy one. You could use an old pizza box for a base, and clothespins for figures, find something junky looking for trees, dribble paint on it—you get the point.

Make your project as bad as you possibly can. As Julia Cameron advises, "You must be willing to be a bad artist. . . . By being willing to be a bad artist you have a chance to *be* an artist."[15]

Why do you do this? Because it's very freeing. Why? Because it's fun. You know you're not going to turn this in. You also *know* this is not your best work—it's not even close—so you'll have a very strong tendency not to judge yourself. *The combination of this freedom and nonjudgment is play.* When you play, guess what? You get ideas, you get energy. You start to think of things you hadn't thought about to add to your project. You go "where no creative person has gone before."

This is a tried-and-true method. In fact, this is how I wrote this book. I'd never written a book before. I had some guidance, but really, where was I supposed to put all the stuff I had in my head? Plus there were times I had no ideas, or I had lousy ones. So I did what I told you: I simply wrote stuff—not good stuff a *lot* of the time—just stuff about creativity. My ideas bounced around, they fit in different chapters, they seemed repetitive and stupid, but I kept writing. I shut up the critical voice and kept typing. Every day I typed three pages. Were they Shakespeare? Certainly not! They reflected what was going on in my head each time (and a lot of the time there wasn't anything really bright going on up there). I didn't worry about it. I just kept typing. Somehow, after I got a lot of material (because you need a lot in a book), the book got better. I figured out ways to write my ideas better. (Plus I got *a lot* of help from my editors.)

Go ahead; make bad creative projects—art, writing, music, websites, and so on—and see what happens. (Remember what Ira Glass said in chapter 2 about working a lot so you progress from not-so-good to mastery.) "To live a creative life we must lose our fear of being wrong."[16]

CREATIVITY AND YOUR FUTURE

The Big Picture

A better title for this section of the chapter might be "Creativity Will Help Your Future." If you asked them, most working adults would say that they either already have a sense of purpose and identity in their jobs (or career) or they would like to have one. It's becoming increasingly less acceptable in society (U.S. society anyway) to have a job simply to earn a paycheck. Now, being a teen, that doesn't mean you're going to immediately land your first job that will match your purpose in life. That may be partly because you're not sure of your purpose. (You're still establishing your identity, remember? It's absolutely fine not to know your purpose yet.)

It is absolutely no stretch of the truth, however, to claim that creative skills will be essential to your future. Repeat: *Creativity skills will be essential to your future.*

Check out the list of movers and shakers on page 176. Is this enough to convince you that creativity is necessary now and will be even more so in the future? You may not have realized this yet, but *there is a direct correlation between the creativity you will use in your work* and *how much job satisfaction you will have in working.*

If you use creativity—which means solving problems in whatever field you're in—you will be able to find more work, whether you work for another company or establish your own. The more polished your creative skills are (meaning you've practiced them), the more valuable you will be to yourself, your clients, students, patients, coworkers, and your future employers.

Daniel Pink describes this process very well in his book *Drive: The Surprising Truth about What Motivates Us.*[1] He refers to Abraham Maslow's hierarchy of human needs, which are often illustrated in a pyramid: on the bottom level are physiological needs such as food, water, shelter, and sleep. As the elevator of humanity rises, its needs morph into safety, such as an environment free of day-to-day hazards (second floor), and then love and belonging, known as social needs

Who's Been Saying That Creativity Is Essential to Your Future?

Teresa M. Amabile, PhD (contemporary), professor in the Entrepreneurial Unit, Harvard Business School, creativity researcher, creativity author

Martha Beck (1962–), sociologist, author, life coach

Julia Cameron (1948–), teacher, playwright, journalist, filmmaker, composer, author of *The Artist's Way* and sequels

Roger L. Firestien, PhD (contemporary), Creative Problem Solving (CPS) consultant and author

Bill Gates (1955–), inventor, cofounder of MicroSoft, philanthropist

Malcolm Gladwell (1963–), sociologist, journalist, author of *Outliers: The Story of Success*

Steve Jobs (1955–2011), inventor, entrepreneur, cofounder of Apple, Inc.

Michael Michalko (contemporary), creativity expert, creativity author

Daniel Pink (contemporary), author, *A Whole New Mind; Drive*

Gerard J. Puccio, PhD (contemporary), chair and professor of International Center for Studies in Creativity at Buffalo State College, CPS consultant, author of books and articles on creativity and CPS, creator of FourSight measure

Sir Ken Robinson (1950–), international education adviser on arts, speaker, author on creativity and education[a]

(third floor). Maslow called the needs in the lower three levels "deficiency needs," meaning these needs *had* to be met for a human being to be able to function well on the other levels.[2]

On the fourth level are self-esteem needs and at the tip of the pyramid (the attic) are six self-actualization needs. Two of these are *problem solving* and *creativity*.[3]

Pink claims that the need to survive is very strong and so is the need for safety, and therefore they require little support. We are also social creatures, and humans have had many eons' experience dealing with other people. (All mammals need other mammals not only for survival, but for play.)[4]

When we get to levels 4 (self-esteem) and 5 (self-actualization and creativity needs), however, we ourselves need to support these levels.[5] These are more delicate needs that require a nurturing, positive environment in order to develop and flourish. Pink calls these levels Motivation 2.0.[6]

Operating under Motivation 2.0 means that we want to put more meaning into our lives, we are becoming intrinsically motivated to spend our time in activities that we excel in and that we want to improve. Motivation 2.0 is a restatement of Amabile's work on intrinsic motivation and Csikszentmihalyi's research into the conditions of flow, one of which is the desire to be occupied in activities that take creativity and lead us closer to self-actualization.

The person with the world's highest recorded IQ from the 1986 to 1989 *Guinness Book of World Records*, columnist and author Marilyn vos Savant, claims that engineers who have contributed the most to our societies have often been underappreciated for their influence. In centuries past they would have been toolmakers, blacksmiths, makers of clocks and navigational instruments, aqueduct and road builders, as well as architects and builders of pyramids, castles, bridges, and cathedrals. Nowadays we often call engineers, inventors, and techies "geeks" or "nerds," although we've also recognized how valuable they are. Vos Savant rightly claims that without the inventiveness of engineers, we would not have tools, roads, plumbing systems, vehicles (starting with the wheel, which led to carts, buggies, chariots), boats and ships, trains, planes, medical equipment, electricity, hydroelectric power, rockets, satellites, space ships, and space stations. If you're reading this between the covers of a book, a "techie" had to invent the printing press (Johann Gutenberg, 1448). If you're reading this on a laptop or iPad, engineers and technologists invented all the computers, operating systems, software, tinier computers (calculators, cell phones, DVDs and players, iPods, iPhones, MP3 players, Pac-Man, PlayStation, Xbox, Wii, video games, and apps).[7]

To achieve all this progress took creativity.

Although, as Daniel Pink has said—along with many others who have studied creativity—that being creative is not solely about creating products or getting and keeping a job, creativity will help you do exactly that.[8]

Because the need for creativity, its study, its use, its importance in every field, not only for art, science, or business—is not in the future. It is *now*.

One teen (name withheld) who answered the question of how creativity would affect the future, answered, "I don't think it matters, but my skills will help me get through life alone for a bit." Sorry to contradict this teen. This view is not correct—at least the part that creativity doesn't matter. However, it is true that anyone can get by on his or her own skills (minus creativity) "for a bit" of time—only not for long.

The truth is, you already have the "drive" to be creative. Now allow your creativity to grab the wheel. You'll be steering a lot of the time, but at points you'll have to go on automatic pilot. You'll have to let your creative drive take over and lead you to "where no one has gone before."[9]

Creativity is one of your highest needs; however, let's look at some other needs in the lower levels of Maslow's hierarchy of needs pyramid to see what might get in the way of your being creative.

It used to be in America that some of the stuff on the bottom levels was "duh." I mean, most people didn't have to ask, "Got enough food? Got a warm bed? Got a secure place to stay?" In the past few years, there have been many people, some of them teens, who haven't had these basic needs met. These were considered so basic to the American lifestyle they were hardly discussed. With the housing crisis and the Wall Street shenanigans, there have been plenty of teens who haven't had food or a place to live, or have been nervous about losing that place. And it's hard to be creative with those situations hanging over your head.

Six New Senses

In a book called *A Whole New Mind*, Daniel Pink (great last name, huh?) talks about how six "senses" will be important in the future.[10] Actually, they're extremely important now. He claims that we have left the information age and have emerged into the conceptual age.[11] The six senses, which Pink says are "fundamental human attributes," are design, story, symphony, empathy, play, and meaning.[12]

So what do these senses mean for you? Well, let's look at each of them.

Design

This can mean anything—the art of anime and manga, the art production in movies such as *The Dark Knight*, the cleverness and beauty in everyday objects we use.

So, you say, "I'm not a designer." Actually, though you might not be able to draw a straight or crooked line, you are. First, you're a consumer, so you're well aware of design. If you have a cell phone cover, a good part of the reason you bought it was its cool design. You wear your favorite clothes mostly because you like their design. Your friends are the same. Design made a huge difference in popular games such as Angry Birds, Minecraft, Grand Theft Auto, and

Six New Senses Needed for the Twenty-First Century

Design: the nature of humans to make and shape the environment in ways not found in nature in order to serve human needs and give meaning to life.

Story: "narrative imaging"—how humans think, organize, and remember (e.g., it's much easier to recall facts in stories rather than lists).

Symphony: the ability to put together the pieces; the capacity to synthesize, to see relationships between seemingly unrelated fields, to see broad patterns.

Empathy: the ability to imagine yourself in someone else's situation and sense what that person is feeling.

Play: the ability to involve self in exercise or activity for amusement and recreation; fun or jest. It's important for personal physiological health and marketplace success.

Meaning: the need to have purpose in one's life.[b]

Wolfenstein, and in their game systems: Xbox, PlayStation, and Wii, which all have been successful applications of design. In the world of entertainment, CGI (computer-generated imagery) has allowed filmmakers to create cinematic worlds never before possible. Whether you like Lady Gaga or not, design made a huge difference in her success.

What happens when the impact of design is minimized? The poor design of the butterfly ballots in Palm Beach County, Florida, affected the outcome of the 2000 presidential election.[13] The failure of the O-ring's design led to the *Challenger* disaster on January 28, 1986, and contributed to the *Columbia* catastrophe on February 1, 2003.[14] There are many other issues of poor or dangerous design, some fatal like brake systems failing in cars; others only a nuisance, such as when your earbuds broke only two days after you bought them.

The magnitude of and need for design will only get more intense. The more products—and services—in the global market, the more vital that they be distinguished by elegant, amusing, and/or creative design.

You are going to (and may already be) the next generation of designers—not only for products, but for how you work and play. The world of work is changing; designing systems and processes in your field will become more significant.[15] Also important is how you will use design in building, maintaining, and furnishing your own homes.

Currently, when you have to put together a presentation, you already know from the Torrance Incubation Model that you'll sway your audience more if you use design, including enticing backgrounds, color and fancy fonts, cartoons, and YouTube videos. There'll be more ways to put design in presentations in the future: some of you are going to create them. Another plus: American design usually isn't outsourced to other countries, which means more jobs for all of you.[16]

Story

We all love stories; it's a very human need to want story in our lives. Many of you have loved the *Twilight* series, *The Hunger Games*, the *Divergent* series, *The Fault in Our Stars*, and the movies made from these books. These stories are about teens, so of course they've been popular. Maybe you think this "story" stuff doesn't fit you. Maybe verbal intelligence is not high on your list, so you have no interest in any kind of writing. Don't concern yourself—story in the conceptual age means much more than writing them. It means that you *want* stories when you see ads, and you can best communicate with each other with stories about your lives. Some of you are regular bloggers. Most of you update your social media sites daily; those posts tell people your life stories in mini-chapters.

It will be important for you to *continue* communicating in story. At some time in your life (it's probably happened already) you'll have to stand up in front of people and inform them, persuade them, even ask them to help. The best way to do this is through stories. You're probably already adding YouTube clips and cartoons, maybe jokes or true stories to your presentations. So you already know their value. (You might even want to consider getting storytelling training.)[17]

As for the future, you're going to be the ones who make the next films (blockbusters or sleepers), write the next books, create the next comic routines, run for the next local, state, congressional, and presidential offices. You'll be selling the next lines of cars or computers, clothing, or marketing ideas. You'll be selling you and your ideas and you'll need story to do this.

Symphony

This sense is not about music per se, though it can be. Symphonies are grand pieces of music that are composed for many instruments so they are symbolic for synthesizing many elements.[18] By that definition, a collage is a symphony. For you, symphony will be combining components from whatever field(s) in which you excel. You will need to tap into your ability to put together pieces of your projects in unaccustomed ways. You'll need to *synthesize* rather than compartmentalize. (Computers do the last task very well; they're not so hot on synthesis.) You'll need to see relationships in categories that seem unrelated. Finally, you'll need to detect broad patterns in your work—not to mention in your life.

Thank the fact that you have been pals with the Internet and the World Wide Web all your lives. Because you've had a worldview since you could read, this view gives you more ability to be in "symphony." You do—and will continue to—cross boundaries; for instance, many of you will excel in a technical or managerial field *and* in one of the arts. You entrepreneurs will be able to synthesize the skills from both into your own businesses.

Now is the time for you to expand your worldview and integrate the pieces of it into creative products and services.

Empathy

This is an easy concept for you to grasp. Teens, as a rule, want to see the world become a better place. You care about the environment, disenfranchised people, and your siblings (even if they annoy you a lot), your parents (ditto), and of course, your friends. Currently, it is becoming more vital for people in the world to empathize with each other, and not solely because of global warming. Anything you can do creatively to demonstrate empathy in the world is a double win—for you and for everyone else. You'll also need empathy in your job(s) or career because it won't be enough to do the tasks of your job well. Since consumers are so used to e-tail, when they venture to shop in brick-and-mortar places, they need more positive connections with flesh-and-body people, like you at your job. For medicine, the trend is for empathy to be an important part of a doctor's success. Medical students are now being evaluated in schools on how well they communicate with and respond to their patients.[19]

Some of you will be building more socially conscious businesses—and even if you don't, you'll tend to buy products from those that follow this model. So even if you only think of empathy as a component of business, it's important to pay attention to its impact.

Play

Remember that Dr. Jaak Panksepp discovered that play is a basic emotion? This means human beings are hardwired for play. Already you play video games such as

Minecraft and maybe online Sudoku or Words with Friends. Some of you might be on sports teams; others in the theater. So you already play, but how can you expand your play *beyond* the screen, smartphone, and sports fields? Remember that many of the techniques in the Torrance Incubation Model are playful.[20] Those of you who are naturally funny already play more than most. Those who lack the knack for humor can use their imaginations to add fun to chores and study (PEPS can help you there—see chapter 11).

Besides increasing your capacity for play in your own life, you could be a contributor to expanding how humans play. What will that look like? No one's sure, but the planet could definitely use more playful means to solve problems. Maybe it'll be playing at cleaning up the environment (like Mom and kids cleaning up the kids' room). Maybe it'll be creating playful negotiation. Maybe it'll be substituting war games for real war. (Wouldn't *that* be *amazing*?) Play with the possibilities!

Meaning

One of the easiest ways to see the shift into the *importance* of meaning is by observing that people greatly desire—even demand—to work in jobs that are meaningful. It's not enough—even in bad economic times—to simply work to get paid and survive. People want their work to count for something. This desire is easy for you to understand because most teens feel this way about life. You're impatient with the aspects of the world that seem to make no sense—like rules at school (endless testing—yechh!), why bad events happen in the world, why leaders simply don't agree to work together on environmental problems, or myriad other issues.

Look at the number of people—teens included—who are attempting to find meaning outside their lives. Teens are joining churches, or if already members, are participating in Bible study and youth groups. Or teens are studying yoga and getting involved in community projects. (Although some community service is required in schools, it often results in teens like you continuing to contribute long after you've fulfilled the class requirement.)

With greater transparency through the Internet, Twitter, and other social networks, as well as through phones, you know more of what's happening in the world, so you have an opportunity to understand other situations and points of view. You see that we are all on the same planet (and better clean it up and stop fighting). Thus you have more chances to empathize with others who are not of your race, religion, nationality, sexual orientation, or politics (yes, even that). Keep building that empathetic muscle; the world needs it now and will need it more in the future.

Creativity and Your Personal Future

Creativity will also help your career because you will be able to identify in which areas of your life you tend to be most creative. Everyone has them. *No* one is creative in all areas of human endeavor (not even if you are a direct descendent of Leonardo da Vinci). We all have special bents or talents[21] that we feel more comfortable in than others, so we tend to spend more time in those; therefore, we have more ability to tap into our creativity in those areas. It becomes a "luscious circle."[22] If you recall what Malcolm Gladwell claimed (chapter 2), spending a long time on any one pursuit (the estimates are 10,000 hours or ten years) means you will become a master of that pursuit. So by the time you leave high school (or get your GED), you will have spent a long time in what you love doing. You will have developed your own tools for bringing out your creativity. You will know

Teen Views on Creativity and their Future

Question 10: "How do you think creativity could play a role in your future?"

"I want to be a director for movies, TV, and theater. I attend [a technical film school] and I have so many ideas I want to bring life to. It will always be something near and dear to my heart. Just walking down the street I come up with new stories."—Kyle, 19, Florida

"It could help me create things that could help people."—James, 15, California

"I want to become a recording artist and performer and singer-songwriter."—Skye, 18, California

"I can use my gift to get a good job or get into a great college like schools Harvard and MIT, but I do plan to see how far it can take me in the future."—Thomas, 13, Virginia

"I think creativity can play a huge role in my future with my ideas, mindset, and thoughts. I feel it can also impact me and the others around me."—Alicia, 16, California

"I think it can play a role in my future if I might want to become a teacher I can show kids that you can learn in school by having a creative mind."—Analyse, 16, California

"Creativity in my future would be coming up with unorthodox solutions to solve issues that affect my everyday life."—Sam, 16, California

"I wanna be an actor so it's up to me to be creative on stage."—A.J., 16, California

"I think technology is taking away from a lot of creativity. It will be less needed in the future." —Meagan, 16, California

"Creativity will play a large role in my life because architecture requires lots of thinking in your own way."—Sylvana, 16, California

"You need creativity to save the world. I'm going to save the world. Creativity is my future."—Justice, 17, California

"Creativity is my future, not just a role."—Arianna, 18, California

"Considering the career I want, musical theatre, creativity is imperative. Even now creativity is something I can't live without."—Glennon, 17, California

"It can play an important role when I need to come up with a solution to diagnose a disease."—Shai, 16, California

"By enabling me to come up with solutions and new experiments that will answer my questions as a scientist (physicist)."— Sofia, 17, Minnesota

"Ultimately, in the future, I want to be happy, and in life sometimes you need to get creative to get what you want to be happy, because maybe it's never been done before. I want to live in the country and work with animals, and to achiev [*sic*] this goal [as a city girl], I might have to be creative."—Nina, 15, New York[c]

how to "unstick" yourself. That mastery will be an invaluable "insert" into your career.

Also, even if you are not focused on the area you've mastered, by spending time playing around with supposedly "silly stuff," you will have gotten comfortable with the creative process and how it works. You will know creativity's ambiguity and uncertainty, its murky ways and doubtful outcomes, and you will be able to navigate its unmarked road to attaining your goals. It takes courage to be in those places; to be, if not comfortable, at least familiar with indeterminate feelings, and to allow them to help you reach solutions. Those people who have not allowed their creative bicycle out for a ride will be afraid to fall. When they do fall, they will not know how to get back up. You know there's no GPS to creativity. You will learn how to make your own map, which will put you in a much more advantageous position to get jobs, find and keep clients, and make a difference in whatever arena you choose.

Census Fantasy

Here's an intriguing question—*why* does no one know the *exact* number of artists in the general population? Why can't we tally the exact number of inventors? (Refer to circles in chapter 1.) We know so many other facts about the human race. Why don't we have more information about people's creative endeavors?

You're all familiar with data mining from polls and surveys—in person and online. These provide information on your gender and age, your address and phone number (land and cell lines), e-dresses, websites, number of pets, and children under eighteen in your household. If you ever revealed your ethnicity or your religious affiliation, it's in a file somewhere. Although people often change jobs, it's easy to find an employment history. Someone's educational history (where you went to school or are planning to go, whether you graduated and how often) is even easier to access. Even medical information, though protected, is available. Plus, almost all serious polls contain questions about your income. The IRS certainly knows what yours is! And unfortunately, unscrupulous sorts can hack our financial information. [23]

Returning to the question about who is creative and inventive, the U.S. Patent Office does have *some* idea how many inventions exist; however, not everyone registers their invention. At any rate, there is no "creative clearinghouse" with numbers indicating who's creative (and how) and who isn't, because so far the government, business, and most people don't think this knowledge is important.

As noted, the Census Bureau gathers a lot of this information (and more) every ten years, but its methods are amateurish compared to online data miners. These professionals know what car(s) you drive, your preferences in books and hobbies, what you bought last year, last month, last week, yesterday, and today. They know how many you bought and how much you paid for it and *how* you paid.[24]

Let's indulge in looking at a future when knowing about people's creativity is essential to a functioning society. Imagine a census taker asking about creativity . . .

The Future: A Creativity Census Scenario

A census taker, whose last job was as an auctioneer, is on the first day at the job. The census taker is speaking to a homeowner in a doorway.

> Census taker: Now back to your profession. You said you were an artist?
> You: Yes.
> Census taker: What have you produced artistically in the last ten years? Has it been drawings? Works on paper? Paintings? Etchings? Collages? Sculpture (stone, wood, ceramic, marble, bronze/snot/fingernails/cat fur)? Mobiles/Stabiles? Animation? Anime? Claymation? Photography? Cinephotography? Cartography? Cubism? Triangulism? Abstract impressionism of the New York school? Ego realism of the Fargo school? Tattoo artist? *Taboo* artist?
> You: What?
> Census taker: Or are you an actor? (Stage? Film? Zombie?) Musician? Composer? (Guitar? Piano? Violin? Zither? Spoons? Oboe? Bassoon? Buffoon?) Are you a vocalist? (Opera? Rock? Rap? Whistler? Yodeler?) Maybe you're a dancer? (Ballerina? Clogger? Stripper?) Puppeteer? (Do you use socks? Or paper bags? Make animal balloons?) Or are you a filmmaker (Art director? Best boy? Best girl?) Circus performer? (Acrobat? Aerialist? Juggler? Clown? Mime? Unicyclist? Stiltwalker? Fire breather?)
> You: Huh?
> Census taker: Or maybe you're a designer? Let's do these alphabetically. Costume? Fashion? Flooring? Furniture? Goth? Graphic? Interior? Landscape set? Or you might be an inventor. Have you invented anything in the past ten years? Mechanical? Automotive? Porta-Potty? Electrical? Software? Chemical? (Be careful how you answer that one.) A monster?
> You: Can you repeat the questions?

Of course, because not everyone is a professional creative, census takers would also have to ask questions about people's hobbies. They'd have to count the numbers of crafters, scrapbookers, jewelry makers, quilters, miniature makers, woodcarvers, seamstresses, and semptors (term for a male who sews), and people engaging in any craft you could mention.

Is There Really a Need for Creativity?

It's hard to imagine this kind of poll, isn't it? Do you wonder why there aren't questions like this on a census? It's because until recently, creativity wasn't considered important. It was considered a side dish on the menu of life.

However, for centuries, in every culture on earth, creativity has been put mostly in the hands of visual and performing artists, craftspeople, and writers. Recognition was also given to certain game-changing scientists, engineers, and inventors. Everyone else's creative capabilities or interests were essentially ignored. Until . . .

Creativity and Innovation in One Millennium and through Another

In the last thirty years, however, the attitude toward creativity has started to change. (If it hadn't, you wouldn't be reading this book.) The change was due, like so many other societal changes, to the explosion of the Internet. Prior to the nineties, the Internet was an information exchange among science geeks in laboratories, military personnel on bases, and academics at universities. Hardly anyone else was on the Internet and *no one* was making a profit from it.

Then, in 1976, the personal computer was invented. In the mid-1980s, Apple was marketing a popular personal computer called the Macintosh, and the Windows operating system, a program for personal computers, was introduced by Microsoft. Soon the fad to own one became a trend, meaning computers were here to stay. It was inevitable that an entrepreneurial businessperson would realize the Internet's potential for marketing and sales. Internet markets (or e-tail) became national quickly, and because there were no travel or brick-and-mortar costs, these markets grew globally almost as fast. Because there were more global markets, there was more need for products. To remain competitive, businesses had to produce better products and newer ones, many of which needed to be attractive globally. New products only come from innovation, so innovation was in white-hot demand. *Innovation* became the "in" term. It still is.

When business focuses on an aspect of human endeavor—in this case, innovation—all too often the cynical version of the Golden Rule emerges: "Those with the gold make the rules." (Innovation basically means "creativity plus money.")[25]

One of these "golden" rules dictates since creativity led to innovation, and innovation led to profit, *now* creativity was important. In the last thirty years, creativity has traveled beyond the world of art, music, theater, and literature, landing smack in the middle of the business boardroom and in whatever wild places entrepreneurs operate.

All of which explains why you hear the word *creativity* so much today (very often followed by the words *and innovation*).

I am sorry to contradict what sixteen-year-old Meagan from California wrote, "I think technology is taking away from a lot of creativity. It will be less needed in the future." Actually, there will be *more* need for creativity as we travel further into the twentieth-first century.

People who have the ability to apply creative thinking skills in twenty-first-century organizations (schools, financial or art institutions, major corporations,

Leaping into your creative future.

"I am young and part of our future. If I can sustain my creativity and imagination, I can create something worthwhile. It can be hard not caring what other people think, but we can't be afraid of doing what we want and feel. That freedom is creativity and how I choose to live my life."
— Hannah, 18, New York

and consulting firms) to generate useful, practical, and novel solutions to actual problems are, and will continue to be, in great demand. In fact, there is a universal need for creative thinking and creative problem solving. The rise of diversity also demands the skills to develop groups' potential, especially in problem solving. Problems in the world are complex, and as you've learned, often the "identified" problem does not end up being the actual problem. Knowing how to identify the correct problem is an essential skill key to developing creative solutions. Leaders will especially need to know how to use creativity in effecting change and in steering people through all the imminent technological, social, and cultural changes in first- through fourth-world countries. Leaders will need to be adept in assisting others to generate creative solutions and put those solutions into action. Some of this leadership will be in managing diverse groups to facilitate problem solving.[26] Some of these change leaders with creative skills are going to be you.

Glossary

Definitions include people associated with the terms.

algorithm: a method to solve problems that uses specific steps in a specified order; a formula. Creativity does not use algorithms.

bisociation: the concept that creativity comes from the interaction of two dissimilar frames of reference, that is, experimenting with unusual combinations. (Arthur Koestler)

brainstorming: a divergent technique to generate ideas in a nonjudgmental atmosphere; must follow four rules; results in many ideas, some novel. (Alex Osborn)

brainwriting: a divergent group technique similar to brainstorming. Sticky notes are placed in three rows of three on printer paper. Each person in the Resource Group fills in one row on a brainwriting sheet and passes it to the next person and the next until all rows are filled. (The number of brainwriting sheets depends on the size of the Resource Group.) The notes are removed and the selection process begins. (Blair Miller, Jonathan Vehar, Roger L. Firestien)

Card Sort: a convergent thinking tool designed to help prioritize options. (Blair Miller, Jonathan Vehar, Roger L. Firestien)

chindogu: the Japanese category of useless inventions that must abide by ten tenets (rules).

Client: in Creative Problem Solving (CPS), the person who requests the problem solving session, is accountable for the challenge, and responsible for taking action.

convergent: thinking that aims at a single and correct solution (inside the box).

creative: the environment, both physical and emotional, that either nurtures or hinders *climate* creativity.

Creative Problem Solving (CPS): a three-phase process utilized to solve a client's problem, which includes (1) Exploring the Problem, (2) Generating Ideas, and (3) Planning for Action. CPS is led by a facilitator and includes a Resource Group to help generate (CPS) ideas. (Alex Osborn, Sidney Parnes, et al.)

creativity: novelty that is useful (or appropriate). This is the most accepted definition, although many others are also valid.

design: one of six "senses" needed in the twenty-first century; the nature of humans to make and shape the environment in ways not found in nature in order to serve human needs and give meaning to life. (Daniel H. Pink)

divergent: thinking that's designed to generate multiple answers (outside the box).

drive: beyond biological drive to survive (1.0), Drive 2.0 is, more broadly, to seek reward and avoid punishment. (Daniel H. Pink)

elaboration: in creativity, how much detail a person provides about an idea, whether verbal or figural. More elaboration is preferred. (E. Paul Torrance)

empathy: one of six "senses" needed in the twenty-first century: the ability to imagine yourself in someone else's situation and sense what that person is feeling. (Daniel H. Pink)

Enneagram: a personality measure consisting of nine types, that is, the helper, the observer. (Renee Baron and Elizabeth Wagele)

everyday creativity: ordinary creativity that is meaningful. (Frank X. Barron)

extrinsic motivation: engaging in an activity for reasons that do not originate from a person's own desire, but for some outside reason (i.e., for money, praise, or to be part of a competition). This is counterproductive to creativity. (Teresa M. Amabile)

Facilitator: in CPS, the person who manages the process for the client.

flow: the experience of being deeply occupied in a pursuit that is balanced between skill level and challenge. In this state a person experiences well-being or happiness; also known as being in the "zone" or "groove." (Mihaly Csikszentmihalyi)

fluency: in creativity, the number of ideas an individual (or team) generates. (E. Paul Torrance)

Forced Connections: a divergent CPS tool using images to stimulate the generation of ideas. Images can be photos (generic pictures of animals, scenery, food, shapes, design—without words or people) in notebooks, on a computer screen, or projected onto a large screen; also known as visual connections.

FourSight: an assessment to measure an individual's thinking approach to creative problem solving; a valuable tool for team building. (Gerard J. Puccio).

genius: an exceptional natural capacity of intellect (not the same as creativity).

giftedness: an exceptionally high intelligence in many areas; broader than talent (also not the same as creativity).

heuristics: a trial-and-error method of problem solving; guidelines for increasing creativity.

highlighting: in CPS, a convergent tool used to select the most appropriate ideas; can highlight these ideas with a dot marker, colored dots, stars, and so on.

incubation: one of three creative skills: taking a break from actively working on a problem; often results in an insight or breakthrough on the problem.

intrinsic motivation: a person's desire to engage in an activity solely for personal reasons by outside factors, that is, money, praise, or for competition. (Teresa M. Amabile)

judgment: assertions about the truth of things or the wisdom of a course of action; relies on evidence. People have a right to challenge your judgment. (Vincent Ryan Ruggio)

Kirton Adaption-Innovation Inventory (KAI): an assessment designed to measure how a person is creative on a continuum of adaption to innovation; has been proven to be valid and reliable. (Michael J. Kirton)

meaning: one of six "senses" needed in the twenty-first century: purpose, significance. (Daniel H. Pink)

multiple intelligences: a measure designed to widen the traditional IQ tests that only measure verbal and mathematical abilities; includes seven other intelligences: spatial (artistic) musical, bodily-kinesthetic, interpersonal, intrapersonal, naturalistic, existential. (Howard Gardner)

Myers-Briggs Type Indicator (MBTI): an assessment based on Carl G. Jung's archetype theory of personality, which describes sixteen personality types. Proven to be a valid and reliable assessment for over a half century—the gold standard in personality assessment. (Isabel Briggs Myers, Katharine Cook Briggs)

person: one of the four Ps: the generator of creativity.

Personal Strengths Survey: an assessment which indicates how people's strengths manifest in four categories; useful information for individuals and for forming teams. (Gary Smalley, John Trent)

persuasion: a necessary link between creativity and leadership; an addition to the four Ps: person, process, product, and press.

play: one of six "senses" needed in the twenty-first century: the ability to involve self in exercise or activity for amusement and recreation; fun or jest, important for personal health and marketplace success. (Daniel H. Pink) Play is also one of seven emotions. (Jaak Panksepp)

PPCO: also known as Praise First; a four-step process for assessing an idea, product, project, or action. PPCO contains four steps: P = Pluses, P = Potentials, C = Concerns, O = Overcoming Concerns.

press: one element of the four Ps: the environment (climate) in which a person creates, which can cultivate or crush creativity.

process: one element of the four Ps: the activity of creating.

Process Buddy—in CPS sessions, the person who assists the Facilitator by handling logistics (i.e., room set-up, handing out supplies, keeping large sheets of Client's CPS notes in order). (Blair Miller, Jonathan Vehar, Roger L. Firestien)

product: one element of the four Ps: the artifacts of creativity.

Productivity Environmental Preferences Survey (PEPS): an assessment to determine an individual's optimal environment for learning and working. (Gary E. Price, Rita Dunn, Kenneth Dunn)

Resource Group: in CPS, the five to seven people who help the Client generate ideas and options. The group also provides insight, enthusiasm, and energy to solve the Client's challenge. (Blair Miller, Jonathan Vehar, Roger L. Firestien)

SCAMPER: acronym for Substitute, Combine, Adapt, Modify, Put to other uses, Eliminate, Rearrange. SCAMPER is a divergent thinking tool that aids in generating ideas. (Robert F. Eberle)

Statement Starters: in CPS, phrases that the Resource Group uses to begin sentences when generating ideas; examples: H2 = How to, HM = How might, IWWM = In what ways might, WMBAT = What might be all the . . . , IWBGI = It would be great if . . . , WISMD = What I see myself doing . . .

story: one of six "senses" needed in the twenty-first century: "narrative imaging"; how humans think, organize, and remember (it is much easier to recall facts in stories rather than lists). (Daniel H. Pink)

StrengthsQuest (SQ): an assessment of personal strengths, also known as "themes." SQ is being used at many colleges and in the business world. There are thirty-four themes. The Top Five are the most important to understand. (Donald O. Clifton, Edward Anderson)

symphony: one of six "senses" needed in the twenty-first century: the ability to put together the pieces; the capacity to synthesize, to see relationships between seemingly unrelated fields, to see broad patterns. (Daniel H. Pink)

talent: a special natural ability or aptitude in one area; often confused with genius, though it can refer to genius in one area.

taste: an internal state or preference. Since it is personal, no need to defend one's taste. (Vincent Ryan Ruggio)

tolerance of ambiguity: one of three creative skills: the ability to accept uncertainty without knowing a direction; to avoid premature closure in finding a solution.

tolerance of complexity—one of three creative skills: the ability to maintain direction while deferring judgment possibilities; momentarily accepting all options.

Torrance Incubation Model (TIM): a model for making presentations; includes eighteen techniques: for example, Make It Ring, Make It Swing; Highlight the Essence; Look at It Another Way. (E. Paul Torrance)

Torrance Tests of Creative Thinking (TTCT): verbal and figural (drawing) assessments that measure a person's fluency (quantity), originality, and elaboration (detail) of ideas. (E. Paul Torrance)

True Colors: an assessment to measure an individual's personality; uses four colors to represent four categories of personality.

Vision Quest: a divergent thinking technique that looks at a problem at both a micro and macro level. (Martha Beck)

Notes

Introduction

a. Aryna Ryan, "Teen Views on Creativity" (questionnaire), 2012.

Chapter 1

1. *Dictionary.com*, s.v. "myth," dictionary.reference.com/browse/myth?s=t (accessed May 8, 2014).
2. Mark Twain, quoted on The Quotations Page, www.quotationspage.com/quote/23633.html (accessed May 12, 2014).
3. Vladimir Lenin, quoted on The Quotations Page, www.quotationspage.com/quote/838.html (accessed May 12, 2014).
4. G. E. R. Lloyd, ed., *Hippocratic Writings*, Penguin Classics reprint ed., translated [from the Greek] by J. Chadwick and W. N. Mann, et al. (Harmondsworth, England: Penguin, 1983), 262.
5. Michael H. Hart, *The 100: A Ranking of the Most Influential Persons in History* (New York: Citadel Press, 1992), 274.
6. Hart, *The 100*, 274.
7. Gary A. Davis, *Creativity Is Forever*, 5th ed. (Dubuque, IA: Kendall/Hunt Publishing, 2004), 44.
8. Carl G. Jung, *Psychological Types* (New York: Harcourt, 1933); Davis, *Creativity Is Forever*, 48, 52.
9. Jung, *Psychological Types*, 581, 609, cited in Davis, *Creativity Is Forever*, 52.
10. Homerus Epic, Odyssea, Book 24, Line 60 (circa BCE 799).
11. Robert S. Albert and Mark A. Runco, "A History of Research on Creativity," in R. J. Sternberg, ed., *Handbook of Creativity* (New York: Cambridge University Press, 1999), 6.
12. Susan P. Besemer and Donald J. Treffinger, "Analysis of Creative Products: Review and Synthesis," *Journal of Creative Behavior* 15 (1981), 158–178.
13. Michael J. Kirton, *Adaptation and Innovation: In the Context of Diversity and Change* (New York: Routledge, 2003); Gerard J. Puccio and Chris Grivas, *The Innovative Team: Unleashing Creative Potential for Breakthrough Results* (San Francisco: Jossey-Bass, 2012).
14. Teresa M. Amabile, "How to Kill Creativity," *Harvard Business Review*, September–October 1998, 1–12.
15. *Dictionary.com*, s.v. "eccentric," dictionary.reference.com/browse/eccentric?s=t (accessed May 8, 2014).
16. Donald J. Treffinger and Roger L. Firestien, "Ownership and Converging: Essential Ingredients in Creative Problem Solving," *Journal of Creative Behavior* 17, no. 1 (1983), 32–38.
17. Treffinger and Firestien, "Ownership and Converging," 32–38.

18. Bonnie Badenoch, *Being a Brain-Wise Therapist: A Practical Guide to Interpersonal Neurobiology* (New York: W. W. Norton, 2008), 47.

19. *Star Trek: The Next Generation,* television series, Rick Berman, executive producer, and Peter Lauritsen, co-producer (Hollywood, CA: Paramount Television, 1987–1994).

20. Eben Alexander, *Proof of Heaven: A Neurosurgeon's Journey into the Afterlife* (New York: Simon and Schuster, 2012), 85.

21. Carl G. Jung, *The Archetypes and the Collective Unconscious: Collected Works* (New York: Pantheon, 1959); Davis, *Creativity Is Forever,* 44.

22. Davis, *Creativity Is Forever,* 44.

23. Samuel T. Coleridge, *Biographia Literaria,* 1817. Cited in William Safire, "On Language: Suspension of Disbelief," *New York Times,* October 7, 2007.

24. Stanley S. Gryskiewicz, "Targeted Innovation: A Situational Approach," in Stanley S. Gryskiewicz, ed., *Creativity Week III Proceedings* (Greensboro, NC: Center for Creative Leadership, 1981), 77–103.

25. Otto Rank, *Art and Artist* (New York: Knopf, 1932/1989), 369; Mel Rhodes, "An Analysis of Creativity," *Phi Delta Kappan* 42, no. 7 (1961), 307–308; Mel Rhodes, "An Analysis of Creativity," quoted in S. G. Isaksen, ed., *Introduction: An Orientation to the Frontiers of Creativity Research: Beyond the Basics* (Buffalo, NY: Bearly Limited, 1987). Rhodes and Isaksen are cited in Davis, *Creativity Is Forever,* 42-44, 47–48.

26. Davis, *Creativity Is Forever,* 83.

27. Davis, *Creativity Is Forever,* 87.

28. Davis, *Creativity Is Forever,* 85–87.

29. Davis, *Creativity Is Forever,* 86–87.

30. Davis, *Creativity Is Forever,* 87.

31. Davis, *Creativity Is Forever,* 83.

32. Abraham Maslow, *Motivation and Personality* (New York: Harper, 1954).

33. Carl R. Rogers, "Toward a Theory of Creativity," in S. J. Parnes and H. F. Harding, eds., *A Source Book for Creative Thinking* (New York: Scribners, 1962), 65–66.

34. Donald J. Treffinger, S. G. Isaksen, and Roger L. Firestien, *Handbook of Creative Learning* (Sarasota, FL: Center for Creative Learning, 1982), 1.

35. Davis, *Creativity Is Forever,* 44–46.

36. Davis, *Creativity Is Forever,* 90.

37. Robert Garvey and Geof Alred, *Mentoring and the Tolerance of Complexity* (London: Elsevier Academic Press, 2001).

38. *Dictionary.com,* s.v. "incubation," dictionary.reference.com/browse/incubation?s=t (accessed May 2, 2014).

39. Microsoft Word Thesaurus, s.v. "incubate" (accessed May 2, 2014).

40. Microsoft Word Thesaurus, "incubate."

41. Microsoft Word Thesaurus, s.v. "incubation" (accessed May 2, 2014).

42. Davis, *Creativity Is Forever,* 47.

43. Davis, *Creativity Is Forever,* 48.

44. Billy Joel, "Pressure," YouTube video, www.youtube.com/watch?v=Iyv905Q2omU (accessed May 27, 2014). Lyrics also available at www.metrolyrics.com/pressure-lyrics-billy-joel.html.

45. Davis, *Creativity Is Forever,* 11; Amabile, "How to Kill Creativity," 1–12.

46. PEPS Learning Style, www.collegesuccess1.com/PEPS.htm (accessed June 4, 2014).

47. Dorothy Parker, quoted on The Quotations Page, www.quotationspage.com/quote/457.html (accessed June 7, 2014); I added the italics.

48. Albert Einstein, quoted on The Quotations Page, www.quotationspage.com/quote/9316.html (accessed June 7, 2014).

49. David Silverstein, "Curiosity and Creativity," *Leadership and Business*, July 15, 2014, www.leadershipandbusiness.com/2013/08/curiosity-and-creativity.html (accessed June 3, 2014).

50. Silverstein, "Curiosity and Creativity."

51. Silverstein, "Curiosity and Creativity."

---

a. Aryna Ryan, compilation of nine myths about creativity. Myths 1, 2, 5, 6, and 7 are based on Gary A. Davis, *Creativity Is Forever*, 5th ed. (Dubuque, IA: Kendall/Hunt Publishing, 2004) (Myth 1, mysterious, p. 42; Myth 2, "just happens," p. 29; Myth 5, who's creative, p. 42; Myth 6, artists only, p. 10; Myth 7, special talents, pp. 5–8). Myth 3—muses, divine inspiration—is based on Homerus Epic, Odyssea Book 24, Line 60 (circa BCE 799), and Robert S. Albert and Mark A. Runco, "A History of Research on Creativity," in R. J. Sternberg, ed., *Handbook of Creativity* (New York: Cambridge University Press, 1999), 6. Myth 4—measuring—is based on Susan P. Besemer and Donald J. Treffinger, "Analysis of Creative Products: Review and Synthesis," *Journal of Creative Behavior* 15 (1981), 158–178; Michael Kirton, *Adaptation and Innovation: In the Context of Diversity and Change* (New York: Routledge, 2003); Gerard J. Puccio and Chris Grivas, *The Innovative Team: Unleashing Creative Potential for Breakthrough Results* (San Francisco: Jossey-Bass, 2012); and Teresa M. Amabile, "How to Kill Creativity," *Harvard Business Review*, September–October 1998, 1–12. Myth 8—eccentric—is based on *Dictionary.com*, s.v. "eccentric," dictionary.comhttp:/dictionary.reference.com/browse/eccentric?s=t (accessed May 8, 2014). Myth 9—airy-fairy—is based on Blair Miller, Jonathan Vehar, and Roger L. Firestien, *Creativity Unbound: An Introduction to Creative Process*, 3rd ed. (Williamsville, NY: Innovation Resources, 2001), 21.

b. Davis, *Creativity Is Forever*.

c. Davis, *Creativity Is Forever*, 84.

d. Donald W. MacKinnon, "Creativity in Architects," in Donald W. MacKinnon, ed., *The Creative Person* (Berkeley: The Institute of Personality Assessment and Research, University of California, 1961); Donald W. MacKinnon, "Educating for Creativity: A Modern Myth?" In Gary A. Davis and J. A. Scott, eds., *Training Creative Thinking* (Melbourne, FL: Krieger, 1978); Robert J. Sternberg, ed., *Handbook of Creativity* (New York: Cambridge University Press, 2006), 47–48.

e. Abraham H. Maslow. *The Farther Reaches of Human Nature* (New York: Viking Press, 1971), 7.

f. *Dictionary.com*, s.v. "ambiguity," dictionary.reference.com/browse/ambiguity (accessed June 2, 2014); Mark A. Runco, *Creativity Theories and Themes: Research, Development, and Practice* (San Diego, CA: Elsevier Academic Press, 2007): 297; Aryna Ryan and Cynthia A. Hedge, "How to Slay Your Critical Dragon and Rescue Your Creativity" (presentation, April 18, 2011).

g. Davis, *Creativity Is Forever*, 86, 90; Robert Garvey and Geof Alred, *Mentoring and the Tolerance of Complexity* (London: Elsevier Academic Press, 2001).

h. Davis, *Creativity Is Forever*, 122.

i. Chindogu, www.chindogu.com/tenets.html; Weird Asian News, "Chindogu: Weird and Useless Japanese Inventions," www.weirdasianews.com/2009/10/19/chindogu-weird-useless-japanese-inventions/ (accessed June 1, 2014).

j. Gordon Ekvall, "Organizational Climate for Creativity and Innovation," *European Journal of Work and Organizational Psychology* 5 (1996), 105–123, in Gerard J. Puccio, Mary C. Murdock, and Marie Mance, *Creative Leadership: Skills That Drive Change* (Thousand Oaks, CA: Sage Publications, 2007), 237–239.

Chapter 2

1. Logan LaPlante, "Hackschooling Makes Me Happy," YouTube video (University of Nevada: Tedx, 2014), www.youtube.com/watch?v=h1lu3vtcpaY&utm_source=newsletter_109&utm_medium=email&utm_campaign=newsletter-07172014 (accessed July 29, 2014).
2. Erik H. Erikson, *Childhood and Society* (New York: W.W. Norton, 1950).
3. Daniel J. Siegel, *Brainstorm: The Power and Purpose of the Teenage Brain* (New York: Jeremy P. Tarcher/Penguin, 2013), 4, 11.
4. Siegel, *Brainstorm*, 6.
5. Siegel, *Brainstorm*, 1, 6.
6. Siegel, *Brainstorm*, 90.
7. Bonnie Badenoch, *Being a Brain-Wise Therapist: A Practical Guide to Interpersonal Neurobiology* (New York: W.W. Norton, 2008), 8.
8. Jeffrey Jensen Arnett, *Adolescence and Emerging Adulthood* (Boston: Pearson Education, 2013), 64–65.
9. *Dictionary.com*, s.v. "creativity," dictionary.reference.com/browse/creativity?s=t (accessed May 3, 2014).
10. Siegel, *Brainstorm*, 6.
11. David Dobbs, "Beautiful Brains," *National Geographic* 220, no. 4 (October 2011), 43.
12. Siegel, *Brainstorm*, 6.
13. Siegel, *Brainstorm*, 22.
14. James Clear, "What Every Successful Person Knows but Never Says" (interview with Ira Glass on taste and failure), jamesclear.com/ira-glass-failure; Ira Glass, "Ira Glass on Storytelling," YouTube video, www.youtube.com/watch?v=BI23U7U2aUY (accessed June 9, 2014).
15. Siegel, *Brainstorm*, 1, 6.
16. Malcom Gladwell, *Outliers: The Story of Success* (New York: Little, Brown, 2011), 39, 41, 42, 47, 49, 50, 55.
17. Gladwell, *Outliers*, 42; I added the italics.
18. Glass, "Ira Glass on Storytelling."
19. Gladwell, *Outliers*, 39, 41, 42, 47, 49, 50, 55.
20. "Apprenticeship Indenture," Cambridge University Library Archives (Luard 179/9), March 18, 1642.
21. "Apprenticeship Indentures 1604–1697," Cambridge St. Edward Parish Church Archives (KP28/14/2).
22. "Apprenticeship Indentures 1604–1697."
23. Adam Smith, *Wealth of Nations: An Inquiry into the Nature and Causes of the Wealth of Nations* (London: W. Strahan and T. Cadell, 1776).
24. Sir Robert Harry Inglis Palgrave, *Dictionary of Political Economy* (London: Macmillan and Co., 1896), 4.91.
25. Palgrave, *Dictionary*, 491.
26. Palgrave, *Dictionary*, 492.
27. "Apprenticeship Indentures 1604–1697."

28. "Apprenticeship Indentures 1604–1697."
29. Palgrave, *Dictionary*, 492.
30. Michael Howe, *Genius Explained* (Cambridge: Cambridge University Press, 1999), 3.
31. Howe, *Genius Explained*, 3.
32. Howe, *Genius Explained*, 3.

a. Aryna Ryan, synopsis of Daniel J. Siegel's book *Brainstorm: The Power and Purpose of the Teenage Brain* (New York: Jeremy P. Tarcher/Penguin, 2013).
b. Teens' definitions of creativity, author's questionnaire, 2012.
c. Bruce Horovitz, "After Gen X, Millenials, What Should the Next Generation Be?" *USA Today*, May 4, 2014, usatoday30.usatoday.com/money/advertising/story/2012-05-03/naming-the-next-generation/54737518/1 (accessed November 6, 2014).
d. Siegel, *Brainstorm*, 94.
e. Teens' views on their creativity as children, author's questionnaire, 2012.
f. Vincent Ryan Ruggio, *The Art of Thinking: A Guide to Critical and Creative Thought* (New York: Pearson/Longman, 2006), 34.

Chapter 3

1. Władysław Tatarkiewicz, *A History of Six Ideas: An Essay in Aesthetics*, trans. Christopher Kasparek (The Hague: Nijhoff, 1980), 244; Robert S. Albert and Mark A. Runco, "A History of Research on Creativity," in R. J. Sternberg, ed., *Handbook of Creativity* (New York: Cambridge University Press, 1999).
2. Gary A. Davis, *Creativity Is Forever*, 5th ed. (Dubuque, IA: Kendall/Hunt Publishing, 2004), 9.
3. Albert and Runco, "A History," 4–5.
4. Michael H. Hart, *The 100: A Ranking of the Most Influential Persons in History* (New York: Citadel Press, 1992), 67.
5. Albert and Runco, "A History," 6.
6. Tatarkiewicz, *A History*.
7. John Dacey, "Concepts of Creativity: A History," in Mark A. Runco and Steven R. P. Pritzker, *Encyclopedia of Creativity*, vol. 1 (New York: Elsevier, 1999).
8. Davis, *Creativity Is Forever*, 64–65.
9. Davis, *Creativity Is Forever*, 2–4.
10. International Center for Studies in Creativity, "History," creativity.buffalostate.edu/history (accessed May 12, 2014).
11. J. P. Guilford, "Three Faces of Intellect," *American Psychologist* 14, no. 8 (1959), 469.
12. Alex F. Osborn, *Applied Imagination: Principles and Procedures of Creative Problem-Solving* (New York: Charles Scribner's Sons, 1953).
13. Alex F. Osborn, *How to Think Up* (New York: Charles Scribner's Sons, 1942).
14. International Center for Studies in Creativity, "History."
15. Creative Education Foundation, "What Is CPSI?" www.creativeeducationfoundation.org/what-we-do/cpsi-conference/what-is-cpsi (accessed May 15, 2014).
16. International Center for Studies in Creativity, "History."
17. Edward De Bono, *Six Thinking Hats* (New York: Little, Brown, 1985).
18. Arthur Koestler, *The Act of Creation* (London: Pan Books, 1964).

19. Margaret Boden, *The Creative Mind: Myths and Mechanisms* (New York: Routledge, 2004).

20. Robert J. Sternberg, "A Three-Faceted Model of Creativity," in Robert J. Sternberg, ed., *The Nature of Creativity* (New York: Cambridge University Press, 1988), 125–147.

21. Mark A. Runco, "Implicit Theories," in M. A. Runco and S. R. Pritzker, eds., *Encyclopedia of Creativity* (San Diego: Elsevier Academic Press, 1999), 145.

22. Dean K. Simonton, "Creativity, Leadership, and Chance," in Robert J. Sternberg, ed., *The Nature of Creativity* (New York: Cambridge University Press, 1988), 409–420.

23. "'Father of Creativity' Honored with Annual Distinguished Lecture Series," *Columns* (online newspaper), November 5, 2007, columns.uga.edu/news/fulltext/father-of-creativity-honored/ (accessed November 6, 2014).

24. E. Paul Torrance, *Torrance Tests of Creative Thinking: Norms-Technical Manual. Figural (streamlined) Forms A and B* (Bensenville, IL: Scholastic Testing Service, 1990).

25. Kendra Cherry, "What Is Longitudinal Research?" About Education, psychology.about.com/od/lindex/g/longitudinal.htm (accessed April 28, 2014).

26. E. Paul Torrance and Carl H. Rush, Jr., *Factors in Fighter-Interceptor Pilot Combat Effectiveness* (Lackland Air Force Base, TX: Personnel Research Lab, 1957).

27. Blair Miller, Johnathan Vehar, and Roger L. Firestien, *Creativity Unbound: An Introduction to Creative Process*, 3rd ed. (Williamsville, NY: Innovation Resources, Inc., 2001), 12; Davis, *Creativity Is Forever*, 257.

---

a. Graham Wallas, *Art of Thought* (New York: Harcourt, 1926).

b. Alfred North Whitehead, *Process and Reality: An Essay in Cosmology: Gifford Lectures Delivered in the University of Edinburgh during the Session 1927–28*, corrected ed. New York: Free Press, 1928/1978.

c. Gary A. Davis, *Creativity Is Forever*, 5th ed. (Dubuque, IA: Kendall/Hunt Publishing. 2004), 24.

d. James C. Kaufman and Ronald A. Beghetto, "Beyond Big and Little: The Four C Model of Creativity," *Review of General Psychology* 13, no. 1 (2009), 1–12. doi:10.1037/a0013688.

Chapter 4

1. Gary A. Davis, *Creativity Is Forever*, 5th ed. (Dubuque: IA, Kendall-Hunt Publishing, 2004), 275.

2. Davis, *Creativity Is Forever*, 275.

3. Davis, *Creativity Is Forever*, 275.

4. *Dictionary.com*, s.v. "assessment," dictionary.reference.com/browse/assessment?s=t (accessed May 15, 2014).

5. Mel Rhodes, "An Analysis of Creativity," *Phi Delta Kappan* 42 (1961), 305–310.

6. FourSight website, foursightonline.com (accessed May 18, 2014).

7. FourSight website.

8. FourSight website.

9. Kirton Adaption-Innovation Inventory, creativity.murli.com/person/kai (accessed June 3, 2014).

10. Kirton Adaption-Innovation Inventory.

11. Smithsonian National Air and Space Museum, "Perfecting the Control System," airandspace.si.edu/exhibitions/wright-brothers/online/fly/1902/perfecting.cfm (accessed June 4, 2014).

12. Orville Wright, "Telegram from Orville Wright in Kitty Hawk, North Carolina, to His Father Announcing Four Successful Flights, 1903 December 17," World Digital Library, December 17, 1903, www.wdl.org/en/item/11372/ (accessed July 21, 2014).

13. Author's personal experience with the KAI.

14. Author's personal experience with the KAI.

15. Kendra Cherry, "What Is Longitudinal Research?" "About Education," psychology.about .com/od/lindex/g/longitudinal.htm (accessed July 22, 2014).

16. Torrance Tests of Creative Thinking, Scholastic Testing Service website, ststesting.com/ 2005giftttct.html (accessed July 22, 2014).

17. True Colors, "What Is True Colors and What Can It Do for Me?" truecolorsintl.com/about -us/ (accessed July 22, 2014).

18. Author's personal experience with True Colors in a group.

19. Author's personal experience with StrengthsQuest.

20. StrengthsQuest website, www.strengthsquest.com/home.aspx (accessed July 29, 2014).

21. StrengthsQuest website.

22. StrenthsQuest, "About," www.strengthsquest.com/content/141728/index.aspx (accessed July 29, 2014).

23. StrenthsQuest, "About."

24. StrengthsQuest, "Students," www.strengthsquest.com/content/143780/Students.aspx (accessed July 29, 2014).

25. Renee Baron and Elizabeth Wagele, *Enneagram Made Easy: Discover the Nine Types of People* (San Francisco: Harper, 1994); Helen Palmer and Paul B. Brown, *The Enneagram Advantage: Putting the Personality Types to Work in the Office* (New York: Random House, 1998).

26. Brown and Wagele, *Enneagram Made Easy*, 5–6.

27. Doc Childre and Howard Martin, with Donna Beech, *The HeartMath Solution* (San Francisco: Harper, 1999), 10.

28. Childre and Martin, with Beech, *HeartMath Solution*, xv.

29. Childre and Martin, with Beech, *HeartMath Solution*, 47–48.

30. Childre and Martin, with Beech, *HeartMath Solution*, 67.

31. Childre and Martin, with Beech, *HeartMath Solution*, 187.

32. Childre and Martin, with Beech, *HeartMath Solution*, 213–214.

33. Gary Smalley and John Trent, *The Two Sides of Love* (Colorado Springs, CO: Focus on the Family Publishing, 1992), 35.

a. Teens' views on measuring creativity, author's questionnaire, 2012.

b. Select teen views on measuring creativity, author's questionnaire, 2012.

c. FourSight, foursightonline.com (accessed May 18, 2014); KAI, creativity.murli.com/person/ kai (accessed June 3, 2014); and TTCT, ststesting.com/2005giftttct.html (accessed June 4, 2014).

d. True Colors, "About," truecolorsintl.com/about-us/ (accessed July 22, 2014); StrengthsQuest website, www.strengthsquest.com/home.aspx (accessed July 29, 2014); Enneagram Institute website, www.enneagraminstitute.com (accessed July 30, 2014).

e. Helen Palmer and Paul B. Brown, *The Enneagram Advantage: Putting the Personality Types to Work in the Office* (New York: Random House, 1998), 282.

f. SimilarMinds website, similarminds.com/jung.html (free site); Center for Applications of Psychological Type website, www.capt.org/take-mbti-assessment/mbti.htm ($150, $15 additional for a career report; accessed November 8, 2014).

g. Sara Paddison, *The Hidden Power of the Heart* (Boulder Creek, CA: Planetary Publications, 1988), 294.

Chapter 5

1. Ruth Richards, ed., *Everyday Creativity and New Views of Human Nature: Psychological, Social, and Spiritual Perspectives* (Washington, D.C.: American Psychological Association, 2007), 5.
2. Richards, *Everyday Creativity*, 5.
3. Richards, *Everyday Creativity*, 5.
4. Julia Cameron, *The Artist's Way: A Spiritual Path to Higher Creativity* (New York: Jeremy P. Tarcher/Putnam, 1992/2012), 20–21.
5. Dorothy Lehmkul and Dolores Cotter Lamping, *Organizing for the Creative Person* (New York: Three Rivers Press, 1993), 135, 138.
6. Emile-Auguste Chartier (1868–1951), French philosopher, journalist, pacifist. Quoted on Tendenci, tendenci.com/quotes/60/ (accessed November 7, 2014).
7. Robert J. Sternberg, ed., *Handbook of Creativity* (New York: Cambridge University Press, 2006), 26.
8. Donald J. Treffinger and Roger L. Firestien, "Ownership and Converging: Essential Ingredients in Creative Problem Solving," *Journal of Creative Behavior* 17, no. 1 (1983), 32–38.
9. *Dictionary.com*, s.v. "play," dictionary.reference.com/browse/play?s=t (accessed May 3, 2014).
10. "3-D Printing: What You Need to Know," *PCMag.com*, www.pcmag.com/slideshow_viewer /0,3253,l=289174&a=289174&po=1,00.asp (accessed November 8, 2014).
11. Tom Robbins, quoted on The Quotations Page, www.quotationspage.com/quote/880.html (accessed May 14, 2014).
12. Pamela Weintraub, "Discover Interview: Jaak Panksepp Pinned Down Humanity's Seven Primal Emotions," *Discover* Magazine, May 2012, discovermagazine.com/2012/may/11-jaak -panksepp-rat-tickler-found-humans-7-primal-emotions (accessed April 8, 2014).
13. Weintraub, "Discover Interview," 1.
14. Weintraub, "Discover Interview," 4.
15. Weintraub, "Discover Interview," 5.
16. Weintraub, "Discover Interview," 5.
17. Doc Childre and Howard Martin, with Donna Beech, *The HeartMath Solution* (San Francisco: Harper, 1999), 158.
18. Cameron, *Artist's Way*, 18–20.
19. Cameron, *Artist's Way*, 20–21.
20. Samuel T. Gladding, *The Creative Arts in Counseling*, 4th ed. (Alexandria, VA: American Counseling Association, 2011), 156–158; Karla D. Carmichael. *Play Therapy: An Introduction* (Upper Saddle River, NJ: Pearson Education, 2006), 2.
21. *Dictionary.com*, s.v. "confront," dictionary.reference.com/browse/confront?s=t (accessed May 16, 2014).
22. Suzanne Collins, *The Hunger Games* (New York: Scholastic Press, 2008), 19.
23. Bonnie Badenoch, *Being a Brain-Wise Therapist: A Practical Guide to Interpersonal Neurobiology* (New York. W.W. Norton, 2008), 294.
24. Carmichael, *Play Therapy*, 2.
25. Gladding, *Creative Arts*, 168.

26. Gladding, *Creative Arts*, vii.
27. Cathy A. Malchiodi, *The Art Therapy Sourcebook*, 2nd ed. (New York: McGraw-Hill, 2007), 9.
28. Gladding, *Creative Arts*, 91.
29. Malchiodi, *Art Therapy Sourcebook*, 35.
30. Gladding, *Creative Arts*, 91; Malchiodi, *Art Therapy Sourcebook*, 165.
31. Barbara Labowitz Boik and E. Anna Goodwin, *Sandplay Therapy: A Step-by-Step Manual for Psychotherapists of Diverse Orientations* (New York: W. W. Norton, 2000), 17.
32. Boik and Goodwin, *Sandplay Therapy*, 17.
33. Boik and Goodwin, *Sandplay Therapy*, 19–51.
34. Boik and Goodwin, *Sandplay Therapy*, 2–3.
35. Boik and Goodwin, *Sandplay Therapy*, 54, 58.
36. Boik and Goodwin, *Sandplay Therapy*, 58.
37. Boik and Goodwin, *Sandplay Therapy*, 58.
38. Boik and Goodwin, *Sandplay Therapy*, 67–70.
39. Boik and Goodwin, *Sandplay Therapy*, 79–80.
40. Gladding, *Creative Arts*, 22–29.
41. Gladding, *Creative Arts*, 26.
42. Gladding, *Creative Arts*, 32–33.
43. Gladding, *Creative Arts*, 52.
44. Gladding, *Creative Arts*, 47.
45. Gladding, *Creative Arts*, 52.
46. Gladding, *Creative Arts*, 140–141, 148.
47. Gladding, *Creative Arts*, 142–144.
48. Garry L. Landreth, *Innovations in Play Therapy* (New York: Routledge, 2001), 66–67, 89; Boik and Goodwin, *Sandplay Therapy*, 215.

---

a. Frank X. Barron, *Creative Person and Creative Process* (New York: Holt, Rinehart & Winston, 1969). Quoted in Ruth Richards, ed., *Everyday Creativity and New Views of Human Nature: Psychological, Social, and Spiritual Perspectives* (Washington, D.C.: American Psychological Association, 2007), 5.
b. Julia Cameron website, juliacameronlive.com and juliacameronlive.com/books-by-julia/ (accessed July 23, 2014); author's experience teaching from *The Artist's Way*.
c. George Bernard Shaw, quoted on The Quotations Page, www.quotationspage.com/quotes/George_Bernard_Shaw/21 (accessed June 5, 2014).
d. Daniel H. Pink, *A Whole New Mind: Why Right-Brainers Will Rule the Future* (New York: Riverhead Books/Penguin Group, 2006), 187.
e. Michele Cassou and Stewart Cubley, *Life, Paint and Passion: Reclaiming the Magic of Spontaneous Expression* (New York: Jeremy P. Tarcher/Putnam, 1995), 37–40.
f. Pamela Weintraub, "Discover Interview: Jaak Panksepp Pinned Down Humanity's Seven Primal Emotions," *Discover* Magazine, May 2012, discovermagazine.com/2012/may/11-jaak-panksepp-rat-tickler-found-humans-7-primal-emotions (accessed April 8, 2014).
g. Teens' views on creativity and play, author's questionnaire, 2012.
h. Quote is attributed to George Bernard Shaw at BrainyQuote, www.brainyquote.com/quotes/quotes/g/georgebern120971.html (accessed November 8, 2014).
i. Tom Robbins, quoted on The Quotations Page, www.quotationspage.com/quote/880.html (accessed September 1, 2014).
j. Author's imagination.

k.   Arnold Toynbee, quoted on The Quotations Page, www.quotationspage.com/quote/4819
     .html; Martha Beck, *The Joy Diet: Ten Daily Practices for a Joyful Life* (New York: Crown/
     Random House, 2003), 138; Martin Buber, quoted on BrainyQuote, www.brainyquote.com/
     quotes/authors/m/martin_buber.html (accessed May 19, 2014).

Chapter 6

1.   Teresa M. Amabile, "How to Kill Creativity," *Harvard Business Review*, September–October
     1998, 1–12.
2.   Julia Cameron, *The Artist's Way: A Spiritual Path to Higher Creativity* (New York: Jeremy P.
     Tarcher/Putnam, 1992/2012), 29, 43, 44, 49.
3.   Cameron, *Artist's Way*, 49, 119–120, 124, 164.
4.   Amabile, "How to Kill Creativity," 1, 3, 6–7, 10.
5.   Cameron, *Artist's Way*, 29–31, 43.
6.   Cameron, *Artist's Way*, 88–89.
7.   Cameron, *Artist's Way*, 152–156, 163–169, 188; Amabile, 5–6.
8.   Amabile, "How to Kill Creativity," 6.
9.   Amabile, "How to Kill Creativity," 3–4, 8.
10. Amabile, "How to Kill Creativity," 6–7, 9.
11. Cameron, *Artist's Way*, 154–157.
12. Amabile, "How to Kill Creativity," 3–10.
13. Amabile, "How to Kill Creativity," 3–4, 8.
14. Teresa M. Amabile. *Creativity in Context: Update to "The Social Psychology of Creativity"*
     (Boulder, CO: Westview Press, 1996), 117.
15. Amabile, "How to Kill Creativity," 8.
16. Amabile, "How to Kill Creativity," 3–4, 8.
17. Amabile, "How to Kill Creativity," 7–8; Cameron, *Artist's Way*, 172–174.
18. Cameron, *Artist's Way*, 7, 29, 43.
19. Amabile, "How to Kill Creativity," 7–8.
20. Cameron, *Artist's Way*, 109–110, 143.
21. Blair Miller, Jonathan Vehar, and Roger L. Firestien, *Creativity Unbound: An Introduction to
     Creative Process*, 3rd ed. (Williamsville, NY: Innovation Resources, 2001), 21.
22. Lee Silber, *Career Management for the Creative Person: Right-Brain Techniques to Run Your
     Professional Life and Build Your Business* (New York: Three Rivers Press, 1999), 18.
23. Alex F. Osborn, *Applied Imagination: Principles and Procedures of Creative Problem-Solving*
     (New York: Charles Scribner's Sons, 1953).
24. Cameron, *Artist's Way*, 72.
25. Cameron, *Artist's Way*, 72.
26. Terence Hanbury (T. H.) White, *The Once and Future King*, reprint ed. (New York: Ace,
     1987).
27. *The Sword in the Stone* (based on T. H. White's *The Once and Future King*), Wolfgang Reither-
     man, director, and Bill Peet, writer (Burbank, CA: Walt Disney Productions, 1963).

a.   Teens' views on what stops their creativity, author's questionnaire, 2012.
b.   Julia Cameron, *The Artist's Way: A Spiritual Path to Higher Creativity* (New York: Jeremy P.
     Tarcher/Putnam, 1992/2012), 72.
c.   Cameron, *Artist's Way*, 73.

Chapter 7

1. Teresa M. Amabile, *Growing Up Creative: Nurturing a Lifetime of Creativity*, 2nd ed. (Buffalo, NY: Education Foundation, 1992), 72.
2. Julia Cameron, *The Artist's Way: A Spiritual Path to Higher Creativity* (New York: Jeremy P. Tarcher/Putnam, 1992/2012), 69.
3. Michela Massimi, *Pauli's Exclusion Principle* (New York: Cambridge University Press, 2005).
4. Amabile, *Growing Up Creative*, 54; Cameron, *Artist's Way*, 110–111, 153, 157.
5. John M. Gottman, *The Marriage Clinic: A Scientifically Based Marital Therapy* (New York: W. W. Norton, 1999), 105.
6. Gottman, Marriage Clinic, 88.
7. Carol S. Dweck, *Mindset: The New Psychology of Success* (New York: Random House, 2007), 6–7.
8. Bonnie Badenoch, *Being a Brain-Wise Therapist: A Practical Guide to Interpersonal Neurobiology* (New York: W. W. Norton, 2008), 8.
9. Badenoch, *Being a Brain-Wise Therapist*, 280.
10. Daniel J. Siegel, *Brainstorm: The Power and Purpose of the Teenage Brain* (New York: Jeremy P. Tarcher/Penguin, 2013), 121, 126, 251.
11. Dweck, *Mindset*, 6–7.
12. Cameron, *Artist's Way*, 73.
13. Cameron, *Artist's Way*, 18–20.

---

a. Author's heartfelt suggestion.
b. John M. Gottman, *The Marriage Clinic: A Scientifically Based Marital Therapy* (New York: W. W. Norton, 1999), 105.
c. Julia Cameron, *The Artist's Way: A Spiritual Path to Higher Creativity* (New York: Jeremy P. Tarcher/Putnam, 1992/2012), 70–72.
d. Aryna Ryan, based on information in Doc Childre and Howard Martin, with Donna Beech, *The HeartMath Solution* (San Francisco: Harper, 1999), 122–126, and Cameron, Artist's Way, 75.
e. Author, based on information in *The HeartMath Solution* and *The Artist's Way*.
f. Carol S. Dweck, *Mindset: The New Psychology of Success* (New York: Random House, 2007), 6–7.
g. Teresa M. Amabile, *Growing Up Creative: Nurturing a Lifetime of Creativity*, 2nd ed. (Buffalo, NY: Education Foundation, 1992), 43–50.

Chapter 8

1. Clark Gesner, composer, lyricist, playwright, from "Happiness." *You're A Good Man, Charlie Brown* (musical), 1967.
2. Jeanne Nakamura and Mihaly Csikszentmihalyi, "The Concept of Flow," in C. R. Snyder and Shane J. Lopez, eds., *The Handbook of Positive Psychology* (Oxford: Oxford University Press, 2002), 94.
3. Mihaly Csikszentmihalyi and Reed Larson, "Validity and Reliability of the Experience-Sampling Method," *Journal of Nervous and Mental Disease* 175, no. 9 (1987), 526–536; Mihaly Csikszentmihalyi, *Finding Flow: The Psychology of Engagement with Everyday Life* (New York: Basic Books, 1997), 15; Nakamura and Csikszentmihalyi, "The Concept of Flow," 90.

4. Csikszentmihalyi and Larson, "Validity and Reliability," 526–536; Csikszentmihalyi, *Finding Flow*, 1997, 15; Nakamura and Csikszentmihalyi, "The Concept of Flow," 89.
5. Mihaly Csikszentmihalyi, *Flow: The Psychology of Optimal Experience* (New York: Harper & Row Publishers, 1990), 66, 61.
6. Csikszentmihalyi, *Flow*, 33, 72.
7. Csikszentmihalyi, *Finding Flow*, 29.
8. Csikszentmihalyi, *Flow*, 76.
9. Csikszentmihalyi, *Flow*, 29.
10. Csikszentmihalyi, *Flow*, 44; Csikszentmihalyi, *Finding Flow*, 29.
11. Csikszentimihalyi, *Finding Flow*, 30.
12. Csikszentmihalyi, *Finding Flow*, 29.
13. Csikszentmihalyi, *Finding Flow*, 29.
14. Csikszentmihalyi, *Flow*, 63.
15. Csikszentmihalyi, *Finding Flow*, 30.
16. Nakamura and Csikszentmihalyi, "The Concept of Flow," 90.
17. Csikszentmihalyi, *Flow*, 66.
18. Csikszentmihalyi, *Flow*, 68.
19. Csikszentmihalyi, *Flow*, 48.
20. Laura Grace Weldon, "Accepting Challenges, Embracing Mistakes," *Laura Grace Weldon* (blog), June 30, 2011, lauragraceweldon.com/2011/06/30/accepting-challenges-embracing -mistakes/ (accessed August 4, 2014); Celeste Kidd, Steven T. Piantadosi, and Richard N. Aslin, "The Goldilocks Effect: Human Infants Allocate Attention to Visual Sequences That Are Neither Too Simple Nor Too Complex." *PLoS ONE* 7, no. 5 (2012), e36399. doi:10.1371/. www.plosone.org/article/info%3Adoi%2F10.1371%2Fjournal.pone.0036399 (accessed August 31, 2014).
21. Tara Brach, *Radical Acceptance: Embracing Your Life with the Heart of a Buddha* (New York: Bantam Books, 2003), 60.
22. Csikszentmihalyi, *Finding Flow*, 30.
23. Csikszentmihalyi, *Flow*, 69.
24. Teresa M. Amabile, "How to Kill Creativity," *Harvard Business Review*, September–October 1998, 3.
25. Lee Silber, *Career Management for the Creative Person: Right-Brain Techniques to Run Your Professional Life and Build Your Business* (New York: Three Rivers Press, 1999), 36–37.
26. Teresa M. Amabile, *Growing Up Creative: Nurturing a Lifetime of Creativity*, 2nd ed. (Buffalo, NY: Education Foundation, 1992), 46.
27. Csikszentmihalyi, *Flow*, 68.
28. Career valuation tool, www.onetonline.org (accessed July 5, 2014).
29. Csikszentmihalyi, *Finding Flow*, 31.
30. John M. Gottman, *The Marriage Clinic: A Scientifically Based Marital Therapy* (New York: W.W. Norton, 1999), 88.
31. William James, *Principles of Psychology* (New York: Henry Holt, 1890), quoted in Csikszent- mihalyi *Finding Flow*, 23.
32. Joe Kita, "Failure Can Enhance Your Brain," *Reader's Digest*, May 2009, http://www.readers digest.ca/health/healthy-living/failure-can-enhance-your-brain/ (accessed May 10, 2014).
33. Biz Stone, *Things a Little Bird Told Me: Confessions of the Creative Mind* (New York: Grand Central Publishing, 2014), 94.
34. John (Jack) L. Ryan, personal conversation with author, November 16, 2013.

35. Shunryu Suzuki, *Zen Mind, Beginner's Mind* (San Francisco: Shambhala, 2011).
36. Aryna Ryan, "Build Your Own Heart" (unpublished poster paper, November 2011, presented at International Association of Social Work Groups Conference [IASWG], 34th Annual International Symposium, Adelphi College, Long Island, NY, June 14–17, 2012).
37. A. Ryan, "Build Your Heart."
38. A. Ryan, "Build Your Heart."

---

a. Kendra Cherry, "Mihaly Csikszentmihalyi Biography," About Education, psychology.about.com/od/profilesal/p/mihaly-csikszentmihalyi-biography.htm (accessed August 7, 2014).
b. Teens' feelings about their creativity, author's questionnaire, 2012.
c. Xomba, "Your 5 Core Strengths: Marcus Buckingham & the Gallup Clifton Strengths Finder Test," June 16, 2009, free-cracker-4-jack.xomba.com/your_5_core_strengths_markus_buckingham_gallup_clifton_strengths_finder_test (accessed July 29, 2014).
d. The definitions of *self-esteem*, *self-worth*, and *self-image* came from a conversation with Dr. Mike King, psychologist, March 12, 2002; the definitions of *self-concept* and *self-confidence* came from *Dictionary.com*, s.v. "self-concept," dictionary.reference.com/browse/self-concept?s=t, and s.v. "self-confidence," dictionary.reference.com/browse/self-confidence (accessed May 2, 2014).
e. Antoine Bechara, www.usc.edu/programs/neuroscience/faculty/profile.php?fid=70 (accessed May 10, 2014); Joe Kita, "Failure Can Enhance Your Brain," *Reader's Digest*, May 2009, www.readersdigest.ca/health/healthy-living/failure-can-enhance-your-brain/ (accessed May 10, 2014).
f. Julia Cameron, *The Artist's Way: A Spiritual Path to Higher Creativity* (New York: Jeremy P. Tarcher/Putnam, 1992/2012), 30.

Chapter 9

1. H. L. Mencken, quoted on The Quotations Page, www.quotationspage.com/quote/282.html (accessed April 8, 2014).
2. Alex F. Osborn, *How to Think Up* (New York: Charles Scribner's Sons, 1942).
3. Joy Paul (J. P.) Guilford, *The Nature of Human Intelligence* (New York: McGraw-Hill, 1967).
4. OmniSkills, "Creative Problem Solving," www.creativeproblemsolving.com/tools/cps_summary.pdf (accessed September 13, 2014).
5. Blair Miller, Jonathan Vehar, and Roger L. Firestien, *Creativity Unbound: An Introduction to Creative Process*, 3rd ed. (Millersville, NY: Innovation Resources, 2001), 26–27.
6. Osborn, *How to Think Up*.
7. Miller, Vehar, and Firestien, *Creativity Unbound*, 28–29.
8. R. F. Eberle, *Scamper: Games for Imagination Development* (Buffalo, NY: DOK Publishing, 1971), in Miller, Vehar, and Firestien, *Creativity Unbound*, 32–33.
9. Gary A. Davis, *Creativity Is Forever*, 5th ed. (Dubuque, IA: Kendall/Hunt Publishing, 2004), 45.
10. Miller, Vehar, and Firestien, *Creativity Unbound*, 30; Andrew Zenyuch, "The Creative Problem Solving Process," andrewzenyuch.com/the-creative-problem-solving-process-step-4-idea-finding/ (accessed August 31, 2014).
11. Liz Vaccaviello, ed., "See the World . . . Differently," *Reader's Digest*, June 2014, 136–139.

12. Miller, Vehar, and Firestien, *Creativity Unbound*, 44; Scott G. Isaksen, K. Brian Dorval, Donald J. Treffinger, eds., *Creative Approaches to Problem Solving: A Framework for Innovation and Change*, 3rd ed. (Thousand Oaks, CA: Sage Publications, 2010), 78.

13. Miller, Vehar, and Firestien, *Creativity Unbound*, 48; Gerard J. Puccio, Mary C. Murdock, and Marie Mance, *Creative Leadership: Skills That Drive Change* (Thousand Oaks, CA; Sage Publications, 2007), 168.

14. Miller, Vehar, and Firestien, *Creativity Unbound*, 48.

15. Miller, Vehar, and Firestien, *Creativity Unbound*, 48; Puccio, Murdock, and Mance, *Creative Leadership*, 168.

16. Miller, Vehar, and Firestien, *Creativity Unbound*, 53.

17. Miller, Vehar, and Firestien, *Creativity Unbound*, 53, 77.

18. SUNY Buffalo State, "Applying Creativity: Card Sort: How to Rank Options," YouTube video, www.youtube.com/watch?v=aN2ALf2f6Lk (accessed August 27, 2014).

---

a. Teens' views on problem solving, author's questionnaire, 2012.

b. Gary A. Davis, *Creativity Is Forever*, 5th ed. (Dubuque, IA: Kendall/Hunt Publishing, 2004), 45.

c. Blair Miller, Jonathan Vehar, and Roger L. Firestien, *Creativity Unbound: An Introduction to Creative Process*, 3rd ed. (Williamsville, NY: Innovation Resources, 2001), 28–29.

d. Robert F. Eberle, *Scamper: Games for Imagination Development* (Buffalo, NY: DOK Publishing, 1971); Litemind, "Creative Problem Solving with SCAMPER," litemind.com/scamper/ (accessed June 11, 2014); Michael Michalko, *Cracking Creativity: The Secrets of Creative Genius* (Berkeley, CA: Ten Speed Press, 2001), 95–100.

e. Martha Beck, *The Joy Diet: Ten Daily Practices for a Joyful Life* (New York: Crown/Random House, 2003), 144–147.

Chapter 10

1. Alex F. Osborn, *Applied Imagination: Principles and Procedures of Creative Problem-Solving* (New York: Charles Scribner's Sons, 1953).

2. Blair Miller, Jonathan Vehar, and Roger L. Firestien, *Creativity Unbound: An Introduction to Process*, 3rd ed. (Williamsville, NY: Innovation Resources, 2001), 64–67.

3. Miller, Vehar, and Firestien, *Creativity Unbound*, 61.

4. Miller, Vehar, and Firestien, *Creativity Unbound*, 60.

5. Creative Education Foundation, "What Is Creative Problem Solving," www.creativeeducationfoundation.org/our-process/what-is-cps (accessed June 7, 2014).

6. Miller, Vehar, and Firestien, *Creativity Unbound*, 8.

7. Miller, Vehar, and Firestien, *Creativity Unbound*, 98–104.

8. Author's and others' personal experiences as CPS Facilitators and members of CPS Resource Groups.

9. Miller, Vehar, and Firestien, *Creativity Unbound*, 62.

10. Miller, Vehar, and Firestien, *Creativity Unbound*, 61.

11. Author's experience with CPS sessions.

12. Miller, Vehar, and Firestien, *Creativity Unbound*, 64–67.

13. Miller, Vehar, and Firestien, *Creativity Unbound*, 26.

14. Miller, Vehar, Firestien, *Creativity Unbound*, 63, 73, 77, 78.

15. Miller, Vehar, and Firestien, *Creativity Unbound*, 30.
16. Miller, Vehar, and Firestien, *Creativity Unbound*, 44.
17. Miller, Vehar, and Firestien, *Creativity Unbound*, 63.
18. Miller, Vehar, and Firestien, *Creativity Unbound*, 63, 73, 77, 78.
19. Miller, Vehar, and Firestien, *Creativity Unbound*, 79.
20. Author's and others' personal experiences as CPS Facilitators and members of CPS Resource Groups.

---

a. Blair Miller, Jonathan Vehar, and Roger L. Firestien, *Creativity Unbound: An Introduction to Process*, 3rd ed. (Williamsville, NY: Innovation Resources 2001), 71.
b. Skills You Need, "Investigating Ideas and Solutions," www.skillsyouneed.com/ips/problem-solving3.html (accessed May 10, 2014). "Brainstorming: A Creative Problem-Solving Method," unido.org/fileadmin/import/16953_Brainstorming.pdf (accessed May 10, 2014); Marlene K. Rebori, "Problem Solving Techniques: Community Board Development: Series 3," University of Nevada, www.unce.unr.edu/ publications/files/cd/other/fs9854.pdf (accessed May 10, 2014).
c. Miller, Vehar, and Firestien, *Creativity Unbound*, 63, 65, 72–73, 77–78.
d. Miller, Vehar, and Firestien, *Creativity Unbound*, 87– 89.

Chapter 11

1. Joy Paul (J. P.) Guilford, Speech to American Psychological Association, 1950.
2. Ken Robinson, *Out of Our Minds: Learning to Be Creative* (Chichester, West Sussex, England: Capstone Publishing, 2011), 79.
3. *Educarenow* blog, educarenow.wordpress.com (accessed November 7, 2014); *Dictionary.com*, s.v. "create," dictionary.reference.com/browse/create?s=t (accessed November 7, 2014); *Dictionary.com*, s.v. "educate," dictionary.reference.com/browse/educate?s=t (accessed November 7, 2014).
4. Gilbert K. Chesterton, quoted on The Quotations Page, www.quotationspage.com/quote/41856.html (accessed September 1, 2014).
5. Ken Robinson, "How Schools Kill Creativity," TED Talk, February 2006, www.ted.com/talks/ken_robinson_says_schools_kill_creativity (accessed August 13, 2014).
6. Robinson, *Out of Our Minds*, 49.
7. Daniel H. Pink, *A Whole New Mind: Why Right-Brainers Will Rule the Future* (New York: Riverhead Books/Penguin Group, 2006), 25–26.
8. Peter Gray, "Schools Don't Have to Fail. Here's How We Fix Education," Salon.com, September 7, 2013, www.salon.com/2013/09/07/schools_dont_have_to_fail_heres_how_we_fix_education/ (accessed June 9, 2014).
9. Pink, *Whole New Mind*, 26.
10. Pink, *Whole New Mind*, 21.
11. Pink, *Whole New Mind*, 22.
12. Pink, *Whole New Mind*, 22.
13. Peter Gray, "School Is a Prison and Damages Our Kids," *Reader's Digest*, January 2014, 118.
14. Sudbury Valley School, "About SVS," www.sudval.com/01_abou_01.html (accessed May 10, 2014).

15. Sudbury Valley School, "About SVS."

16. Ansel Adams, quoted from PBS.org, "Primary Sources: The Education of Ansel Adams," www.pbs.org/wgbh/amex/ansel/filmmore/ps_child.html (accessed November 6, 2014).

17. Logan LaPlante, "Hackschooling Makes Me Happy," YouTube video (University of Nevada: TEDx, 2014), www.youtube.com/watch?v=h11u3vtcpaY&utm_source=newsletter_109&utm _medium=email&utm_campaign=newsletter-07172014 (accessed August 4, 2014).

18. Laura Grace Weldon, "Five Ways to Transcend the School Mindset," Alternatives to School, alternativestoschool.com/2014/08/06/five-ways-transcend-school-mindset/ (accessed August 11, 2014).

19. Robinson, "How Schools Kill Creativity."

20. Laura Grace Weldon, "Accepting Challenges, Embracing Mistakes," www.education revolution.org/blog/accepting-challenges-embracing-mistakes/ (accessed August 11, 2014); Celeste Kidd, Steven T. Piantadosi, and Richard N. Aslin, "The Goldilocks Effect: Human Infants Allocate Attention to Visual Sequences That Are Neither Too Simple Nor Too Complex," *PLoS ONE* 7, no. 5 (2012), e36399. doi:10.1371/journal.pone.0036399 (accessed August 11, 2014); Mihaly Csikszentmihalyi, *Flow: The Psychology of Optimal Experience* (New York: Harper & Row, 1990), 52.

21. Marcus Buckingham, *Now, Discover Your Strengths* (New York: The Free Press/Simon & Schuster, 2001), 123.

22. LaPlante, "Hackschooling."

23. Laura Grace Weldon, "How the '10,000 Hour' Rule Can Benefit Any Child," *Laura Grace Weldon* (blog), January 10, 2012lauragraceweldon.com/2012/01/10/how-the-10000-hour -rule-can-benefit-any-child/ (accessed August 11, 2014).

24. Mark Twain, quoted on The Quotations Page, www.quotationspage.com/quote/23671.html (accessed June 19, 2014).

25. VARK (visual/audio/read-write/kinesthetic), "The VARK Questionnaire," www.vark-learn .com/english/page.asp?p=questionnaire (accessed August 2, 2014).

26. VARK assessment download, www.genieo.com/macsolution/?campaign=ads_dcomac&gclid =CIXWmfjDh8ACFSpo7AodmTcA9w (accessed August 2, 2014).

27. "The Education Issue," *iPhone Life* 6, no. 5 (September–October 2014), 35–64.

28. Linda Suskie, *Five Dimensions of Quality: A Common Sense Guide to Accreditation and Accountability* (San Francisco: Jossey-Bass, 2014), 122.

29. Principal Voices, "Biography: Ken Robinson," www.principalvoices.com/voices/ken-robinson -bio.html (accessed August 3, 2014); Robinson, *Out of Our Minds*, 79.

a. Ken Robinson biography, sirkenrobinson.com/?page_id=10 (accessed August 30, 2014).

b. Teens' views on the role of creativity in education, author's questionnaire, 2012.

c. Sudbury Valley School, Framingham, Massachusetts, sudval.org (accessed May 10, 2014).

d. Peter Gray biography, www.bc.edu/schools/cas/psych/people/affiliated/gray.html (accessed August 30, 2014).

e. Laura Weldon, "Five Ways to Transcend the School Mindset," Alternatives to School, alternativestoschool.com/2014/08/06/five-ways-transcend-school-mindset/ (accessed August 11, 2014).

f. Howard Gardner biography, howardgardner.com/biography/ (accessed August 30, 2014).

g. Howard Gardner, *Intelligence Reframed: Multiple Intelligences for the 21st Century* (New York: Basic Books, 1999).

h. Gary E. Price, Rita Dunn, and Kenneth Dunn, *PEPS Manual* (Lawrence, KS: Price Systems, 1979, 1982), humanesources.com/site/PEPS-learning-style-preferences/ and learn.humane sources.com/online.html (accessed July 12, 2014).

Chapter 12

1. *Dictionary.com*, s.v. "leadership," dictionary.reference.com/browse/leadership?s=t (accessed March 28, 2014).
2. Peter G. Northouse, *Leadership Theory and Practice*, 3rd ed. (Thousand Oaks, CA: Sage Publications, 2007), 3.
3. Gary A. Davis, *Creativity Is Forever*, 5th ed. (Dubuque, IA: Kendall/Hunt Publishing Co., 2004), 41.
4. Gerard J. Puccio, Mary C. Murdock, and Marie Mance, *Creative Leadership: Skills That Drive Change* (Thousand Oaks, CA: Sage Publications, 2007), xv.
5. Puccio, Murdock, and Mance, *Creative Leadership*, xvi.
6. Alex F. Osborn, *Your Creative Power: How to Use Imagination* (New York: Charles Scribner's Sons, 1952), 307.
7. Russell A. Wheeler, "Alex F. Osborn: The Father of Brainstorming," RussellAWheeler.com, russellawheeler.com/resources/learning_zone/alex_f_osborn/ (accessed August 3, 2014).
8. Abraham Zaleznik, "Managers and Leaders: Are They Different?" *Harvard Business Review on Leadership* 1977 (1998), 61–88. In Puccio, Murdock, and Mance, *Creative Leadership*, 6.
9. *Dictionary.com*, s.v. "power," dictionary.reference.com/browse/power?s=t (accessed July 21, 2014).
10. *Dictionary.com*, s.v. "power."
11. Puccio, Murdock, and Mance, *Creative Leadership*, 8–10.
12. Mariam G. MacGregor, *Everyday Leadership: Attitudes and Actions for Respect and Success (a Guidebook for Teens)* (Minneapolis, MN: Free Spirit Publishing, 2007), 31–33.
13. Puccio, Murdock, and Mance, *Creative Leadership*, 153.

a. Teens' views on leadership, author's questionnaire, 2012.
b. Warren G. Bennis, communicationleadership.usc.edu/people/distinguished_fellow/warren _bennis.html (accessed June 8, 2014); quoted on BrainyQuote, www.brainyquote.com/quotes/quotes/w/warrenbenn121715.html (accessed June 19, 2014).
c. Gerard J. Puccio, Mary C. Murdock, and Marie Mance, *Creative Leadership: Skills That Drive Change* (Thousand Oaks, CA: Sage Publications, 2007), 95–97.
d. Rick Barnes, Carl Creasman, Mark Hartley, et al., *Ten Keys to Extraordinary Leadership* (Keller, TX: TopLeader Publishing, 2009), 8–10.
e. Maxwell, John C., *Leadership Gold: Lessons I've Learned from a Lifetime of Leading* (Nashville, TN: Thomas Nelson, 2008), xi.

Chapter 13

1. Gary Smalley and John Trent, *The Two Sides of Love* (Colorado Springs, CO: Focus on the Family Publishing, 1992), 32.

2. Ruth B. Noller, *Scratching the Surface of Creative Problem Solving: A Bird's-Eye View of CPS* (Buffalo, NY: DOK Publishing, 1979).

3. Bonnie Thomas, *Creative Expression Activities for Teens: Exploring Identity through Art, Craft, and Journaling* (London: Jessica Kingsley Publishers, 2011), 27.

4. Amy P. Ryan-Rued, personal conversation with author, May 14, 2014.

5. Lee Silber, *Career Management for the Creative Person* (New York: Three Rivers Press, 1999), 36.

6. Silber, *Career Management*, 37.

7. Webb Smith, animator, creator of storyboard at Walt Disney Studios, 1933.

8. Casey Cole Corbin, *Expressive Art Therapy for Problem Solving and Getting Past Your Past* (Lexington, KY: Author, 2013), 20–21; CreateArtTherapy.weebly.com and www.facebook.com/CreateArtTherapy (accessed May 12, 2014).

9. Julia Cameron, *The Artist's Way: A Spiritual Path to Higher Creativity* (New York: Jeremy P. Tarcher/Penguin, 1992/2012), 114.

10. Centers for Disease Control and Prevention, "U.S. Public Health Service Syphilis Study at Tuskegee," www.cdc.gov/tuskegee/timeline.htm (accessed July 19, 2014).

11. Michell Cassou and Stewart Cubley, *Life, Paint and Passion: Reclaiming the Magic of Spontaneous Expression* (New York: Jeremy P. Tarcher/Putnam, 1995), 37–40.

12. E. Paul Torrance and Tammy Safter, *Making the Creative Leap Beyond* (Hadley, MA: Creative Education Foundation Press, 2005), 38–41; Mary C. Murdock and Sue Keller-Mathers, "Teaching for Creativity: Where There's a Will, There's a Way," *National Association of Gifted Children Celebrate Creativity* 12, no. 2 (2002), 3–4.

13. Torrance and Safter, *Making the Creative Leap Beyond*, 39; Murdock and Keller-Mathers, "Teaching for Creativity," 3–4.

14. Daniel H. Pink, *A Whole New Mind: Why Right Brainers Will Rule the Future* (New York: Riverhead Books/Penguin, 2006), 101, 103.

15. Cameron, *Artist's Way*, 30.

16. Joseph Chilton Pearce, quoted in Cameron, *Artist's Way*, 29.

---

a. E. Paul Torrance and Tammy Safter, *Making the Creative Leap Beyond* (Hadley, MA: Creative Education Foundation Press, 2005); Mary C. Murdock and Sue Keller-Mathers, "Teaching for Creativity: Where There's a Will, There's a Way," *National Association of Gifted Children Celebrate Creativity* 12, no. 2 (2002), 3-4.

Chapter 14

1. Daniel H. Pink, *Drive: The Surprising Truth about What Motivates Us* (New York: Riverhead Books/Penguin Group, 2012).

2. Kendra Cherry, "Maslow's Needs Hierarchy," About Education, psychology.about.com/od/theoriesofpersonality/ss/maslows-needs-hierarchy.htm (accessed July 29, 2014).

3. Pink, *Drive*, 7.

4. Pink, *Drive*, 7.

5. Pink, *Drive*, 7; Cherry, "Maslow's Needs Hierarchy."

6. Pink, *Drive*, 7.

7. Daniel H. Pink, *A Whole New Mind: Why Right-Brainers Will Rule the Future* (New York: Riverhead Books/Penguin, 2006), 192.

8. Pink, *Whole New Mind*, 65–66.
9. *Star Trek: The Next Generation*, television series, Rick Berman, executive producer, and Peter Lauritsen, co-producer (Hollywood, CA: Paramount Television/Paramount Pictures, 1987–1994), www.imdb.com/title/tt0092455/fullcredits?ref_=tt_ov_st_sm (accessed June 2, 2014).
10. Pink, *Whole New Mind*, 65–67.
11. Pink, *Whole New Mind*, 2, 49–51, 246–247.
12. Pink, *Whole New Mind*, 65–67, 68, 100, 129, 158, 185, 216.
13. Pink, *Whole New Mind*, 84–85.
14. Alan J. McDonald with James R. Hansen, *Truth, Lies, and O-Rings: Inside the Space Shuttle Challenger Disaster* (Gainesville: University Press of Florida, 2009).
15. Pink, *Whole New Mind*, 86.
16. Pink, *Whole New Mind*, 86.
17. National Storytelling Network, "How to Become a Storyteller," www.storynet.org/resources/howtobecomeastoryteller.html (accessed August 3, 2014); also see www.storynet.org and www.storyteller.net (accessed August 3, 2014).
18. Pink, *Whole New Mind*, 130.
19. Liz Kowalczyk, "Empathy Gap in Medical Students: Stress Can Harden Students' Attitude towards Patients, but Medical Schools are Trying to Change That," *Boston Globe,* March 25, 2013, www.bostonglobe.com/lifestyle/health-wellness/2013/03/24/medical-students-empathy-drops-just-they-start-caring-for-patients/rWqFiVVsr9oze6EWRLwzwN/story.html (accessed May 15, 2014); Charmaine Mutucumarana, "Empathy in Medical Schools: Improving Medical Students' Empathy," sites.duke.edu/empathyinmedicalschoolcurricula/improving-medical-students-empathy/ (accessed May 15, 2014).
20. E. Paul Torrance and Tammy Safter, *Making the Creative Leap Beyond* (Hadley, MA: Creative Education Foundation Press, 1999), 38–41; Mary C. Murdock and Sue Keller-Mathers, "Teaching Creativity: Where There's a Will, There's a Way," *National Association of Gifted Children Celebrate Creativity* 12, no. 2 (2002), 3–4.
21. Howard Gardner, *Intelligence Reframed: Multiple Intelligences for the 21st Century* (New York: Basic Books, 1999).
22. Author's term.
23. Jeffrey Deaver, *The Broken Window* (New York: Simon & Schuster/Pocket Star Books, 2009), 121–125.
24. Deaver, *Broken Window*, 121–125.
25. Author's cynical observation.
26. International Center for Studies in Creativity, "Why Study Creativity?" creativity.buffalostate.edu/why-study-creativity-0 (accessed August 2, 2014).

a. All other contributors except Bill Gates and Steve Jobs have been previously cited in this book. On Bill Gates: Tamar Amashukeli, "Bill Gates—Using Creativity and Innovation to Make an Impact," Idolium, September 3, 2012, www.idolium.com/idol/publication/bill-gates-using-creativity-and-innovation-make-impact (accessed July 9, 2014). On Steve Jobs: Stephen Searer, "How Steve Jobs Encouraged Creativity and Collaboration," *Turnstone* (blog), myturnstone.com/blog/how-steve-jobs-encouraged-creativity-and-collaboration/ (accessed July 9, 2014).
b. Daniel H. Pink, *A Whole New Mind: Why Right-Brainers Will Rule the Future* (New York: Riverhead Books/Penguin Group, 2006), 65–67, 81–82, 100, 142, 173, 188, 219.
c. Teens' views on creativity and their future, author's questionnaire, 2012.

Resources for Teens

Websites/Links

This list of links and assessment costs was current as of summer 2014.

Chindogu at uselessinvention@designboom.com (Ten Rules for creating useless inventions)

    Japanese Cost: Free

Enneagram

    To read *and* take assignment: www.enneagraminstitute.com

FourSight

    To read what FourSight measures: foursightonline.com
    To take the assessment: i.foursightonline.com/assessments/1da18a95bd2cfb0
       2537193c6d453cf56
    Cost: $25

Kirton Adaption-Innovation Inventory (KAI): www.bmgi.com/webinars/kai-theory

    A not-too-technical KAI article: www.breakoutofthebox.com/kai.htm
    Cost: Unknown. Must contact a certified KAI professional, who buys the KAI indexes in batches of fifty and can set own price for administering and scoring the KAI to an individual.

Productivity Environmental Preferences Survey (PEPS)

    Five categories (sixteen components) of learning style and productivity: www.collegesuccess1.com/PEPS.htm
    Learning Style and Productivity Preferences: humanesources.com/site/PEPS-learning-style-preferences/; cost is $12.95

Get a free two-week pass (as of Summer 2014): learn.humanesources.com/online.html

StrengthsQuest: Discover and Develop Your Strengths in Academics, Career, and Beyond by Donald O. Clifton and Edward Anderson: www.strengthsquest.com

Cost: $50–55 for *new* copy with StrengthsQuest (SQ) code (as of August 2014). Do *not* buy a used copy—SQ code can only be used *once*. Can also buy codes and books separately on website.

For a different perspective on the StrengthsQuest assessment, check out www.tmbc.com, on which Marcus Buckingham, author of *First, Break All the Rules* (1991) and *Now, Discover Your Strengths* (2001), outlines how knowing your strengths applies to work situations, especially when forming teams. Buckingham also discusses how your knowledge of strengths contributes to effective leadership (tmbc.com and tmbc.com/resources/books)

TED Talk—Sir Ken Robinson: "Do Schools Kill Creativity?" www.youtube.com/watch?v=iG9CE55wbtY&list=PL70DEC2B0568B5469 (most-watched TED Talk as of September 2014)

TED Talk—Sir James Dyson: "Failures Are Interesting," January 24, 2014. www.sciencefriday.com/segment/01/24/2014/james-dyson-failures-are-interesting.html

Torrance Test of Creative Thinking (TTCT). ststesting.com/2005giftttct.html

Figural TTCT and Verbal TTCT
Cost: $7.10 for Figural TTCT per student booklet and scoring; $8.75 for Verbal TTCT per student booklet and scoring

True Colors

To read how True Colors works: truecolorsintl.com
To take the assessment: truecolorsintl.com/assessments/
Cost: $34.50

Schools/Institutes

Creative Problem Solving Institute (CPSI): www.acronymfinder.com/Creative-Problem-Solving-Institute-(CPSI).html. Sponsors the longest-running creativity conference in the world.

Creative Education Foundation (CEF). Established in 1954 by Alex Osborn, in Buffalo, NY. CEF was original publisher of the *Journal of Creative Behavior*.

Future Problem Solving Program International: www.fpspi.org. Founded by E. Paul Torrance, "Father of Creativity." FPSPI offers students necessary thinking and problem solving skills for now and the future. Also see www.coe.uga .edu/torrance/creativity-resources/ for information about the Torrance Center for Creativity and Talent Development.

International Center for Studies in Creativity (ICSC), Buffalo State College (State University of New York), Buffalo, NY: creativity.buffalostate.edu

ICSC Programs: creativity.buffalostate.edu/programs
- Graduate Certificate in Creativity and Change Leadership (18 hours), distance and local
- MS in Creativity and Change Leadership (33 hours), distance and local
- Minor in Creative Studies (18 hours), local
- Minor in Leadership (18 hours), local

ICSC Publications—*Journal of Creative Behavior*: creativity.buffalostate.edu

Sudbury Valley School: www.sudburyvalleyschool.com. Original school was founded in Framingham, Massachusetts, in 1968, and is still open. Nineteen other schools in US are based on the original Sudbury model. On the Sudbury home page menu, click "About SVS" tab and learn about the school's structure and philosophy. Back on the home page, click on "Articles" tab and select any articles you wish to get a deeper sense of how the Sudbury model works from the points of view of the founders, parents, and students.

Books

As mentioned in the introduction, there are over 418,000 books on creativity and related topics. The following is a suggested list, divided into categories of interest, and includes the most interesting books!

Creativity Books/Journals

This category is for you who want to delve deeper into the topic of creativity itself. If you're going to buy a few creativity books, I recommend these first five. (If you are too broke to buy these, ask your aunts, uncles, grandparents, and other adults to them for holidays and birthday gifts. Adults *love* buying teens books; they want you to learn and want to be a part of your success.)

Julia Cameron. *The Artist's Way: A Spiritual Path to Higher Creativity*. New York: Jeremy P. Tarcher/Putnam, 1992/2012.

Julia Cameron. *Walking in This World: The Practical Art of Creativity*. New York: J.P. Tarcher/Penguin, 2003. Cameron's books will help you break through your emotional blocks to being not only an artist, but a creative person in any field. Though not scientifically based (more of a twelve-step model as promoted by Alcoholics Anonymous), the insights, exercises, and the author's compassion are invaluable.

Gary A. Davis. *Creativity Is Forever*. 5th ed. Dubuque, Iowa: Kendall/Hunt Publishing Co., 2004. In my humble opinion, this is the best overall book on the subject of creativity. Yes, it's an academic book with references; it'll give you a thorough overview of the history of creativity, the major and minor players, all the big and little theories (with drawings), lots of black-and-white photos, plus creativity exercises. This book also provides an excellent introduction to Creative Problem Solving (CPS), an update to the author's 2000 book. It's also fairly easy to read and contains lots of humor. Make *sure* to get the fifth edition!

Donald Treffinger, Scott Isaksen, and Brian Stead-Doval. *Creative Problem Solving: An Introduction*. 4th ed. Waco, TX: Prufrock Press. 2005.

The next two books are also excellent and written for teens.

Daniel J. Siegel. *Brainstorm: The Power and Purpose of the Teenage Brain*. New York: Jeremy P. Tarcher/Penguin, 2013. Siegel has written a book about and for teens (twelve to twenty-four years old), in which he explains the changes in and benefits of the teenage brain.

Bonnie Thomas. *Creative Expression Activities for Teens: Exploring Identity through Art, Craft, and Journaling*. London: Jessica Kingsley Publishers, 2011. This book has many easy original art and writing activities. (It is the source for the body art activity in chapter 13.)

Art Books

Laura Bowley. *Brave Intuitive Painting-Let Go, Be Bold, Unfold! Techniques for Uncovering Your Own Unique Painting Style*. Beverly, MA: Quarry Books, 2012.

Tracie Bunkers. *The Art Journal Workshop*. Beverly, MA: Quayside/Quarry Books, 2011.

Michele Cassou and Stewart Cubley. *Life, Paint, and Passion: Reclaiming the Magic of Spontaneous Expression*. New York: Jeremy P. Tarcher/Putnam, 1995. It is the source for the painting tool "Life, Paint, and Passion: Just Play" in chapter 13.

Stephanie Corfee. *Creative Doodling and Beyond.* Irvine, CA: Walter Foster Publishing, 2011.

Meredith Dillman. *Fantasy Fashion Art Studio.* Cincinnati, OH: F&W Media/Impact Books, 2013.

Jenny Doh. *Art Saves: Stories, Inspirations and Prompts Sharing the Power of Art.* Cincinnati, OH: F&W Media/North Light Books, 2011.

Jim Henson. *Doodling with Jim Henson: Guided Art Journal.* Irvine, CA: Walter Foster Publishing, 2014.

642 Things to Draw Journal. San Francisco: Chronicle Books, 2010.

Craft Books

Isaac Anderson, Joe Martino, Mark Mendez, and Bette McIntire. *Mixed Media: A Multi-Faceted Approach to Creating Unique Works of Art Step by Step.* Irvine, CA: Walter Foster Publishing, 2012.

Amy Barickman. *Indygo Junction's Fabric Flowers: 25 Flowers for Fashion and Home.* Holley, NY: QuiltWoman.com/Amy Barickman, 2012.

Betty Edwards. *Drawing on the Right Side of the Brain: The Definitive, Fourth Edition.* New York: Jeremy P. Tarcher/Penguin, 2012.

Kooler Design Studio. *Party Favors (Leisure Arts #4770).* Little Rock, AR: Leisure Arts, 2009.

Leisure Arts. *Learn to Make Jewelry.* Little Rock, AR: Leisure Arts, 2013.

Elyse Major. *Tinkered Treasures.* London: CICO Books, 2013.

Kathleen McCafferty. *Making Mini Books: Big Ideas for 30+ Little Projects.* Asheville, NC: Lark Crafts, 2012.

Darlene Olivia McElroy and Sandra Duran Wilson. *Mixed Media Revolution: Creative Ideas for Reusing Your Art.* Cincinnati, OH: F&W Media/North Light Books, 2012.

Darlene Olivia McElroy and Sandra Duran Wilson. *Surface Treatment: Explore 45 Mixed-Media Techniques.* Cincinnati, OH: F&W Media/North Light Books, 2011.

Matthew Mead. *Flea Market Finds.* New York: Time Lifestyle Group/Oxmoor House, 2012.

Richela Fabian Morgan. *Tape It and Make It: 101 Duct Tape Activities.* Hauppauge, NY: Barron's Educational Series, 2012.

Lisa Occhipinti. *The Repurposed Library: 33 Craft Projects That Give Old Books New Life.* New York: Abrams/Stewart, Tabori, and Chang, 2011.

Linda Peterson. *Art and Life Combined: 35 Mixed-Media Projects to Inspire Your Inner Artist.* London: CICO Books, 2012.

Linda Scott. *How to Be the Best Bubble Writer in the World Ever!* London: Laurence King Publishing, 2011.

Jeannine Stein. *Re-Bound: Creating Handmade Books from Recycled and Repurposed Materials*. Beverly, MA: Quayside/Quarry Books, 2009.

Manga and Zentangle Books

Supittha Bunyapen. *Shojo Wonder Manga Art School: Create Your Own Cool Characters and Costumes with Markers*. Cincinnati, OH: F&W Media/Impact Books, 2011.

Sandy Steen Bartholomew. *Yoga for Your Brain: A Zentangle Workout*. East Petersburg: PA, Fox Chapel Publishing/Design Originals, 2011.

Margaret Bremner, Norma J. Burnell, Penny Raile, and Lara Williams. *The Art of Zentangle: 50 Inspiring Drawings, Designs & Ideas for the Meditative Artist*. Irvine, CA: Walter Foster Publishing, 2013.

Mark Crilley. *Mastering Manga: 30 Drawing Lessons from the Creator of Akiko*. Cincinnati, OH: F&W Media/Impact Books, 2012.

Kass Hall. *Zentangle Untangled: Inspiration and Prompts for Meditative Drawing*. Cincinnati, OH: F&W Media, 2012.

Beckah Krahula. *One Zentangle A Day: A 6-Week Course in Creative Drawing, Relaxation, and Fun*. Beverly MA: Quarry Books, 2012.

Suzanne McNeill and Cindy Shepard. *The Beauty of Zentangle: Inspirational Examples from 137 Gifted Tangle Artists Worldwide*. East Petersburg: PA, Fox Chapel Publishing/Design Originals, 2013.

Jeanne Paglio and Michael Hale. *Zentangle from the Heart*. New York: Barnes and Noble/CreateSpace Independent Publishing Platform, 2013.

Tatyana Williams. *Zentangle Basics: Get Creative with Zentangle Patterns, Shapes, and Art*. Kindle Book, Amazon Digital Services.

Sewing Books

Marina Druker. *Enchanting Art Dolls and Soft Sculptures*. Lafayette, CA: C&T Publishing, 2012.

Tone Finnange. *Tilda's Fairytale Wonderland: Over 25 Beautiful Sewing and Papercraft Projects*. Cincinnati, OH: F&W Media/David & Charles, 2013.

Austen Gilliland and Karen Kirk, eds. *Create, Update, Remake: DIY Projects for You, Your Family, and Your Home*. Toronto, Ontario: Canadian Living, 2011.

Rayna Gilman. *Create Your Own Free-Form Quilts: A Stress-Free Journey to Original Design*. Lafayette, CA: C&T Publishing, 2011.

Nancy Halvorsen. *Sew Necessary (Art to Heart)*. Layton, UT: Art to Heart, 2009. Nancy Halvorsen has written many books on sewing projects.

Jean Wells. *Journey to Inspired Art Quilting: More Intuitive Color and Design.* Lafayette, CA: C&T Publishing, 2012.

Writing Books

Constance Hardesty. *The Teen-Centered Writing Club: Bringing Teens and Words Together.* Westport, CT: Greenwood Publishing Group/Libraries Unlimited (Professional Guides for Young Adult Librarians Series), 2008.

Gabriele Lusser Rico. *Writing the Natural Way: Using Right-Brain Techniques to Release Your Expressive Powers.* Los Angeles: J.P Tarcher, 1983.

San Francisco's Writers' Grotto. *642 Things to Write Journal.* San Francisco: Chronicle Books, 2014.

Leadership Books

Mariam G. MacGregor. *Everyday Leadership: Attitudes and Actions for Respect and Success (A Guidebook for Teens).* Minneapolis: Free Spirit Publishing, 2006.

Mariam G. MacGregor. *Everyday Leadership Cards: Writing and Discussion Prompts.* Minneapolis: Free Spirit Publishing, 2006.

Miscellaneous Books

Renee Baron and Elizabeth Wagele. *The Enneagram Made Easy.* San Francisco: HarperCollins Publishers, 1984.

Martha Beck. *The Joy Diet: Ten Daily Practices for a Joyful Life.* New York: Crown/Random House, 2003.

Casey Cole Corbin. *Expressive Art Therapy for Problem Solving and Getting Past Your Past.* Lexington, KY: Author, 2013. CreateArtTherapy.weebly.com; www.facebook.com/CreateArtTherapy.

Grace Dobush. *The Crafty Superstar Ultimate Craft Business Guide.* Cincinnati, OH: F&W Media Ink/North Light Books, 2012.

Carol S. Dweck. *Mindset: The New Psychology of Success.* New York: Random House, 2007.

Howard Gardner. *Intelligence Reframed: Multiple Intelligences for the 21st Century.* New York: Basic Books, 1999.

Peter Gray. *Free to Learn: Why Unleashing the Instinct to Play Will Make Our Children Happier, More Self Reliant, and Better Prepared for Life.* New York: Basic Books, 2013.

Elizabeth Foy Larsen, Joshua Glenn, Heather Kasunick, and Mister Reusch. *Unbored: The Essential Field Guide to Serious Fun*. New York: Bloomsbury USA, 2012.

Dorothy Lehmkuhl and Dolores Cotter Lamping. *Organizing for the Creative Person*. New York: Three Rivers Press, 1993.

Daniel H. Pink. *A Whole New Mind: Why Right-Brainers Will Rule the Future*. New York: Riverhead Books/Penguin Group, 2006.

Cate Prato. *Inside the Creative Studio: Inspiration and Ideas for your Art and Craft Space*. Cincinnati, OH: F&W Media/Interweave, 2011.

Lee Silber. *Career Management for the Creative Person: Right-Brain Techniques to Run Your Professional Life and Build Your Business*. New York: Three Rivers Press, 1999.

Lee Silber. *Self-Promotion for the Creative Person: Getting the Word Out about Who You Are and What You Do*. New York: Three Rivers Press, 2001.

Lee Silber. *Time Management for the Creative Person*. New York: Three Rivers Press, 1998.

Gary Smalley and John Trent. *The Two Sides of Love*. Colorado Springs, CO: Focus on the Family Publishing, 1992.

Biz Stone. *Things a Little Bird Told Me: Confessions of the Creative Mind*. New York: Grand Central Publishing, 2014.

Bonnie Thomas. *Creative Expression Activities for Teens: Exploring Identity through Art, Craft, and Journaling*. London: Jessica Kingsley Publishers, 2011.

Magazines

Craft Magazines

Apprentice: Artful Building Blocks
Cloth, Paper, Scissors
Craft & Click: The Essential Guide to Crafting Online
Greencraft
Just Cards!
Paper: Creative Paper Crafting

Event Creativity Magazines

Handmade Wedding
Mingle: Creative Ideas for Unique Gatherings
Real Weddings

Scrapbooking Magazines

Somerset Studio: The Art of Paper and Mixed Media
Take Ten (cards)

Writing Magazines

Journaling Somerset Studio

Author's Sources

Since the study of creativity is comparatively new and relatively rare, I have included the sources I used in this book.

Albert, Robert S. and Mark A. Runco. "A History of Research on Creativity." In Robert J. Sternberg, ed., *Handbook of Creativity*, 6. New York: Cambridge University Press, 1999.

Alexander, Eben. *Proof of Heaven: A Neurosurgeon's Journey into the Afterlife.* New York: Simon and Schuster, 2012.

Amabile, Teresa M. *Growing Up Creative: Nurturing A Lifetime of Creativity.* 2nd ed. Buffalo, NY: Education Foundation, 1992.

Amabile, Teresa M. "How to Kill Creativity." *Harvard Business Review*, September–October, 1998.

Badenoch, Bonnie. *Being a Brain-Wise Therapist: A Practical Guide to Interpersonal Neurobiology.* New York: W.W. Norton, 2008.

Barnes, Rick, Carl Creasman, Mark Hartley, Shelley Marie, Stacy Andeau, Stan Pearson, Jessica Pettitt, Kevin Snyder, Shane Windmeyer, and Duane Zobrist. *Ten Keys to Extraordinary Leadership.* Keller, TX: TopLeader Publishing, 2009.

Baron, Renee and Elizabeth Wagele. *The Enneagram Made Easy.* San Francisco: HarperOne, 1984.

Beck, Martha. *The Joy Diet: Ten Daily Practices for a Joyful Life.* New York: Crown/Random House, 2003.

Besemer, Susan P. and Donald J. Treffinger. "Analysis of Creative Products: Review and Synthesis." *Journal of Creative Behavior* 15 (1981), 158–178.

Brach, Tara. *Radical Acceptance: Embracing Your Life with the Heart of a Buddha.* New York: Bantam Books, 2003.

Buckingham, Marcus. *Now, Discover Your Strengths.* New York: The Free Press/ Simon & Schuster, 2001.

Cameron, Julia. *The Artist's Way: A Spiritual Path to Higher Creativity.* New York: Jeremy P. Tarcher/Putnam, 1992/2012.

Cassou, Michele and Stewart Cubley. *Life, Paint, and Passion: Reclaiming the Magic of Spontaneous Expression.* New York: Jeremy P. Tarcher/Putnam, 1995.

Childre, Doc and Howard Martin, with Donna Beech. *The HeartMath Solution.* San Francisco: HarperCollins, 1999.

Clear, James. "What Every Successful Person Knows but Never Says." Interview with Ira Glass on taste and failure. jamesclear.com/ira-glass-failure (accessed January 23, 2014).

Clifton, Donald O., Edward "Chip" Anderson, and Laurie A. Schreiner. *Strengths-Quest: Discover and Develop Your Strengths in Academics, Career, and Beyond.* 2nd ed. New York: Gallup Press, 2006.

Coleridge, Samuel T. "Biographia Literaria, 1817." In William Safire. "On Language: Suspension of Disbelief." *New York Times*, October 7, 2007.

Collins, Suzanne. *The Hunger Games.* New York: Scholastic Press, 2008.

Corbin, Casey Cole. *Expressive Art Therapy for Problem Solving and Getting Past Your Past.* Lexington, KY: Author, 2013.

Csikszentmihalyi, Mihaly. *Creativity: Flow and the Psychology of Discovery and Invention.* New York: HarperCollins, 1996.

Csikszentmihalyi, Mihaly. *Finding Flow: The Psychology of Engagement with Everyday Life.* New York: Basic Books/Harper Collins, 1997.

Dacey, John. "Concepts of Creativity: A History" In Mark A. Runco and Steven R. Pritzer, *Encyclopedia of Creativity.* New York: Elsevier, 1999.

Davis, Gary A. *Creativity Is Forever.* 5th ed. Dubuque IA: Kendall/Hunt Publishing, 2004.

Dobbs, David. "Beautiful Brains." *National Geographic* 220, no. 4 (October 2011), 36–59.

Dweck, Carol S. *Mindset: The New Psychology of Success.* New York: Random House, 2007.

Eberle, Robert F. *Scamper: Games for Imagination Development.* Buffalo, NY: DOK Publishing, 1971.

Edwards, Betty. *Drawing on the Right Side of the Brain.* Definitive 4th ed. New York: Jeremy P. Tarcher/Penguin, 2012.

Gardner, Howard. *Intelligence Reframed: Multiple Intelligences for the 21st Century.* New York: Basic Books, 1999.

Garvey, Robert and Geof Alred. *Mentoring and the Tolerance of Complexity.* London: Elsevier Academic Press, 2001.

Gladwell, Malcolm. *Outliers: The Story of Success.* New York: Little, Brown, 2011.

Gottman, John M. *The Marriage Clinic: A Scientifically Based Marital Therapy.* New York: W.W. Norton, 1999.

Gray, Peter. *Free to Learn: Why Unleashing the Instinct to Play Will Make Our Children Happier, More Self Reliant, and Better Prepared for Life.* New York: Basic Books, 2013.

Gray, Peter. "School Is a Prison—and Damaging Our Kids." Salon.com, August 26, 2013. www.salon.com/2013/08/26/school_is_a_prison_and_damaging_our_kids/.

Guilford, Joy Paul (J. P.). *The Nature of Human Intelligence*. New York: McGraw-Hill, 1967.

Hardesty, Constance. *The Teen-Centered Writing Club: Bringing Teens and Words Together*. Westport, CT: Greenwood Publishing Group/Libraries Unlimited, 2008.

Hart, Michael H. *The 100: A Ranking of the Most Influential Persons in History*. New York: Citadel Press, 1992.

Homerus Epic. Odyssea Book 24, line 60 (circa BCE 799).

Jung, Carl G. *The Archetypes and the Collective Unconscious: Collected Works*. New York: Pantheon, 1959.

Jung, Carl G. *Psychological Types*. New York: Harcourt, 1933.

Kaufman, James C. and Ronald A. Beghetto. "Beyond Big and Little: The Four C Model of Creativity." *Review of General Psychology* 13, no. 1 (2009), 1–12. doi:10.1037/a0013688.

Keirsey, David and Marilyn Bates. *Please Understand Me: Character and Temperament Types*. 3rd ed. Vol. 1 and 2. Del Mar, CA: Prometheus Nemesis Books, 1984.

Kirton, Michael J. *Adaption and Innovation: In the Context of Diversity and Change*. New York: Routledge, 2003.

Kowalczyk, Liz. "Empathy Gap in Medical Students: Stress Can Harden Students' Attitude Towards Patients, but Medical Schools Are Trying to Change That." *Boston Globe*, March 25, 2103. www.bostonglobe.com/lifestyle/health-wellness/2013/03/24/medical-students-empathy-drops-just-they-start-caring-for-patients/rWqFiVVsr9oze6EWRLwzwN/story.html.

Kubie, Lawrence S. *Neurotic Distortion of the Creative Process*. Lawrence: University of Kansas Press, 1958.

Lehmkuhl, Dorothy and Delores Cotter Lamping. *Organizing for the Creative Person*. New York: Three Rivers Press, 1993.

Lloyd, G. E. R., ed. *Hippocratic Writings*, Penguin Classics reprint ed. Translated [from the Greek] by J. Chadwick and W. N. Mann, et al. Harmondsworth, England: Penguin, 1983.

MacGregor, Mariam G. *Everyday Leadership: Attitudes and Actions for Respect and Success: A Guidebook for Teens*. Minneapolis, MN: Free Spirit Publishing, 2006.

Maslow, Abraham. "Hierarchy of Human Needs." www.edpsycinteractive.org/topics/conation/maslow.html; psychology.about.com/od/theoriesofpersonality/ss/maslows-needs-hierarchy.htm.

Massimi, Michela. *Pauli's Exclusion Principle*. New York: Cambridge University Press, 2005.

Maxwell, John C. *Leadership Gold: Lessons I've Learned from a Lifetime of Leading*. Nashville, TN: Thomas Nelson, 2008.

McDonald, Alan J., with James R. Hansen. *Truth, Lies, and O-Rings: Inside the Space Shuttle Challenger Disaster.* Gainesville: University Press of Florida, 2009.

Michalko, Michael. *Cracking Creativity: The Secrets of Creative Genius.* Berkeley, CA: Ten Speed Press, 2001.

Miller, Blair, Jonathan Vehar, and Roger L. Firestien. *Creativity Unbound: An Introduction to Creative Process.* 3rd ed. Williamsville, NY: Innovation Resources, 2001.

Mullainathan, Sendil and Eldar Shafir. *Scarcity Changes How We Think: Why Having Too Little Means So Much.* New York: Times Books/Henry Holt, 2013. www.salon.com/2013/09/08/scarcity_changes_how_we_think/.

Mutucumarana, Charmaine. "Empathy in Medical Schools: Improving Medical Students' Empathy." sites.duke.edu/empathyinmedicalschoolcurricula/improving-medical-students-empathy/.

Noller, Ruth B. *Scratching the Surface of Creative Problem Solving: A Bird's-Eye View of CPS.* Buffalo, NY: DOK Publishing, 1979.

Northouse, Peter G. *Leadership Theory and Practice.* 3rd ed. Thousand Oaks, CA: Sage Publications, 2007.

Osborn, Alex F. *Applied Imagination: Principles and Procedures of Creative Problem-Solving.* New York: Charles Scribner's Sons, 1953.

Osborn, Alex F. *How to Think Up.* New York: Charles Scribner's Sons, 1942.

Osborn, Alex F. *Your Creative Power: How to Use Imagination.* New York: Charles Scribner's Sons, 1952.

Paddison, Sara. *The Hidden Power of the Heart.* Boulder Creek, CA: Planetary Publications, 1998.

Palmer, Helen and Paul B. Brown. *The Enneagram Advantage: Putting the Personality Types to Work in the Office.* New York: Random House, 1998.

Parnes, Sidney J. *Source Book for Creative Problem Solving.* Hadley, MA: Creative Education Foundation Press, 1992.

Pink, Daniel H. *Drive: The Surprising Truth about What Motivates Us.* New York: Riverhead Books/Penguin Group, 2012.

Pink, Daniel H. *A Whole New Mind: Why Right-Brainers Will Rule the Future.* New York: Riverhead Books/Penguin Group, 2006.

Puccio, Gerard J. and Chris Grivas. *The Innovative Team: Unleashing Creative Potential for Breakthrough Results.* San Francisco: Jossey-Bass, 2012.

Puccio, Gerard J. and Mary C. Murdock. *Creativity Assessment: Readings and Resources.* Buffalo, NY: Creative Education Foundation Press, 1999.

Puccio, Gerard J., Mary C. Murdock, and Marie Mance. *Creative Leadership: Skills That Drive Change.* Thousand Oaks, CA: Sage Publications, 2007.

Rank, Otto. *Art and Artist.* New York: Knopf, 1932/1989.

Rhodes, Mel. "An Analysis of Creativity." *Phi Delta Kappan* 42 (1961), 305–310.

Richards, Ruth. "Introduction." In Ruth Richards, ed., *Everyday Creativity and New Views of Human Nature*, 3–22. Washington, D.C.: American Psychological Association, 2007.

Rico, Gabriele Lusser. *Writing the Natural Way: Using Right-Brain Techniques to Release Your Expressive Powers*. Los Angeles: J.P. Tarcher, 1983.

Robinson, Ken. *Out of Our Minds: Learning to Be Creative*. Chichester, West Sussex, England: Capstone Publishing, 2011.

Rugg, Harold. *Imagination: An Inquiry into the Sources and Conditions that Stimulate Creativity*. New York: Harper & Row, 1963.

Ruggiero, Vincent Ryan. *The Art of Thinking: A Guide to Critical and Creative Thought*. New York: Pearson/Longman, 2006.

Runco, Mark A. and Robert S. Albert. "A History of Research on Creativity." In Robert J. Sternberg, *The Handbook of Creativity*, 16–32. New York: Cambridge University Press, 2006.

Ryan, Aryna. "Build Your Own Heart." Presentation, International Association of Social Work Groups Conference 34th Annual International Symposium, Adelphi College, Long Island, NY, June 14–17, 2012.

Ryan, Aryna and Cynthia A. Hedge. "How to Slay Your Critical Dragon and Rescue Your Creativity." Presentation, World Creativity and Innovation Week, LaPorte County Public Library, LaPorte, IN, April 18, 2011.

Ryan, John (Jack) L. Personal conversation with author, November 16, 2013.

Ryan-Rued, Amy P. Personal conversation with author, May 14, 2014.

Siegel, Daniel J. *Brainstorm: The Power and Purpose of the Teenage Brain*. New York: Jeremy P. Tarcher/Penguin, 2013.

Silber, Lee. *Career Management for the Creative Person: Right-Brain Techniques to Run Your Professional Life and Build Your Business*. New York: Three Rivers Press, 1999.

Silber, Lee. *Self-Promotion for the Creative Person: Getting the Word Out about Who You Are and What You Do*. New York: Three Rivers Press, 2001.

Silber, Lee. *Time Management for the Creative Person*. New York: Three Rivers Press, 1998.

Smalley, Gary and John Trent. *The Two Sides of Love*. Colorado Springs, CO: Focus on the Family Publishing, 1992.

Star Trek: The Next Generation. Television series, Rick Berman, executive producer. Peter Lauritsen, co-producer. Hollywood, CA: Paramount Television/Paramount Pictures, 1987–1994.

Sternberg, Robert J., ed., *Handbook of Creativity*. New York: Cambridge University Press, 1999.

Stone, Biz. *Things a Little Bird Told Me: Confessions of the Creative Mind*. New York: Grand Central Publishing, 2014.

Suskie, Linda. *Five Dimensions of Quality: A Common Sense Guide to Accreditation and Accountability.* San Francisco: Jossey-Bass, 2014.

Thomas, Bonnie. *Creative Expression Activities for Teens: Exploring Identity through Art, Craft, and Journaling.* London: Jessica Kingsley Publishers, 2011.

Torrance, E. Paul. *Torrance Tests of Creative Thinking: Norms and Technical Manual. Figural (Streamlined) Forms A and B.* Bensenville, IL: Scholastic Testing Service, 1990. Cited in Gary A. Davis. *Creativity Is Forever.* 5th ed. Dubuque, IA: Kendall/Hunt Publishing, 2004.

Torrance, E. Paul and Tammy H. Safter. *Making the Creative Leap Beyond.* Hadley, MA: Creative Education Foundation Press, 2005.

Treffinger, Donald J. and Roger L. Firestien. "Ownership and Converging: Essential Ingredients of Creative Problem Solving." *Journal of Creative Behavior* 17, no. 1 (1983), 32–38.

Wallas, Graham. *The Art of Thought.* New York: Harcourt, 1926.

Weintraub, Pamela. "Discover Interview: Jaak Panksepp Pinned Down Humanity's 7 Primal Emotions." *Discover* Magazine, May 2012. discovermagazine .com/2012/may/11-jaak-panksepp-rat-tickler-found-humans-7-primal -emotions (accessed May 12, 2014).

Whitehead, Alfred North. *Process and Reality: An Essay in Cosmology: Gifford Lectures Delivered in the University of Edinburgh during the session 1927–28.* Corrected ed. New York: Free Press, 1928/1978.

Zastrow, Charles H. and Karen K. Kirst-Ashman. *Understanding Human Behavior and the Social Environment.* Belmont, CA: Brooks/Cole, 2010.

Index